WORKSHOPS IN COMPUTING
Series edited by C. J. van Rijsbergen

Also in this series

**Women into Computing: Selected Papers
1988–1990**
Gillian Lovegrove and Barbara Segal (Eds.)

3rd Refinement Workshop (organised by
BCS-FACS, and sponsored by IBM UK
Laboratories, Hursley Park and the Programming
Research Group, University of Oxford),
Hursley Park, 9–11 January 1990
Carroll Morgan and J. C. P. Woodcock (Eds.)

Designing Correct Circuits, Workshop jointly
organised by the Universities of Oxford and
Glasgow, Oxford, 26–28 September 1990
Geraint Jones and Mary Sheeran (Eds.)

Functional Programming, Glasgow 1990,
Proceedings of the 1990 Glasgow Workshop on
Functional Programming, Ullapool, Scotland,
13–15 August 1990
Simon L. Peyton Jones, Graham Hutton and
Carsten Kehler Holst (Eds.)

4th Refinement Workshop, Proceedings of the
4th Refinement Workshop, organised by BCS-
FACS, Cambridge, 9–11 January 1991
Joseph M. Morris and Roger C. Shaw (Eds.)

AI and Cognitive Science '90, University of
Ulster at Jordanstown, 20–21 September 1990
Michael F. McTear and Norman Creaney (Eds.)

Software Re-use, Utrecht 1989, Proceedings of
the Software Re-use Workshop, Utrecht,
The Netherlands, 23–24 November 1989
Liesbeth Dusink and Patrick Hall (Eds.)

Z User Workshop, 1990, Proceedings of the Fifth
Annual Z User Meeting, Oxford,
17–18 December 1990
J.E. Nicholls (Ed.)

IV Higher Order Workshop, Banff 1990
Proceedings of the IV Higher Order Workshop,
Banff, Alberta, Canada, 10–14 September 1990
Graham Birtwistle (Ed.)

ALPUK91 Proceedings of the 3rd UK
Annual Conference on Logic Programming,
Edinburgh, 10–12 April 1991
Geraint A.Wiggins, Chris Mellish and
Tim Duncan (Eds.)

Specifications of Database Systems,
1st International Workshop on Specifications of
Database Systems, Glasgow, 3–5 July 1991
David J. Harper and Moira C. Norrie (Eds.)

**7th UK Computer and Telecommunications
Performance Engineering Workshop,**
Edinburgh, 22–23 July 1991
J. Hillston, P.J.B. King and R.J. Pooley (Eds.)

Logic Program Synthesis and Transformation,
Proceedings of LOPSTR 91, International
Workshop on Logic Program Synthesis and
Transformation, University of Manchester,
4–5 July 1991
T.P. Clement and K.-K. Lau (Eds.)

Declarative Programming, Sasbachwalden 1991
PHOENIX Seminar and Workshop on Declarative
Programming, Sasbachwalden, Black Forest,
Germany, 18–22 November 1991
John Darlington and Roland Dietrich (Eds.)

continued on back page...

Philip Gray and Roger Took (Eds.)

Building Interactive Systems:

Architectures and Tools

Published in collaboration with the
British Computer Society

Springer-Verlag London Ltd.

Philip Gray, MSc
Computing Science Department
University of Glasgow
Glasgow G12 8QQ
Scotland, UK

Roger Took, PhD
Department of Computer Science
University of York
York YO1 5DD
UK

ISBN 978-3-540-19736-2   ISBN 978-1-4471-3548-7 (eBook)
DOI 10.1007/978-1-4471-3548-7

British Library Cataloguing in Publication Data
Gray, Philip
  Building interactive systems
   I. Title   II. Took, Roger
004.019

Library of Congress Cataloging-in-Publication Data
Gray, Philip, *1946–*
Building interactive systems: architecture and tools / Philip Gray and Roger Took
      p.   cm. – (Workshops in computing)

1. Interactive computer systems–Congresses.   I. Took, Roger, *1950–*   .
II. Title.   III. Series
QA76.9.I58G73 1992   91-43342
004'.33–dc20   CIP

34/3830-543210 Printed on acid-free paper

Preface

The papers which form this volume are the outcome of two separate day-long meetings. The first of these meetings, entitled 'Architectures for Interactive Systems' and sponsored by the DTI HI Club, was held at the University of York on the 4th of March 1991. The second, 'Object-Oriented Tools for User Interface Construction', was jointly sponsored by the BCS Specialist Groups in HCI and Object-Oriented Programming Systems, and took place at the University of Glasgow on the 5th of April 1991. Although ostensibly covering different topics, both workshops addressed the problems of constructing modern interactive systems and, as it transpired, the contents of the presentations in the two meetings were often complementary or gave different perspectives on the same problem. It seemed only natural, therefore, to combine the proceedings of the two meetings in a single volume.

The papers have been organised into two sections, 'Architectures' and 'Tools', which correspond roughly to the division between the York and Glasgow meetings. However, in some cases it has proved illuminating to place a paper from the Glasgow meeting in the 'Architectures' section and a York paper in the 'Tools' section. Additionally, the editors have included two further papers which were not presented at the workshops but which offer useful additional insights into topics dealt with in the meetings. Some of the papers in this volume are expanded versions of the rather shorter presentations made in March and April. The editors were pleased to accept more lengthy versions when they enhanced the coverage of the topic.

Given the divergence of the contents and arrangement of the papers in this volume from the presentations at the two workshops, the meeting programmes are given below:

Architectures for Interactive Systems,
York University, 4 March 1991

Peter Rosner – A Generalised Mechanism for the Construction of Input Models.
David Duce – Logical Input Devices – An Outdated Concept?
Peter Williams – Surface Interaction: A Universal Paradigm for Persistent Objects.

Alan Burns – Human Interfaces to Real-time Embedded Systems.
Phil Gray – Representing Design Choices in User Interface Management
   Systems.
Ernest Edmonds – An Architecture for Integration.

**Object-Oriented Tools for User Interface Construction,
University of Glasgow, 5 April 1991**

Steve Draper – The Iconographer System.
Trevor Hopkins – Declarative Objects for User Interface Construction.
Harold Thimbleby – HyperCard: An Object-Oriented Disappointment.
Peter Windsor – Separation, Connection and Specialisation: Issues and
   Mechanism for Object-Oriented User Interface Construction.
Alistair George – X-Designer: Abstraction and Visibility in GUI Design.
Cathy Waite – The HyperNeWS System.

The present volume gives the most comprehensive recent account of
UK research into the construction of interactive computer systems. It
addresses concerns both formal and theoretical as well as pragmatic and
practical, academic as well as commercial. The meetings themselves
were lively and stimulating. The editors feel that this collection reflects
the breadth and excitement of the meetings from which it arises, and hope
that it prompts further research into the relationship between architectures
and tools in interactive systems.

November 1991   Philip Gray
                                                     University of Glasgow

                                                          Roger Took
                                                     University of York

Contents

I Architectures 1

The Active Medium: A Conceptual and Practical Architecture for
Direct Manipulation
Roger Took 6

Surface Interaction: A Paradigm for Object Communication
Peter Williams 23

HyperCard: An Object-Oriented Disappointment
Harold Thimbleby, Andy Cockburn and Steve Jones 35

An Architecture for HCI in Real-time Systems
Alan Burns 56

Logical Input Devices – An Outdated Concept?
D.A. Duce, P.J.W. ten Hagen and R. van Liere 69

A Generalised Event Mechanism for Interactive Systems
Peter Rosner, Mel Slater and Allan Davison 85

Generalising MVC to ERID: Orthogonalising Entities,
Representations, and Input Dispatching to Interaction Classes
Ramzan Mohamed and Stephen W. Draper 104

Constructing front-ends to existing software systems
E.A. Edmonds, I. Reid, S.P. Heggie and D.J. Cornali 115

II Tools 129

Correspondence between Specification and Run-Time
Architecture in a Design Support Tool
Philip Gray 133

Incorporating an Incremental Learning Model in the Design of
HyperNeWS2.0
Cathy Waite 151

Declarative Objects for User Interface Construction
Trevor P. Hopkins and Steve K. Wallis 168

X-Designer – Abstraction and Visibility in Graphical User
Interface Design
Alistair George 182

SIRIUS: An Object-Oriented Framework for Prototyping User
Interfaces
Peter Windsor 200

Author Index 243

I Architectures

An architecture is a description or specification of the structural organisation of a system. Stand-alone, one-off, or once-off (i.e. maintenance-free) systems have little need of an explicit architecture. It is only when a system is placed in an environment and is used as a resource that its structural organisation becomes important. In this situation, a system needs to be designed to take account, on the one hand, of operating constraints in its environment, for example, time or space limitations which require the sharing of code or execution. On the other hand, a system used as a resource must also be responsive to the needs of its clients. For example, the client may require the system to behave consistently over changes to the operating or device environment. This can only be ensured by localising such changes in back-end components while preserving the abstract behaviour in independent, higher-level components. Thus the basic principle in the design of an architecture is a separation and factoring of concerns, and the basic mechanisms in its construction are standard software engineering strategies: modularity, levels of independence, extensibility, and component reuse. As a result, the architecture is both an implementation structure, and a commitment to a stable organisation for the benefit of its clients.

We can view an architecture abstractly as consisting of a set of discrete components, linked by a communication structure by which the components are coordinated. Most dynamically, the communication structure may consist of messaging channels. In this case the interpretation of the messages is up to the receiver. This allows flexibility and extensibility in the construction of the architecture. More tightly, the communication structure may consist of invocations or applications of procedural or functional abstractions. This increases the predictability of the system. Most statically, the communication structure may consist of code dependencies such as inheritance hierarchies or included library files. Any one architecture may have a variety of these types of structure.

A rigid architectural structure, however, is not an assurance of usefulness, or even of efficient implementation. The components of the architecture must also encapsulate *appropriate* abstractions or classifications, given the problem domain. These can be used either internally, by other components, or externally, by the client. Thus the architecture should also form a high-level rationalisation or design within the problem domain.

Architectures designed specifically for interactive systems have particular features which distinguish them from embedded architectures. They must at least take account of the obvious separation between the user and the computer. A first-level architectural separation in these systems is therefore clearly between software that manages the user interface, and software that provides the application functionality. Further refinement of this top-level architecture, however, is by no means so simple, as is illustrated by the many structures and stratifications of user interface management systems, object-oriented toolkits, and the input and output languages of the graphics standards from GKS on.

In fact, interactive systems exemplify in a high degree the problems of architectural design and construction. Firstly, in terms of design, these problems centre on the conflict between generality and customisation. There are strong arguments for preserving generality in the functionality provided to client users - domain or implementation bias can limit the expressive freedom of the user. There are many familiar examples of such limitations in user interface systems: rectangular but not polygonal windows; horizontal but not diagonal text. Yet at the same time there are equally strong arguments for preserving user interface consistency by customising the functionality in just such ways. The `look and feel' of an interface house style is thus maintained at the expense of flexibility and originality. Secondly, in terms of construction, architectures for interactive systems must cope with the fundamental problem that both applications and end users are clients of the user interface component. These two types of client have radically different modes of access to the resources provided by the user interface, and yet often have similar requirements. This is especially true if the interface supports interactive objects which are intended to form a medium of communication between the application and the user.

The papers in this section address the problems of architectural design and construction for interactive systems from a number of points of view. Some are broadly theoretical, such as Took and Williams; some make constructive proposals, such as Duce et al and Rosner et al; some describe implemented architecures in more detail, like Mohamed and Draper and Edmonds et al; and Burns elaborates a principle of design, while Thimbleby et al gives a principled critique of an existing system. The use of the term architecture suggests that the structural organisation is itself an object of engineering, and can be abstracted from the content of the current components and applied as an organising principle to other components. This is the premise behind classical, linguistically-based user interface architectures such as the Seeheim architecture, which divides the user interface manager into three components: presentation, dialogue control, and application linkage. Took's paper, `The Active Medium: A Conceptual and Practical Architecture for Direct Manipulation', is also based on this premise of architectural abstraction. It defines a three-component architecture (UMA) in terms of its communication protocols and channels, but does not presuppose any semantic content for the components themselves. In UMA, in contrast to Seeheim, the fundamental separation is between `surface' and `deep' semantics, but these are not defined except in terms of their control requirements. That is, surface interaction takes place entirely between the user and the interactive medium or surface, whereas deep interaction requires the involvement of the application.

The architecture described in Williams' paper, `Surface Interaction: A Paradigm for Object Communication', is also intended to be independent of particular application semantics. However, whereas UMA is heterogeneous, in the sense that the components perform distinct roles, Williams' architecture is homogeneous, since different objects are not distinguished. Rather, Williams paper posits a model that unifies the notions of object and channel. Both maintain constraints between dependent attributes - in objects this implements functionality, whereas in channels it implements communication. Williams borrows the term `surface' to describe that subset of an object's attributes which can also form part of a channel and so be communicated to other objects.

Architectures can differ in the degree of separation of their components. In structured code, the architectural components consist simply of the set of procedures. The communication structure is the calling hierarchy. The separation here is bridged by simple addressing. In object-oriented code, in addition to the objects and their messaging structure, the components also include classes, and the communication structure includes the inheritance hierarchy. Here the separation is stronger, since addressing methods may require searching up the hierarchy. In client-server and other distributed architectures, the separation is between processes, and the architecture is built on the process communication channels. The separation here is over address spaces. Finally, in systems providing levels of device independence and ease of porting, the separation is between physical devices, and the architecture is structured on front- and back-end software.

Thimbleby's paper, `HyperCard: An Object-Oriented Disappointment', emphasises this view of an architecture as an organisation of separate components. A programming language is a generic architecture in the sense that it can be instantiated, by compilation or interpretation, to provide particular programs and execution structures. The abstraction and data manipulation mechanisms of a programming language determine how well these structures can be organised. The particular language that Thimbleby examines, HyperCard, is, moreover, expressly designed for the construction and maintenance of user interfaces. Thimbleby's criticisms show not only how far HyperCard falls short of this goal, they also highlight how criteria from programming language theory can be also used to evaluate user interface architectures.

Architectures may also differ in their lifetimes. An architecture may exist only at design time, as a sketch, for example a schematic layered diagram to guide implementation. It may persist only until writing time, as a static code structuring. It may persist until compile time, as a library of primitives or set of classes which are only then bound in to the code. If objects can be instantiated dynamically from classes, then the architecture persists until run time. Finally, if instantiated objects can be saved independently of the process which allowed them to be created (as for example in user interface editors) then the architectural separation may be preserved permanently.

Burns' paper, `An Architecture for HCI in Real-time Systems', exploits this temporal perspective to propose an architecture which supports the real-time principles of safety and reliability. His system has a persistent architecture which maintains a real-time user interface database. This database not only generates the user interface and mediates the communication between the user and the application, it also holds timing requirements and ensures temporarily correct interaction when the application is safety-critical in real-time.

The architectures described in Duce et al and Rosner et al make a strong separation between input and output, concentrating on input structuring as a dynamically maintained component. Duce et al's paper, `Logical Input Devices - An Outdated Concept?' is written from within the historical context of the development of the standard graphics languages. In this thread of development, input and output have if anything been poorly integrated. Little support has traditionally been provided for input-output linkage other than as facilities for interactive picking of graphical segments. In contrast to the standard flat set of input logical device classes, Duce et al proposes a set of composable input devices which can be built up into a logical hierarchy in which higher devices implement more semantically complex interactions.

The input device hierarchy can thus support arbitrary application functionality. In this architecture the communication structure is based on event messages passing up the hierarchy from triggers and measures in low-level devices to similar processes in higher, more complex, devices.

By contrast, Rosner et al's paper, `A Generalised Event Mechanism for Interactive Systems', is written from within the bitmapped toolkit tradition in which the input routing structure is typically shared with the geometric or dependency structure of the graphical output objects. That is, input events here are usually routed along the composition paths of the interface objects. Rosner et al's contribution is to separate these two structures, and to provide general strategies for the routing of input that decouple input dependencies from output dependencies.

Mohamed and Draper's paper `Generalising MVC to ERID: Orthogonalising Entities, Representations, and Input Dispatching to Interactive Classes' makes a similarly motivated decoupling of the specification of the screen appearance of an interactive object from the specification of its behaviour. It takes as a starting point Smalltalk's MVC architecture, in which, while a model may have many views, typically each view has only a single controller. In the ERID architecture, views may have a number of controllers, determining separate behaviours dependent, for example, on context or location. This decoupling of presentation and behaviour (or view and controller) allows the definition of a small set of generic behaviours which need only be instantiated to provide control for specific presentation views of application models.

Finally in this section, Edmonds et al's paper. `Constructing Front Ends to Existing Software Systems', describes an architecture whose main purpose is not the separation of concerns, but rather their integration. The FOCUS project is an attempt to produce an architecture to harness a diverse variety of applications within a generic, knowledge-based user interface.

The Active Medium: A Conceptual and Practical Architecture for Direct Manipulation[†]

Roger Took

Department of Computer Science,
University of York,
York YO1 5DD, U.K.

Abstract

This paper presents a precise but general architecture (*UMA*) which attempts to resolve two critical and conflicting qualities of graphical user interfaces: *directness* and *separation*. This is achieved by placing central emphasis on the *medium* of interaction, and making this *active* through a dedicated *user agent*. This active medium allows *surface interaction* - application-independent manipulation of medium objects by the user. A major strength of *UMA* is that it is both a conceptual and an implementation architecture, and therefore is both intuitive to the user and the application designer, and effective in rationalising the separate construction and execution of the user interface and the application.

1 Introduction: Surface Interaction

Breaking down an interactive system into a user interface module and application modules is a powerful rationalisation of the cost of building interactive applications, and can enforce consistency over the user interfaces of a range of applications, for example as a standardised 'look and feel.' Much current user interface research focuses on *static* modularisation, in the form of software libraries or classes of toolkit objects that are bound in to the application code. On the other hand, the dominant *run-time* architecture in direct manipulation interactive systems is based on a separation of relatively low-level window and input management from such toolkit-extended applications. The X window environment [17] is a prime example of this.

---

† This paper is reproduced from the Proceedings of HCI '91: *People and Computers VI*, pp 249-264, © Cambridge University Press, 1991, by kind permission of the publishers.

This misalignment between the *conceptual* boundary between user interface and application, and their *architectural* boundary imposed by the run-time environment, leads to application-dominated interaction: most of the possible courses of interaction have to be planned and managed from the application side. This is a burden on the application programmer, and inevitably restricts the user's *independent* control over the objects of interaction. The user, for example, may only have independent control over the size and position of the application window.

A number of alternative architectures have been proposed which allow more of the application to be factored into the interface. The classical UIMS [15] attempts to manage the *dialogue* of interaction separately from applications. However, dialogue is difficult to abstract from the semantics of the application [23]. On the other hand, the NeWS environment [14], and the Blit [16] before it, allow user interface code to be downloaded from the application into a server executing locally to the user. This results in improved local response, but responsibility for most interaction still lies within the application.

[23] proposes a new architecture which separates a presentation *surface* common to all applications. The surface has an *objective* structure (that is, both dynamic and encapsulated) which supports all objects of interaction for all applications. It thus acts as a *medium* of communication between application and user, as well as potentially between different users (thus supporting cooperative work) and between different applications. Critically, the surface is distinguished from window-managed display spaces by the fact that surface objects have *behaviour* which can be accessed directly by the user, without application involvement. This direct independent manipulation of surface objects is referred to as *surface interaction*.

The power of surface interaction as a principle of separation lies in the observation that many manipulations of displayed objects have significance to the user, but none to the application. Moving a dialogue box to another location in order to uncover some hidden information is a typical example: the *position* of the dialogue box may be irrelevant to the application. Interaction can thus be cleanly separated into *surface* actions like textual and geometric manipulation, and *deep* actions which may result in changes to application state and in semantic feedback [10] from there to the surface. With this separation, an application need be informed only of those surface actions which it considers meaningful, while the user may have considerable freedom to manipulate the application's surface objects in ways that are irrelevant to their functionality. Furthermore, if an application *does* place significance on a particular surface manipulation, then, even so, the presentation management of this action can be factored out from the application so long as its *occurrence* is reported back.

Surface objects essentially have textual and graphical content, structure, geometry and behaviour. They are *not* bound to application semantics and are thus generic over all applications. This logical separation is enhanced by the surface's objective structure, which is addressed and modified through a well-defined set of

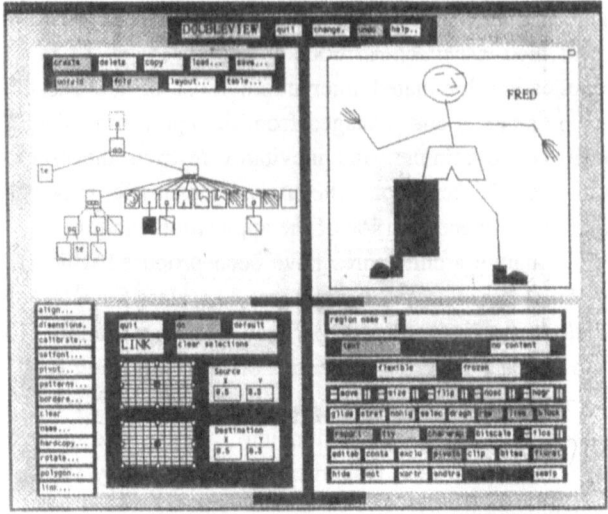

Figure 1. Presenter's interactive surface editor, DoubleView [9]

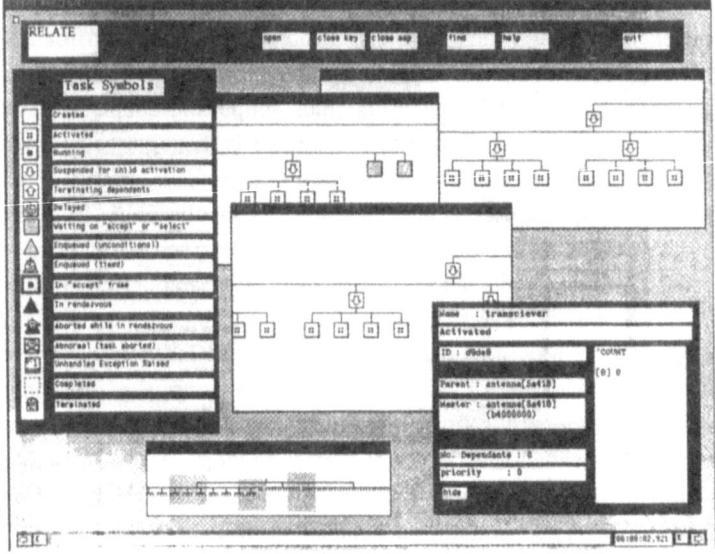

Figure 2. An Ada debugger [1]

commands rather than by static references. The surface can therefore be supported by a separate process in the run-time architecture.

A working system, *Presenter* [22], has been implemented based on surface separation. Figures 1 to 4 show a number of applications already built using *Presenter*.

While the notion of surface separation has conceptual appeal, and while *Presenter* shows that it has practical applicability, there remains a need to account for exactly *how* the user and the application can communicate via such a surface and

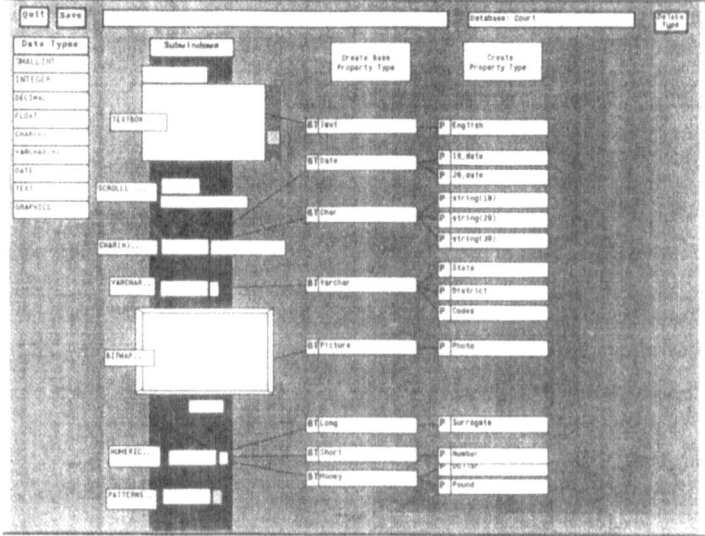

Figure 3. An interactive database management system [2]

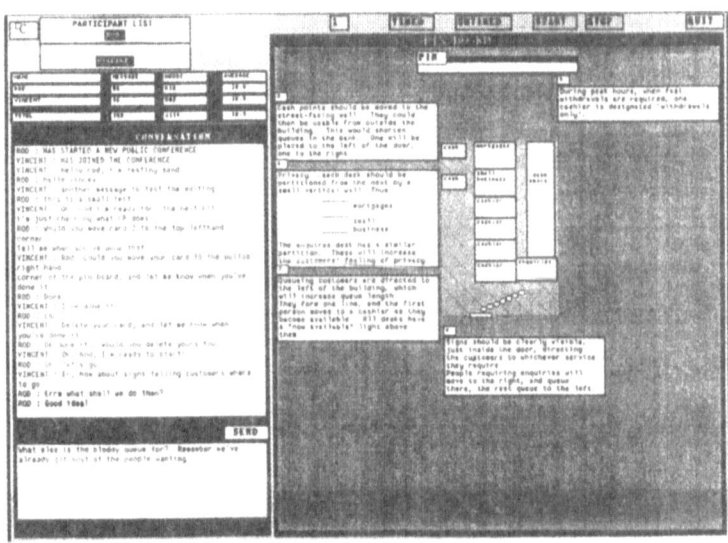

Figure 4. An interactive conferencing system [13]

retain mutual expressive power over surface objects. If this essential communication architecture between surface and deep components can be formulated precisely and abstractly it can form the basis for further implementations [23]. The result is the *UMA* architecture (*User Agent, Medium, Application*), which is presented in this paper.

Two formative requirements were to maximise the separation between surface and deep components, and yet at the same time to support direct manipulation of application objects at the surface.

2 Directness and Separation

There are a number of characterisations of direct manipulation [6, 18, 19, 11]. We use, however, a simple but powerful criterion for directness: that the *same* object is the target of both input and output. At the very least, an object that is the target of input (for example, an icon which is selected by a mouse click) must previously have been output. In the general case, an object may also be the target of interleaved input and output, in the sense that it can be addressed and updated both by the user (using a mouse), and the application (using an internal identifier). For example, a scroll bar may be moved by user input to request a change of document view, or changed in size by application output as the viewed document changes size. On the other hand, textual interaction on a glass teletype is not direct in this sense, since input references to previous output are *symbolic*. For example, removing a file from a displayed list of files involves retyping the filename as an argument to the remove command.

Formal models of interaction [3, 4, 5, 7, 20] often rely on a *semantic interpretation* function of type

$$seq\ I \rightarrow seq\ D$$

which defines the functionality of the application by specifying, for any sequence of input events I, the sequence of output displays D it produces (ignoring other application effects such as hardcopy output or process control). For example, in order to define an application which allows the user to draw lines using the mouse, one such interpretation mapping might be:

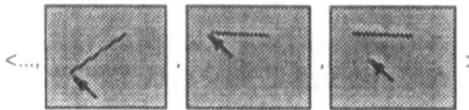

$$<press\ (x_0, y_0),\ drag\ (x_1, y_1),\ release> \mapsto <\qquad,\qquad,\qquad>$$

That is, the particular sequence of input events on the left hand side will generate the sequence of displays on the right. This formalism is capable of expressing directness so long as all information on the state of the display is retained within it. Thus a *further* sequence of input:

$$<..., press\ (x_1, y_1),\ drag\ (x_3, y_3),\ release>$$

could result, for example, in direct selection and repositioning of the line that has already been drawn:

$$<...,\qquad,\qquad,\qquad>$$

Modelling direct manipulation interaction with this type of function is only possible if the application retains knowledge of the physical locations of its objects, for example that the line's endpoint is at (x_1, y_1). This makes the application difficult to separate from its user interface.

In addition, in a multitasking environment, no one application fully controls the display, as this semantic function requires. This is because the display in this case is a *shared resource*, and may also be updated by other applications. Multi-threaded direct manipulation interaction modelled by this type of function, therefore, is only possible if the application uses a protected display space such as a window, which can have no interference from other applications.

Thus there is a fundamental conflict between providing *directness*, which requires both knowledge and control of the display, and *separation*, which requires a level of independence of the display. The resolution adopted here is to create an *intermediate* representation, called the *medium*, which has enough knowledge of the display to provide directness, but which communicates with the application only in terms of symbolic references to display objects. Applications thus control output not by drawing directly on the display, as above, but by sending commands to the medium to change the state of their medium objects.

By itself, however, the medium cannot supply the required separation of *behaviour*.

3 The Functional Architecture

We now describe the functional *types* of the components of the *UMA* architecture.

3.1 The Medium

Since to support directness the medium must retain information about the display, and since the numbers of displayed objects may change dynamically, it is convenient, without at this level being any more specific, to think of the state of the medium as represented by a set of objects. (We can call this the *model* for the display). Consequently, there must be a function which *presents* any particular set of objects (O) onto the display:

$$present: set\ of\ O \rightarrow D$$

Conversely, since directness requires that the user can *address* objects visible on the display using a pointer like the mouse, there must correspondingly be a function which *picks* objects in the model given an input pixel location (a component of events I) on the display:

$$pick: I \rightarrow O$$

We consider the medium essentially to encapsulate *state* (the set of model objects O and the display D) and the *pick* and *present* functions. These can be hid-

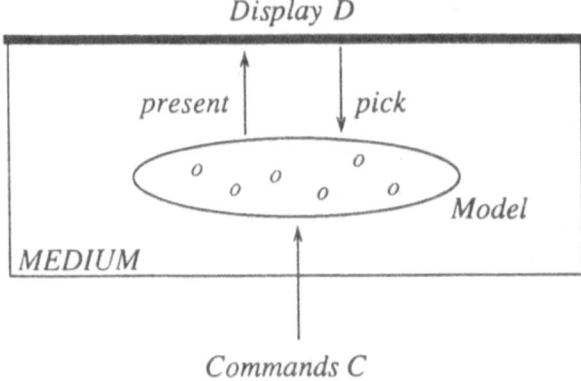

Figure 5. The Medium

den from the application. However, the application must be able to issue commands *C* to create, structure and modify objects in the model. Such a medium is illustrated in Figure 5.

The type of the medium can be expressed:

$$M: seq\ C \rightarrow seq\ D$$

That is, it is a mapping between sequences of commands, and sequences of displays. A typical mapping of this type, which creates a number of objects which can subsequently be referred to in further commands, might be:

$$<create\ (X,\ size_1,\ position_1),\ create\ (Y,\ size_2,\ position_2),\ highlight\ (X)> \mapsto$$

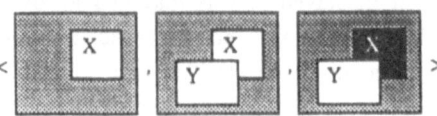

Thus the display is *determined* by the sequence of commands to the model (in practice the medium also needs to generate return values for queries and object creation). Note, however, that the *source* of the command is immaterial, in the sense that the medium can handle interleaved commands from any number of applications.

Clearly, the richness of the model will be critical to the power of the medium to generate displays suitable for a wide variety of applications. In a window manager the objects may simply be windows, but other systems may preserve graphical/textual models of greater complexity and granularity, as for example in *Presenter*.

3.2 The Application

If the medium model has sufficient granularity, all an interactive application needs to know is the current user input i (keypress, mousepush, etc.) and the medium object o upon which the input occurred. Similarly, all the user needs to know *from* the application can in principle be conveyed by the effect of its output commands C. A general application A can therefore be defined as taking sequences of *(input, object)* pairs, and generating commands to the medium:

$$A: seq\ (I \times O) \rightarrow seq\ C$$

For example, given the state of the medium at the end of the above example, the application could determine that a user mouse *press* event on object Y denoted deletion of that object, and so send a *delete* command to the medium:

$$<..., (press, Y)> \mapsto <..., delete\ (Y)>$$

resulting in:

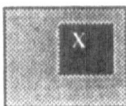

Because the precise display states are hidden from the application, it can ignore the presence of other application objects on the medium.

3.3 The User Agent

Thus we have refined the abstract interaction function into two components, the medium M and the application A. This formulation is deficient, however, in two respects:

- It does not explain from where the application gets *(input, object)* reports.

- It requires the application to manage *all* its interaction, from simple echoing to complex semantic responses.

Although the latter is the case for many window-based applications, one of the main premises of this architecture is that it is possible to make an effective separation in the *behaviour* of objects between that which is caused solely by the user, and that which is caused by the application. In order to effect this separation of behaviour we need to abstract some *control* from the application, and so a third component in the architecture is necessary: the *user agent*. This monitors all user input, and manages

- *surface* interaction by interpreting user actions as direct commands to the medium. Thus a mouse drag may be interpreted as a *move* or *size* command on a medium object, without involving the application.

- *deep* interaction by constructing *(input, object)* pairs from user actions and *picks* on the medium, and reporting these pairs to the application.

We can thus define the type of the user agent (*U*):

$$U: seq \, I \rightarrow seq \, (deep \ll I \times O \gg \, | \, surface \ll C \gg \,)$$

U takes a sequence of user inputs, and generates either *deep* or *surface* actions. The deep actions consist of input reports to the application in the form of *(input, object)* pairs, whereas the surface actions consist of commands to the medium. Together, the medium and the user agent form an *active medium*, or surface.

Even though the principle of surface separation allows some manipulations of surface objects to be performed without involving the application, we cannot know in advance *which* manipulations will be irrelevant to an application. Each application must therefore be able dynamically to determine which input, on which objects, should be reported to it, and conversely which input should be handled autonomously within the surface. At the extreme, it must be possible for an application to request reports of all input, and so take full control of interaction. We therefore allow the application to encode its interactive requirements dynamically as attributes of the surface objects themselves. These attributes are interpreted by the user agent when deciding whether to report input. For example, the application may require that a *move* event on an object representing a slider button be reported to it, but a *move* event on a dialogue box not be reported although its action may go ahead through surface interaction.

We have refined the abstract interaction function given in Section 2 into three essential functional components: a medium *M* interpreting commands as display changes, an application *A* receiving *(input, object)* reports and generating commands to the medium, and a user agent *U* interpreting input in the context of the current display, and either sending input reports to the application, or causing surface interaction by sending commands directly to the medium.

4 The Communication Architecture

The formulation so far tells us simply about the *functionality* of these components. It does not describe any necessary communications or synchronisations between them, for example to ensure that the display against which input is interpreted is the current display, or that input alternates with output. To do this precisely we use a different formalism, CSP [8]. Processes in CSP are modelled simply in terms of the sequences of events (traces) in which they are prepared to engage. Communication is described by an algebra over the traces.

This description of the mechanics of separation using an active medium or surface is therefore completed by a specification of how the functional components communicate with each other, and what sequencing and synchronisation constraints apply. This *UMA* architecture is illustrated in Figure 6.

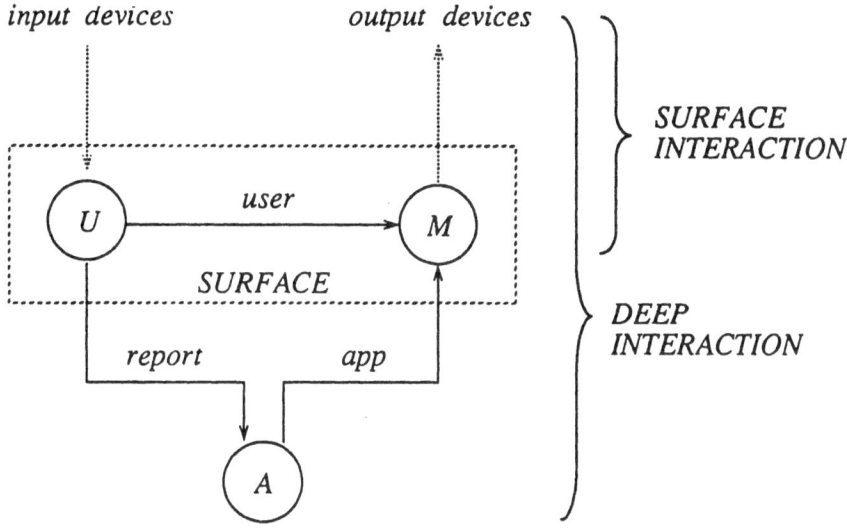

Figure 6. The *UMA* Architecture

The solid arrows here are channels, and show the directions in which communication is initiated. Each communication may also have a reply in the opposite direction, but the synchronisation is such that we do not need an explicit channel for these. Broadly, the diagram illustrates the potential for both surface interaction (input → *user* channel → output) and deep interaction (input → *report* channel → *app* channel → output).

4.1 The Medium *M*

We start by defining the behaviour of the medium *M*:

$$M = user?c \rightarrow r \rightarrow M \mid app?c \rightarrow r \rightarrow M$$

This shows that the medium is purely passive, since it just inputs (? in CSP) commands c (of type C), and then responds with a reply r (of some suitable reply type). This it does repeatedly (the definition is recursive). It accepts commands either from the user agent (via the channel *user*) or from the application (via the channel *app*). These may be arbitrarily interleaved. However, *M* cannot be *interrupted*, since it sends out a reply before it will accept the next command.

4.2 The Application A

In specifying the application we wish to accommodate either user-driven interaction (for example during direct manipulation), or application-driven interaction (for example during animation or process monitoring), or a mixture of these interaction modes:

$$A = report? \ (i, o) \rightarrow \mu X . (app!c \rightarrow r \rightarrow X \ \sqcap \ (i', o') \rightarrow A)$$
$$| \ app!c \rightarrow r \rightarrow A$$

Thus the application A is the process which cycles over two sub-traces:

- it accepts an input report of the form (i, o) from the user agent (along channel *report*). Thereafter it can send (! in CSP) along channel *app* as many commands to the medium as it likes (X is a nested process), before returning the (possibly modified) input report (i', o') to the user agent. *When* it does this is not determined by the readiness of the user agent to receive the report (we see below that the user agent waits for a reply in any case), but by the semantics of the application itself. The choice to reply to the user agent is thus non-deterministic ($\sqcap$), and the application can use this to block the user agent while it makes display changes.

- it spontaneously sends a command c to the medium along channel *app*.

4.3 The User Agent U

Finally, the user agent U has the most complex behaviour. Its activity is always driven by an input event i from the user:

$$U = i \rightarrow user! \ pick(i) \rightarrow o \rightarrow$$
$$(user!c \rightarrow r \rightarrow U \qquad\qquad \text{[surface]}$$
$$\sqcap \ report!(i, o) \rightarrow (i', o') \rightarrow user!c \rightarrow r \rightarrow U) \qquad \text{[deep]}$$

U then sends a *pick* request to the medium with i as a parameter (we assume that $pick(i)$ is one of the commands in C, and that the medium replies in this case with the picked object o). Depending on the attributes of o, U can then initiate either surface or deep interaction. Again, the choice between these is not determined by the readiness of either M or A to receive input, but by the semantics of the user agent, and thus is non-deterministic. The choice is:

- Surface interaction: the attributes of object o determine that input i on it is not to be reported to the application, so U converts i immediately into an appropriate command to the medium.

- Deep interaction: the attributes of object o determine that input i on it must be reported to the application, so U composes an input report (i, o) and sends this along the *report* channel to the application. It then waits for the application's reply *(i', o')*, which might modify either the input or the target object. Upon receipt, *U* interprets this as a command to be sent to the medium. (This specification omits some optimisations. For example, it is unnecessary to make repeated *picks* during a sequence of *drag* events, since the dragged object presumably remains the same.)

In all these definitions, note that the trace types of the CSP processes *U*, *M*, and *A* conform with the types of their associated semantic functions (of the same name) defined in Section 3.

4.4 Behaviour

Communication between these components occurs when they are run in parallel:

$$U \parallel M \parallel A$$

Surface interaction takes place when the user agent sends commands directly to the medium. Deep interaction takes place when the user agent reports input and its *picked* object to the application. The choice between these is determined by the attributes of the *picked* object, as interpreted by the user agent.

Application control of the surface can be achieved by three mechanisms (in order of increasing behavioural separation):

- The application can modify its surface objects by direct commands to the medium. This it can do either spontaneously, for example to create animation, or in response to input reports from the user agent.

- The application can modify the actions of the user agent by modifying the input report it returns. For example, the application can veto user selection of a menu item by returning a null input report to the user agent.

- The application can simply determine the actions of the user agent in advance by making suitable attribute settings on its objects. This sort of control has a declarative nature, implemented by constraints built in to the user agent.

The last mechanism is clearly dependent upon the semantics of the user agent. [23] describes one set of general textual and graphical operations for this. However, the *UMA* architecture is not prescriptive about the semantics of any component.

4.5 Synchronisation

All internal communications in the architecture are *synchronous*, that is, the sender blocks while waiting for a reply. This guarantees the integrity of the internal states of the user agent and the medium, since neither can be interrupted. This is not as restrictive as it may sound. Asynchronous events, either from the user or from the application, can be buffered at the periphery of the architecture. We regard this as an implementation issue rather than as fundamental. If the application or user chooses not to wait for a reply, that is their prerogative. If needed, the application can delegate agents to handle communication queues. On the other hand, the slow-

Figure 7. Dragging an Icon to the Dustbin

ness of synchronous communication between the surface and the application, particularly over a network, is offset by the reduced number of calls that need to be made (see the following example).

When the architecture is extended to allow multiple applications, then the scheduling of input to applications is effectively carried out by the user. Input reports can be routed to the target application by the user agent on the basis of application ownership of a current object, determined by the position of the mouse or by some previous user selection. On the other hand, if there are a number of applications directly communicating to the medium, then their output must be scheduled by the medium in order to ensure fairness (i.e. so that no application hogs the medium).

5 An Example

As an example of surface interaction on an active medium, consider the case of dragging a file icon onto a dustbin, where it is deleted (Figure 7.).

Here the only *deep* action is the deletion of the icon, which may entail deleting a file, for example. The *dragging* of the file icon towards the dustbin icon, on the other hand, is a manipulation that can be carried out entirely at the surface (we assume the medium supports discrete objects and *move* operations on them). The application therefore sets the file icon to be movable, but to report only mouse button *release*.

Traces of this interaction are represented in Figure 8. We assume that the file icon (*f*) starts under the cursor, and that the application already knows the identity of the dustbin icon (*dustbin*). The arrows represent communication. Notice that they form a single linear trace which represents the sequence of events in the interaction of the three components.

These traces show surface interaction taking place initially between the user agent and the medium to highlight and then drag the file icon. The first input report

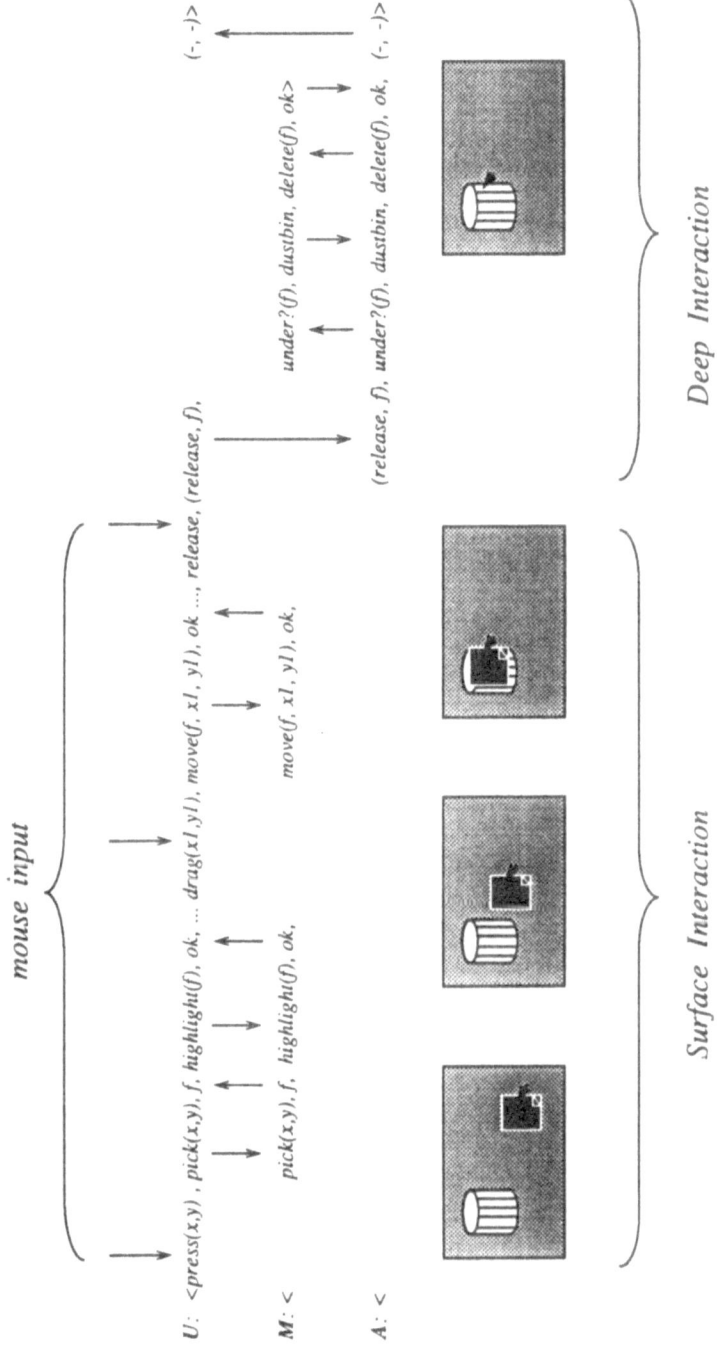

U : ⟨*press(x,y)* , *pick(x,y)*, *f*, *highlight(f)*, *ok*, ... *drag(x1,y1)*, *move(f, x1, y1)*, *ok* ..., *release*, *(release, f)*,   *under?(f)*, *dustbin*, *delete(f)*, *ok*⟩   (-, -)⟩

M : ⟨   *pick(x,y)*, *f*, *highlight(f)*, *ok*,   *move(f, x1, y1)*, *ok*,

A : ⟨   *(release, f)*, *under?(f)*, *dustbin*, *delete(f)*, *ok*,   (-, -)⟩

mouse input

Surface Interaction

Deep Interaction

Figure 8. Surface and Deep Interaction in a Trace of *UMA*

to the application, *(release, f)*, which initiates deep interaction, is on button release. The application then enquires what object is under the file icon *f* using the medium command *under?*. Since this is the dustbin, the application takes the deep decision to delete the file. This also requires deleting the object *f* from the surface, which the application does using a *delete* command to the medium. Finally the application returns a null input report *(-, -)* to unblock the user agent.

6 Conclusions

This paper reconciles the essential requirements of directness and separation within an abstract model of interaction, and thus derives a generic architecture (*UMA*) for constructing effectively modularised direct manipulation systems. The architecture is centred on an *active medium*, which encapsulates a display model, and can (through a specialised user agent) abstract semantically irrelevant behaviour from applications. Thus the active medium has its own semantics and control.

UMA is generic in two senses. Firstly, since only the *types* of the semantic functions for the components are defined, any particular semantics for these could be instantiated in the architecture. This is clearly needed in the case of applications, since we want to accommodate any application semantics. But it also allows different models for the medium and the user agent to be developed. It also gives the capability to describe existing user interface systems. For example, a window manager can be modelled as a medium consisting of windows and operations such as *open* and *close*, and a user agent which routes input either to the desktop or to the application. A UIMS can be modelled in *UMA* by extending the semantics of the user agent to include a dialogue interpreter. Similarly, the medium could be specialised to include a set of toolkit objects.

Secondly, *UMA* is generic in its *behaviour*, since it can accommodate both internal (application-driven) and external (user- or event-driven) modes of interaction [21], as well as full concurrency between application and interface [12].

At the same time, *UMA* is also precise enough to act as a template for implementation. This is borne out by the existing system *Presenter* and its many applications (although *Presenter* does not conform entirely with *UMA*). *UMA*'s modularisation of the behaviour and semantics of the surface into user agent and medium respectively, and the precision of its communication scheme, make it a useful basis for implementation of a wide range of surface models.

Finally, *UMA* allows the surface to be supported by a separate process, distributed from its applications. The surface model can therefore be made *persistent*, in the sense that surface objects are not then tied to the lifetime of the application which creates them. Interactive surface editors like [9], which create interface components for application use, are thus easily built. In theory also surface objects can act as communication tokens between different users and applications. This aspect of the architecture has yet to be explored.

References

[1]   A. P. Cobbett & I. C. Wand, "The Debugging of Large Multi-Task Ada Programs," *Proc Ada UK Conference*, University of York (September 1989).

[2]   W. Daly, "A Graphical Management System for Semantic Multimedia Databases" (PhD Thesis), University of York (1989).

[3]   A. J. Dix & C. Runciman, "Abstract Models of Interactive Systems," *BCS Conference Proc. "People and Computers: Designing the User Interface,"* P. Johnson & S. Cook (eds.), Cambridge University Press (1985), 13-22.

[4]   A. J. Dix, "Formal Methods and Interactive Systems: Principles and Practice"(PhD Thesis), University of York, Dept. of Computer Science (1988).

[5]   A. Dix, "Abstract, Generic Models of Interactive Systems," *People and Computers IV: Proc. HCI '88*, D. M. Jones & R. Winder (eds.), Cambridge (September 1988), 63-77.

[6]   S. W. Draper, "Display Managers as the Basis for User-Machine Communication." *User Centered System Design*, D. A. Norman & S. W. Draper (eds.), Lawrence Erlbaum (1986), 339-352

[7]   M. Harrison & A. Dix, "A State Model of Direct Manipulation in Interactive Systems," *Formal Methods in Human-Computer Interaction*, M. Harrison & H. Thimbleby (eds.), Cambridge (1990), 129-151.

[8]   C. A. R. Hoare, "Communicating Sequential Processes", Prentice-Hall International (1985).

[9]   S. Holmes, "Overview and User Manual For Doubleview," University of York Dept. of Computer Science, Tech. Rep. No. YCS109 (1989).

[10] S. E. Hudson, "UIMS Support for Direct Manipulation Interfaces," *ACM Computer Graphics* 21(2) (April 1987), 120-124.

[11] E. L. Hutchins, J. D. Hollan & D. A. Norman, "Direct Manipulation Interfaces," *User Centered System Design*, D. A. Norman & S. W. Draper (eds.), Lawrence Erlbaum (1986), 87-124.

[12] K. A. Lantz et al., "Reference Models, Window Systems, and Concurrency," *ACM Computer Graphics* 21(2) (April 1987) 87-97.

[13] J. M. McCarthy & V. C. Miles, "Elaborating Communication Channels In Conferencer," *Proc IFIP WG8.4 Conference on Multi-User Interfaces and Applications* (May 1990).

[14] "NeWS Manual", Sun Microsystems (1987).

[15] "User Interface Management Systems," G. E. Pfaff (ed.), Springer-Verlag, Berlin (1985).

[16] R. Pike, "The Blit: a multiplexed graphics terminal," *AT&T Bell Labs technical Journal* 63(8) (October 1984), 1607.

[17] R. W. Scheifler & J. Gettys, "The X Window System," *ACM Trans. Graphics* 5(2) (April 1986), 79-109.

[18] B. Shneiderman, "The Future of Interactive Systems and the Emergence of Direct Manipulation," *Behaviour and Information Technology* **1**(3) (1982), 237-256.

[19] B. Shneiderman, "Direct Manipulation: A Step Beyond Programming Languages," *IEEE Computer* **16**(8) (1983), 57-69.

[20] B. Sufrin & J. He, "Specification, Analysis and Refinement of Interactive Processes," *Formal Methods in Human-Computer Interaction*, M. Harrison & H. Thimbleby (eds.), CUP (1990), 153-200.

[21] J. J. Thomas & G. Hamlin, "Graphical Input Interaction Technique Workshop Summary," *ACM Computer Graphics* **17**(1) (January 1983), 5-30.

[22] R. K. Took, "Surface Interaction: A Paradigm and Model for Separating Application and Interface," *Proc CHI '90* (April 1990), 35-42.

[23] R. K. Took, "Surface Interaction: Separating Direct Manipulation Interfaces from their Applications" (PhD Thesis), University of York Dept. of Computer Science (1990).

Surface Interaction*:
A Paradigm for Object Communication.

Peter Williams
Hewlett-Packard Laboratories
Filton Road, Bristol BS12 6QZ
England

Abstract

When real objects interact, they directly alter each other's state. In graphical user interfaces, users "directly" alter the state of objects in an information system. It is difficult to model "natural" interaction using the techniques of conventional object-oriented programming and systems. This paper proposes a model of object interaction which more closely follows the principles of natural interaction. A uniform treatment of object interaction offers benefits in the description, design and implementation of distributed, multi-user, graphical applications.

* The term "surface interaction" was coined by Roger Took in [1] to describe a user interface architecture which was one of the inspirations for this work.

1 Introduction

Object-oriented design and implementation can simplify the construction of distributed, multi-user office systems. Object behaviour results from user input or messages from other objects, but since objects and users do not communicate in the same way, other objects cannot use the same interfaces as users.

In the real world, objects interact by altering each other's state and (perhaps) inducing a reaction. In object-oriented programming, behaviour is a side effect of one object calling another, and state changes are always an *effect* of behaviour, never a cause. A more "natural" model of object interaction, which treated users as objects, might simplify object design, and create opportunities for new types of object communication and integration.

2 The Object Model

Before we can talk about interactions between objects, we need a consistent notion of object. The model adopted here is simpler than those generally used in object-oriented programming, but provides a better basis for describing a user as an object. It borrows heavily from a formal model of objects developed in [2].

In this model an object is a concrete, uniquely identifiable combination of changeable state and behaviour, with which other objects interact. We can classify objects by their behaviour, but object classes are not, themselves, objects.

2.1 Object State and Behaviour

Objects have properties by which we identify them, and properties are of two types - state properties (or **attributes**) and behavioural properties (or **laws**). The values of an object's attributes collectively comprise its state, and are a key determinant of its future behaviour. The laws of an object define the states it can be in. An object has lawful and unlawful states, and for each unlawful state the laws specify an unique lawful state to which it must change. A set of objects having the same laws is sometimes called a **natural kind** in Ontology, and a **Class** in object oriented programming and systems. Figure 1 depicts an object with its attributes constrained by its laws.

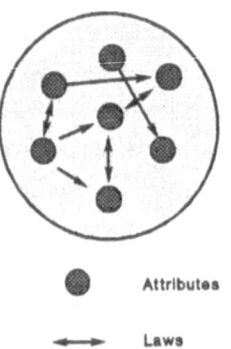

● Attributes

◄—► Laws

Figure 1: An Object

2.2 Interaction

Objects interact by changing each other's state. Two objects which interact have an **interface**. An interface, like an object, has state and behaviour. Its state is "borrowed" from the states of the objects being interfaced, and its laws partition that state into lawful and unlawful states, defining for each unlawful state an unique lawful state. Interaction occurs when one object's state changes in violation of the interface, and the laws of the interface require a change to the state of the second object to render the interface lawful again. Figure 2 is a schematic of an object interface, showing the interface state and the laws of the interface.

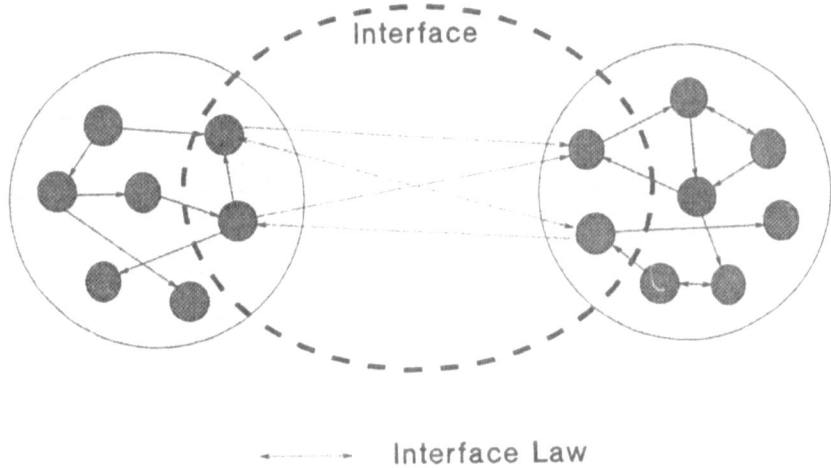

Figure 2: Object Interaction

Objects do not reach unlawful states spontaneously, so object behaviour can only be caused by interaction with other objects. A set of objects closed to interaction will either reach a lawful state or behave in a cyclic manner.

3 Examples

We now use this model to explain two examples of object interaction. The first is from the physical world, the second an interaction between objects in an information system.

3.1 Physical World Example

First, consider a man driving a car about to run over a cat (see figure 3). A man is a complex object, but a car is relatively simple, as is the interface between a man and a car. Let us suppose that the sight of the cat in front of the car puts the man in an unlawful state. The laws of the man require a change to the position of his right foot to render his state lawful.

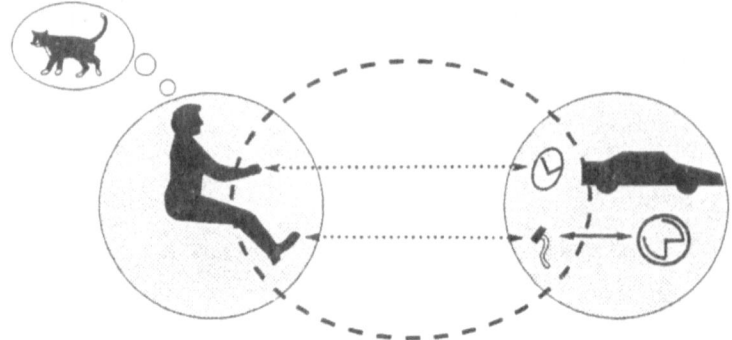

Figure 3: Real World Object Interaction

The attribute "position of right foot" forms part of the man's interface with the car, and the laws of that interface require that the position of the brake pedal and the man's foot be the same. To obey this law the position of the pedal must change - the position of the brake pedal being a property of the car.

The laws of the car now come into play. One of them asserts a relationship between the position of the brake pedal and the pressure on the braking surface. To obey this law, the pressure on the braking surface increases, stopping the car.

3.2 Information System Example

Now consider a spreadsheet of monthly target expenditure which apportions an annual figure over 12 months. If the figure for a given month is explicitly asserted, that month's value is frozen by the spreadsheet, and the remaining budget apportioned to "floating" months. This spreadsheet is an object with state and fairly concisely formulated behaviour.

Suppose we also have a graph object which plots a year's worth of figures by month, and further suppose that this graph has an interface to the spreadsheet whose laws require equality between the monthly figures of the graph and the spreadsheet. When the spreadsheet, the graph and the interface are all in a lawful state, the graph plots the figures in the spreadsheet (see figure 4 below.)

Now suppose that a user moves one of the graph points downwards. This is lawful for the graph, but it renders the interface unlawful, requiring the corresponding spreadsheet value to change. This violates the spreadsheet laws, requiring the budget to be re-apportioned. This, in turn, renders the spreadsheet lawful, but changes 11 properties in the interface, making it unlawful. To render the interface lawful, the corresponding 11 values in the graph change, and the screen display of the graph will alter to show the current budget.

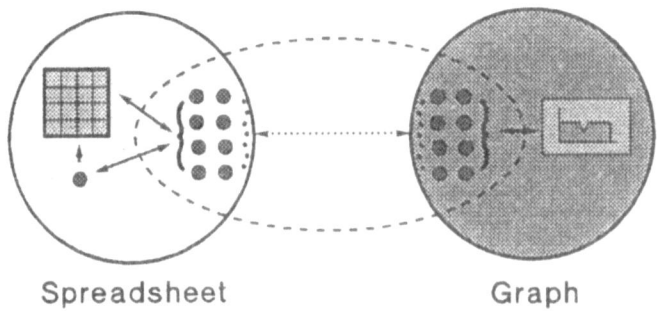

Spreadsheet   Graph

Figure 4: Information Systems Interaction.

3.3 Discussion

The same model has been used to describe information system and real world objects. The model shares some fundamental concepts - such as object, class, instance, state, behaviour and interface - with object-oriented programming [3]. Other programming concepts, such as method, message, and inheritance, do not figure in the model, though they may well be employed in an implementation.

Both of the examples had simple interface laws - selected attributes of one object had their values equated to the values of equivalent attributes in the other. It would simplify implementations of this model if we could always do this.

In general, and certainly in the real world, more complex interface laws are required, but we can build a large class of information systems by limiting interface laws to simple equational constraints. When a system requires more complex interface behaviour, we can define interfacing objects which factor a complex interface into two simple ones, as shown in Figure 5. The physical world abounds with interface objects - simple machines such as levers and pulleys being obvious examples.

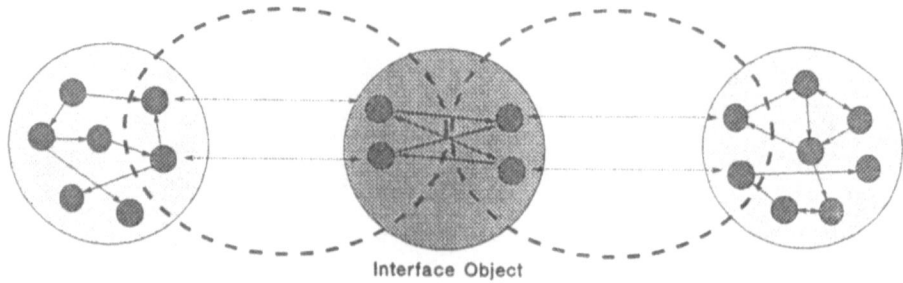

Interface Object

Figure 5: Factoring Interfaces.

4 Surfaces

Every object in this model has a subset of its state devoted to interfaces to other objects. These are the properties whose values can change and be changed by the values of the properties of other objects. We call this subset of an object's state its **surface**. Objects communicate with their environment by changing, and by responding to changes to, their own surfaces. We can think of an object as being "on" the surface of another if there is currently an interface between the two. Figure 6 is a redrawing of figure 2 showing the interface between two objects in terms of their surfaces.

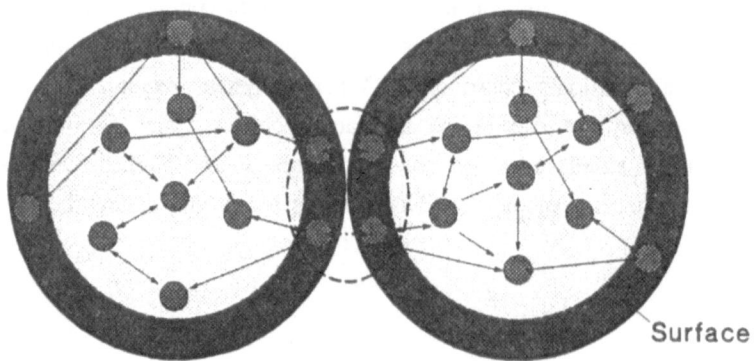

Surface

Figure 6: Object Surfaces

5 User Interfaces

The interface between a user and an object equates properties on the user's surface with properties on the object's surface. A user can now be modelled as an object in the system, with laws which map its surface values to a display, and transducer events (keyboard, stylus, and mouse input for example) to surface changes. Thus it is the user object which converts transducer events to display changes, as well as changing (the surfaces of) objects to which it is interfaced.

The user object and its interface to an application object are shown in figure 7. Note that the surface of the user object is abstract. The function of the user object is to map the physical world of display screens and transducers to and from this abstract surface.

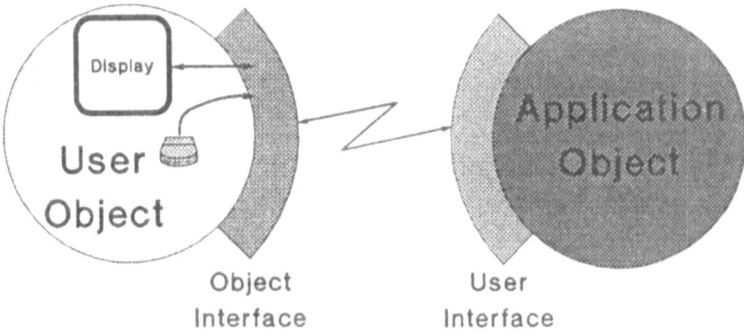

Figure 7: User Interaction through Surfaces

In effect, the screen becomes a medium of communication between user and application objects - other objects do not "see" transducers or displays, they only process changes to their own surfaces induced by changes to the user's. Changes they make to their own surfaces will cause changes to the abstract user surface by virtue of the laws of interface, and hence to the screen by virtue of the laws of the user object.

6 Advantages

Apart from offering a different way to model object interaction, why might this architecture be attractive for user interfacing? There are several reasons:

1. Direct Manipulation and Consistency.
2. Distribution.
3. Multiple users.
4. Rationalisation of Interfaces.

6.1 Direct Manipulation

In a direct manipulation interface, a user controls an object by editing its appearance, *using editing gestures which are independent of the object*, until it looks as he wants it to be. In our model, the set of gestures a user can generate are behavioural properties of the user. The effect of the gestures on their target are determined by the laws of the target object.

In an implementation conforming to our model, therefore, the user changes his own electronic "surface", which induces equivalent changes in objects connected to the user's surface at the point where it is changed. The state and behaviour of user objects is defined by the laws of *users*, and objects which interface to users must have surface properties compatible with user surface properties at the point of connection. This means that the part of an object's surface devoted to its user interface has a "standard" behaviour, and can be implemented once for all objects.

Other user interface architectures propagate transducer events to the application and expect the application to generate compatible visual feedback. In effect, the manipulations a user can perform become properties of the object he is manipulating. Because the feedback can vary from application to application, an important characteristic of direct manipulation - the application independence of the gestures - is at risk. The immediacy of the direct manipulation feedback can also be impaired, an effect which is particularly pronounced in distributed systems.

6.2 Distribution

The main effect of distribution on user interfaces is latency. Latency over a small fraction of a second, or worse still variable latency, changes the nature of an interface. While we may prefer direct manipulation interfaces, they are difficult to achieve over wide area networks.

In a surface interacting system, the user is never remote from his own surface, so any change he makes to it occurs immediately. With other architectures, the visual effect of an action is delayed by the communication network. Anyone who has held down the backspace key to erase a word when editing remotely understands this problem all too well. To be successful, the user has to imagine an effect he cannot see, which fundamentally alters the nature of the interface so that it is no longer "direct." With surface interaction, the visual effect of the changes made by the user appear immediately.

Technically, the network propagating the surface change is itself an object (or rather a very large sequence of objects) whose behavioural impact on the propagation cannot always be ignored. The user changes the surface through which he observes the object of his attention. That object may, of course, be in a different state than he perceives, because of delay to the propagation of its latest change.

6.3 Multiple Users

In a distributed system whose user model is object-oriented we will naturally strive to achieve a measure of "objectivity." If there is an objective world, which is the pragmatic assumption of most of our behaviour, it is possible for several users to observe the same object, and they will believe that they see the object in the same state. For some reason (possibly the technical difficulty of achieving it) this is regarded as a very special and limited requirement in information systems. This may change as so-called "naive" users of systems with an object-oriented user model start to use distributed systems.

Surface interaction isolates the internal behaviour of objects from their environment. All an object does is change its surface and respond to changes made to that surface. A single surface can be connected to many other surfaces - including multiple user surfaces. Surface propagation alone will ensure that all users see a shared object in the same state at the same time, as shown in figure 8.

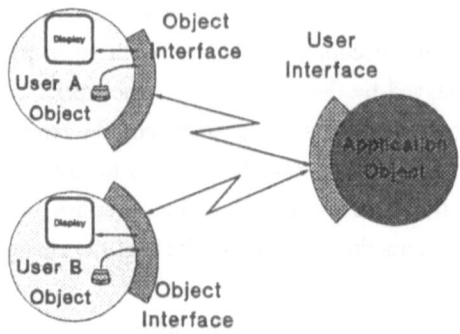

Figure 8: Multiple User Interaction through Surfaces

Architectures which pass transducer events in one direction and drawing primitives in the other are difficult to adapt to this sort of operation. Applications have to keep track of the states of these transducers, and the presumed state of the screen, to provide a direct manipulation interface. It is quite hard to do this for several users simultaneously, because of the need to record multiple user state in the application.

The principles of surface interaction do not deny or avoid the problem of several users making conflicting change to elements of their surfaces which map to common elements of a single object's surface. Suitable augmentation of the protocol used for surface-to-surface propagation only enables such conflicts to be detected. We have found in tests that users do not see this as a problem provided they have some other means of communication (such as a simultaneous telephone conversation) by which to mediate their interactions. This is just as well, since it is not clear that there can be an application independent solution to this problem.

6.4 Rationalised Interfaces

Surface interaction suggests solutions to some important problems in user interface design. The model should, however, apply to all forms of object interaction. If so, then objects other than user objects could connect to those parts of an application's surface devoted to users. Agent objects, using surface interaction, can literally use the same interface as users. Cutting and pasting between applications in windowing environments can be explained in terms of the surface of one object directly changing the surface of another.

More radical is the idea that an object's surface is all user interface(able) - that there are no object interfaces in which a user cannot participate. There are difficulties with this - many, it must be said, to do with adequately simulating current interaction mechanisms using surfaces. The benefit, however, would be enormous, since the surface implementation could be done once for all objects, and writing a new object would be much simpler.

7 Issues and Further Work

If we confine ourselves to user interfaces, surface interaction promises worthwhile benefits. Ideally, we would like to embed user object code into future window managers, but user objects can be built using today's graphical infrastructures. Applying surface interaction to all object interfaces is a more ambitious goal. We have not yet fully tested the hypothesis that surface interaction is sufficient to model all useful classes of object interaction. In particular, we have yet to explain the following phenomena in terms of a surface interaction model:

1. **Navigation** - how do new objects become connected to the user (or any other object's) surface?

2. **Perspective** - how does the user (or any other object) connect different parts of a large or complex object to his surface at different times?

3. **Composition** - how do the surfaces of composite objects connect to each other and to the user's surface?

4. **Binding and Unbinding** - how are compositions formed and re-formed through surface interaction alone?

5. **Creation and Duplication** - how are new objects created through surface interaction?

We have tentative explanations for some of these phenomena, but they continue to provide an interesting research agenda we are keen to pursue and to share with interested parties.

References

[1]   Roger Took, "Surface Interaction: A Paradigm and Model for Separating Application and Interface" in *Human Factors in Computer Systems, CHI '90 Proceedings*, ed. Chew and Whiteside, ACM Press, Seattle, WA. 1990.

[2]   Yair Wand, "A Proposal for a Formal Model of Objects" in *Object-Oriented Concepts, Databases and Applications*, ed. Kim and Lochovsky, Addison-Wesley, Reading, MA. 1988.

[3]   Oscar Nierstrasz, "A Survey of Object-Oriented Concepts", ibid.

HyperCard:
An Object-Oriented Disappointment

Harold Thimbleby* Andy Cockburn, Steve Jones
Stirling University,
STIRLING, Scotland, FK9 4LA.

October 16, 1991

Abstract

Although HyperCard is claimed to be easy to use it has many limitations
and curious features. It is further claimed to be 'object oriented.' This
object orientation is also limited and curious. The disappointment is that
HyperCard's arbitrariness and limitations are technically unnecessary,
indeed result in error prone constructions, slower execution, increased
learning effort. Yet HyperCard is successful: we will never know how
much *more* successful it might have been had its designers employed any
programming language design principles.

1   Introduction

HyperCard is a flexible flat database system with a graphical user interface.
It is user programmable in a proprietary language, HyperTalk, and supports
some object oriented programming possibilities. The purpose of this paper is
to discuss the design of HyperTalk.

For a recent, late 1980s, programming language, HyperTalk is surprisingly
arbitrary, and fails to show any obvious benefit from programming language
design research (see [8] for a tutorial). We can guess: it appears that Hyper-
Talk was implemented by a group of uncoordinated programmers, each being
responsible for his or her own feature, from parsing to implementation. Despite the claims made for HyperCard (in particular in its user manuals which
use 'object oriented' as an explanatory hook), technically, there are no obvious
design rationales.

Following some introductory background material, this paper is structured
first by HyperTalk features, and then it briefly examines HyperTalk's position
with respect to object orientation. To have written the paper 'the other way
around'—to start from object orientation—would have necessitated too many
exceptions and tedious case by case discussion! The lengthy nature of our
criticisms reflects the lack of structure in HyperTalk; and our written criticisms
are by no means exhaustive of its weak features.

---

*Author for correspondence.

1.1 Background

When HyperCard was introduced in 1987 there was a great deal of publicity about the multitude of new possibilities that it presented for Macintosh users. It was ensured a large user-base because it was bundled free of charge with all new Macintosh computers, and was provided at a nominal fee to existing users. So HyperCard has become something of a *lingua franca* among Macintosh users.

HyperCard's roots lie with MacPaint, a painting program, and one of the very first Macintosh applications. Both were designed by Bill Atkinson, indeed HyperCard incorporates the graphical facilities provided by MacPaint, and more: HyperCard also includes facilities for information storage, structuring and recall, which is where its power lies.

> "HyperCard is a new kind of application—a unique information environment for your Apple Macintosh computer. Use it to look for and store information—words, charts, pictures, digitized photographs—about any subject that suits you."
>
> *from the HyperCard user's manual*

HyperCard's innovation was claimed to be the manner in which information could be structured associatively, reflecting human thought patterns (well, that was the idea). The information is presented via a user interface which includes graphics, text, and sound. Various actions can be invoked via mouse clicks, pointing at different parts of the pictures or text, or at *buttons* (which are discussed at greater length below). But the most powerful idea behind HyperCard is that it can be programmed in a fairly simple language, HyperTalk, and a lot of this programming is so simple that the user doesn't think of it as programming. Indeed some common operations can be programmed 'by example' (such as generating the code for a button to link one card to another) and from simple menu choices. More details of the language can be found in [4] and [5].

Thus, when the user's manual says

> "Any piece of information in HyperCard can connect to any other piece of information, so you can find out what you want to know in as much or as little detail as you need."
>
> *from the HyperCard user's manual*

... the "connecting to other pieces of information" is really done by simple bits of program. If a user doesn't like the connections, they can change it—or even get HyperCard to play a little tune instead, or do anything else that the programming language allows.

Interactive systems are notoriously difficult to program well. Casual Macintosh users, therefore, were given the ability to write their own Macintosh programs without much of the time-consuming toil. One of the features of HyperTalk is that it is easy to read: this means that an ordinary user can read other people's working HyperCard programs and very easily convert them to their own purposes.

There are two important practical features in HyperCard to encourage new users. First, much 'programming' can be done by pointing and clicking: the user is 'led' through some programming decisions, and does not need to know the vocabularly and syntax to make simple applications work. More complex features can be provided by coding in HyperCard's language, HyperTalk. Secondly, almost any HyperTalk command can be evaluated interactively (in the *message window*). It's a separate question why *all* commands cannot be executed interactively!

So, creating a graphical interface to demonstrate "what the real system will look like" is as easy in HyperCard as it could be using any system. In addition, interface objects can be made invisible (permanently or under program control), hence letting painted graphics 'show through,' enabling many styles of interaction objects to be simulated if they cannot be programmed directly. We have found that many beginning programmers gain satisfaction from discovering tricks of this sort: in turn, giving HyperCard an enthusiastic following that closer examination of its design does not bear out (see [6] for an example, and [7] for a study).

1.2   HyperCard's interface metaphor

HyperCard is built around a user interface metaphor of a stack of cards (as from a card index). In any stack the cards are the same size, and although real cards are made of stiff paper, it is better to think of HyperCard's as being made from a combination of acetate and paper. A HyperCard card, then, contains picture and text on its transparent 'acetate' layer or *foreground* and picture and text on its opaque 'backing paper' layer, its *background*. The purpose of having two layers is that a background may be shared between several cards, for example, to provide a common graphical theme. The paint graphics in the foreground can be black, white or transparent, so the background can be obscured selectively for particular card designs.

Unlike a real card index, HyperCard's cards may have active objects attached to them, so-called *buttons* and *fields*. In general, an object has associated program, called its *script* which consists of methods, in HyperTalk terms *functions* or *handlers*. In addition to scripts, objects have *properties*, for example, the coordinates of their position on the card.

Mouse actions, such as clicking the mouse button down or up, generate messages that are directed first to the object the mouse is positioned over. This is the primary way in which the user controls a HyperCard system: by moving the mouse over various objects (typically buttons) and clicking.

The card, background and stack itself are also objects. The card is additionally sent messages by HyperCard that are not generated by mouse actions, for example, keystroke messages and general housekeeping messages. Messages pass through the card to its background and then to the stack, and then through a list of stacks, finally to the distinguished stack (*home*) and then to the HyperCard application itself which implements default actions for messages that have not been otherwise processed.

Fields are used for displaying textual information and have several predefined features such as scrolling, opaque, shadow, visible lines. Buttons are more specifically used for carrying out actions when the mouse does something on them (such as being pressed, released, entering their boundaries). As with fields, buttons come from a fixed repertoire of flavours, including rectangular, invisible, iconic (that is, pictorial, and user (but not program!) editable). Fields and buttons can have their size, shape and position manipulated directly with

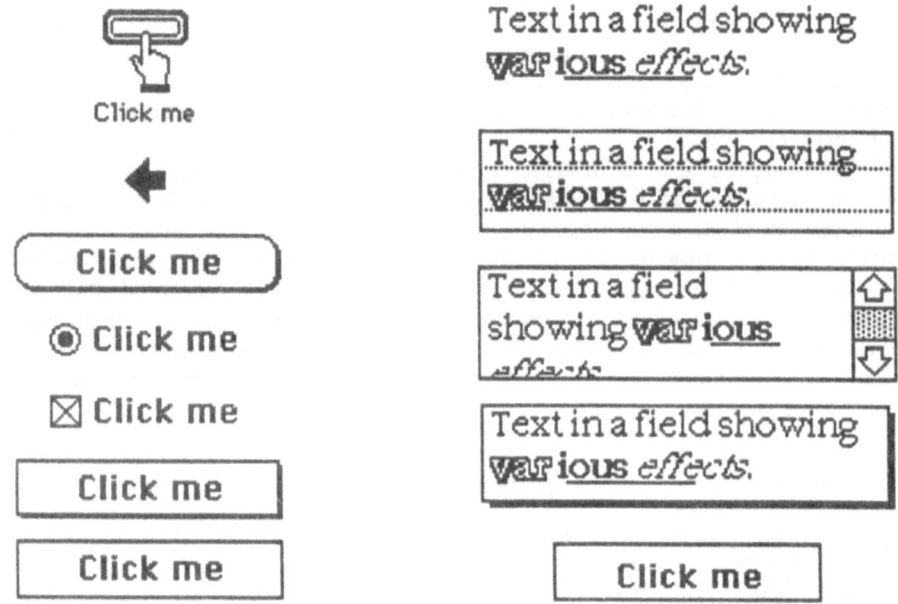

Figure 1: Example styles: button (left) and field (right). Buttons display their name or are entirely graphical (second example from top), fields display arbitary text.

the mouse (in the appropriate editing mode), and if required they can have an associated program, which specifies the actions to do when particular user actions are made.

Note that in the various editing and graphics modes, HyperCard does not send messages, therefore an object cannot know directly that it has been moved or otherwise modified by the user. Of course a development mode is required to debug faulty objects, but the flexibility of direct manipulation for moving objects is intrinsically denied the end user.

Although cards are numbered and arranged sequentially, backgrounds can be shared between non-contiguous cards. The user has various ways to move from card to card, optimised for linear operations (first, previous, next, last) and temporal 'recent' operations, such as 'go back.' Programmers may override this scheme or add alternative methods.

1.3 "Doing things at once"

HyperCard has the advantage that ideas can be added, bit by bit. There is no restrictive idea of 'the' program that has to be got completely right before it can be tried out: the user can change or add bits here-and-there as the fancy takes them, and try them out as they go along. In particular the presentation (graphics, object positions), content (text and/or graphics) and application (programming) can be done in any order, to suit the design process. (Of course this *laisez faire* approach has disadvantages for serious programming.)

A very nice, and distinctive, feature is that everything can be done "at once" [9] (strictly, interleaved, since the user can only do one thing at a time): there is no set order in which a HyperCard program must be written. In contrast, in a conventional programming system, you first have to get the program right, provide its data, and—often the hardest part—design what it looks like. These are three separate and distinct phases of conventional design. Revisions to the overall design plan, motivated by experience or evaluation at any phase, may have unfortunate repercussions on earlier decisions. The problem with a conventional system is that designing what an interactive program should look like is difficult to do until you have had it working and seen (or got prospective users to see) how well it works: maybe it should be changed here or there. And if you do change the program to improve how it looks, this probably upsets some other part of the program. In a conventional programming language, it's easiest not to bother. The result is that interactive programs are often nowhere near as good as they could be. HyperCard, then, provides the opportunity to design better interfaces in an interactive style. A HyperCard programmer is generally happy to modify graphics and layout to suit customers' requirements as they change with experience of use.

1.4   Interaction objects are editable as objects

The amount of time and coding effort required to produce a complete system is greatly reduced because buttons and fields can be copied (including their associated program) between HyperCard stacks and then modified if and where necessary.

There are some example stacks provided with HyperCard and many sources of free and cheap stacks that are easy to obtain. Useful items (buttons, scripts, pictures, and so on) can be copied from them, and work the same way (bugs notwithstanding) in the user's own programs. In these aspects, HyperCard could have been an ideal vehicle for shareware and cooperative program development generally,

2   Syntax

There are many features of HyperTalk which make it attractive for prototyping, that is, getting experimental programs together quickly and easily. The pseudo-English style of HyperTalk attracts experimentation, which makes it easily and quickly mastered; it is vaguely reminiscent of SQL, though less powerful, less systematic and with imperative semantics. Learning HyperTalk doesn't feel the same as learning one of the 'hard' programming languages like C. A typical HyperTalk line might be

```
put "hello" before the first word of customerName
```

On the one hand, the Englishy feel to HyperTalk makes reading scripts very easy; on the other hand, the inevitable fussiness of the "English" means that you never quite know how to say what you mean—there are many little exceptions and idiosyncracies.

You can say **number of cards in this background** but you can't say **number of cards in this stack** (which makes just as much sense). You have to say `number of cards`, since (for some reason) the qualifier 'in this stack' which is allowed in other contexts is not accepted.

2.1 Examples of inconsistent 'English'

- You have to write `item 1 to 5` not `items 1 to 5` as is correct (for English, that is);[1]

- You can refer to the last word of a string s with `last word of s`, you can refer to several words with the form `word 2 to 3 of s`, but you cannot refer to `word 4 to last of s`, which instead has to be written as `word 4 to number of words in s of s`.

- One can say `lock screen` and `unlock screen` and equivalently `set the lockscreen to true` (or `false`); but the recent buffer which can also be locked or unlocked is only controlled by the `set` form. The potential form `lock recent` is not permitted. Similarly for the system message sending (`lockmessages`) for which only a `set` form is provided.

2.2 Examples of inconsistent syntax

Regardless of the claimed 'Englishness' of the syntax, many syntactic forms are internally inconsistent.

A principle that would have made sense is for any expression that takes an index (e.g., `card i` or `card field "x" of card 1`) could be preceded by `number of` and the index (here, `i` and `"x"` respectively) omitted to form `number of cards` or `number of card fields of card 1` respectively; but the latter is not permitted. In conformance with the flavour of HyperTalk, note that we would allow an optional English plural (as in `cards` or `fields`) to improve readability.

This is just one example where orthogonality—a basic syntactic principle—has been lost in favour of *ad hoc* rules. This makes HyperTalk much harder to learn than many other languages. There is no way for the user to generalise his knowledge about the language: each construct *for each class of object* has to be learnt individually. One of the advantages of object oriented languages, polymorphism, is lost even at the syntactic level in HyperTalk.

The operator `number` has other meanings, and this perhaps explains its confusing and limited syntax (though it invites other design questions). Thus if x is an object (rather than an expression) `the number of x` obtains the number of that object. Hence `number of this card` yields a number, being the number of this card within the stack. Yet `number of this card in this background` gives the *same* value as `number of this card`, say 2—despite `go card 2` and `go card 2 of this background` which generally go to different cards! The issue is that `number of` an object gives the value of that property (the number) of that object, which is the same regardless of the expression evaluating to the object. This example shows there is no way to determine the number of a card (that is, its numerical offset) within a background, since the number

---

[1] The selector `menuitem` selects items from menus (since the context is unambiguous, it could have been `item`): however constructs of the form `menuitem 1 to 5` are not permitted.

property of a card gives its offset in the stack regardless. The opportunity for a conceptually simplifying identity law has been lost on HyperTalk.

Again, the **there is** a predicate should be able to work with any object expression, but it cannot. For example, although **go card 10** and **go card 10 of stack x** are both correct expressions, only **there is a card 10** is acceptable.

Dangling else

HyperTalk has 'dangling elses.' There is no need for a modern language to suffer from this confusing problem! HyperTalk suffers with panache.

The syntax of the HyperTalk **if** command is defined as follows:

if *condition* **then** *statement* [**else** *statement*]

if *condition* **then** *statement*
[**else** *statement*]

if *condition* **then**
  statement-list
[**else**
  statement-list]
end if

if *condition* **then**
  statement-list
else *statement*

The reference manual further requires that a nested multiple-line **if** must have its own **end if**. However, this is not a sufficient condition as the following example (which is accepted by the implemented parser) shows:

if c_1 **then**
  if c_2 **then** s_1
else s_2

This, containing a nested *single*-line **if**, has two possible parse trees (one of which is incomplete). Since by definition HyperTalk disambiguates with the rule that **else** associates with the nearest preceding **if**, in this case, depending on the intended meaning, one is required to write either:

    if c_1 **then**   **if** c_1 **then**
      if c_2 **then**   **if** c_2 **then** s_1
        s_1 or   **else**
      end if s_2
    else s_2 **end if**
                            end if

Surprisingly the following example is correct despite the **else** association rule: a comment (taken from the symbol '--' to the end of the line) contributes a 'statement,' making the **else** associate with the first **if**:

```
if c₁ then
  if c₂ then s₁
  --

else s₂
```

The following forms are allowed in practice, as is reasonable, but are not defined in the manual:

```
if condition then statement          if condition
else                                 then statement
   statement-list                    else
end if                                  statement-list
                                     end if
```

2.3 Syntactic sugar

The language definition claims to allow the *f* and *f*() as alternatives, but *only* if *f* is a built-in function (such as time). Yet the long time has no equivalent using the () form! In practice, however, if the user has redefined a built-in function, say time, then time() obtains the value of the user's function but the time still returns the value of the built-in function—so the forms are *not* equivalent. Although the user can override built-in functions like time with their own definitions, they cannot simulate modifiers (like time's long and short).

2.4 Abbreviations and synonyms

Most HyperTalk keywords can be abbreviated. Some synonyms permit US or UK variant spellings, such as hilited and highlighted; on the other hand, sharedhilite has no English variant.

Thus background can be written bkgnd or bg; card can be abbreviated cd. There are a large number of abbreviations, and there is no systematic rule for their derivation. The shortest abbreviation for card is cd; the shortest abbreviation for background is bg; yet the shortest abbreviations for button and field are btn and fld respectively. Finally, some words only occur in a (partially) abbreviated form, such as editBkgnd (but not editbg or editbackground as might be expected from the abbreviations for background). Button is an abbreviation for card button, but field is an abbreviation for background field. Some words are abbreviated one way, others another (the word abbreviated itself can be abbreviated as abbr[ev[iated]]).

Some words are alternatives, e.g., in and of are synonyms in some contexts, for example: word 5 of x can be written word 5 in x. The of in function applications, however, such as number of has no synonym. Or is and = are synonyms (x = 5 and x is 5 are equivalent); yet though 5 is a number is correctly interpreted as true, 5 = a number causes an obscure error.

2.5 Object naming

Although fields and buttons are conceptually very similar HyperCard makes a clear distinction between them, and provides different visual styles for them.

Fields can contain (and display) arbitrary text, whereas buttons can only display their name. A problem for buttons is that their representation to the user has to be the same as their name; one might want, for example, a button either showing 'on' or 'off.' Doing this would mean that the name of the button in the program has to be 'on' or 'off' accordingly, hence encouraging the programmer to refer to it by other, less direct, means.

Since names of objects can be changed, there are several alternative reference mechanisms.

A so-called ID (guaranteed to be unique within scope and over time; IDs are not recycled) can be used, or a number. However, both of these may change as the structure of the HyperCard system develops (even as a program runs), so there is in fact no generally reliable way of referring to objects. For example, card numbers depend on the linear position of a card within a stack, and this is readily changed by resorting or other such operations. The ID of a card may change when it is cut-and-pasted (of course, one or other name inevitably changes when it is *copied*-and-pasted, since this action creates a new object, a copy of the card). Although button and field IDs are supposedly unique per card, the object ID will change when it is pasted to a new card. Curiously, the manual claims only that IDs change when an object is copied.

Apart from the expressions **me** and **target**, then, all object references are variable—and unreliable. Quality programming in HyperCard requires an unusual level of self-imposed programming discipline, either not to change names (which restricts what can be done) or to change them in carefully prescribed ways (which anyway won't be very secure)! Where user requirements call for objects with names that do change (such as the button example mentioned above), there may be no alternative to risky coding.

To confuse matters further, there is no syntactic distinction between object names and numbers: the numeric value 3 is indistinguishable from the character literal "3". Hence **card "3"** refers to a card named 3 yet **card 3** generally refers to card number 3. Consequently if the name of a card is a numeral, ambiguity is inevitable. The obvious work-around is to name objects with non-numeric names, but this can be a problem for some applications (e.g., where a program naturally subscripts the objects), but a constructed name might be used (e.g., X2, which is not a numeral, but can be constructed from an expression such as "X"&n). The problem becomes much more serious when referring to buttons, since the user interface may require a button to be represented to the user as 1, 2, 3: if such names must be visible there is no sensible solution except *ad hoc* simulation using paint graphics.

Clearly both the syntax and semantics of object naming represents a major weakness in HyperCard.

Is there a reliable way to refer to objects? An object can refer to itself using **me**, so long as **me** occurs lexically in the object's script. If the object is a card, background or stack, it can refer to itelf using the form **this card**, **this background** or **this stack**. No other possibilities are reliable.[2]

Further confusion arises since asking for the name of an object that does not have a name initialised instead obtains an expression, and indeed one that cannot be used as a name!

---

[2]The **target** is supposedly the object to which a message is first sent. If a card, however, receives a message, then sends a message to a button, the **target**—whether evaluated in the button or card—incorrectly yields that button.

- First, consider the normal case, when a card has a name, **x**, say. The expression **short name of this card** obtains the value **x**, and this may naturally be used in an expression such as **card short name of this card**. (The alternative form **name of this card** obtains the expression **card "x"**.)

- Now, suppose we have just created a new, as yet unnamed, card. The expression **the short name of this card** obtains a value like 'card ID 4523.' Yet as the expression **card card ID 4523** fails, one asks why the name couldn't have been returned as simply **ID 4523**, or—since there is a method to obtain an ID—that **the short name of this card** should return an empty string: the card supposedly has no name!

In short, the potential identity: **card the short name of this card** ≡ **this card** fails, and, indeed, there is no way to determine whether a card has a name or not. Things are further confused if an object name happens to be, say, **card ID 123**, which would be the outcome of executing **set the name of this card to the name of this card**, or equivalent.[3]

3 Semantics

Such HyperTalk confusions are syntactic; there are plenty of semantic confusions too. For example, and not exhaustively,

- **put x & return after last line of x** loses the return character if **x** contains just one line.

- Dividing by zero results in the value **INF**. For example, **put 1/0 into x** puts the value **INF** into the variable **x**. This value may be used further, with the expected arithmetic results: **put x+1 into x** leaves **x** as **INF**. Yet even though **x = INF** is true directly after executing **put INF into x**, executing **put x+1 into x** results in an error (whereas before it worked)—because the numerical value **INF** generated by arithmetic can be operated on as either a number or string, yet the value denoted by the literal **INF** is not treated as a number. By similar methods we can arrange that **x = y** is true, with **x is a number** unequal to **y is a number**. So much for the equivalence of strings and numerals!

  We might also add that the blank characters **space** and **return** are treated as the numeric value 0 and **is a number** is true of both; yet **tab** is not a number.

- Menus are available as a return separated list of menu items. Hence **line 3 of menu "edit"** yields 'Cut,' since cut is on the third line of this menu. Yet a menu is initialised by a command such as **put "Undo,-,Cut,..." into menu "edit"**—which uses commas, not returns: the entire menu is all, apparently, on line 1!

---

[3]One would normally **put the name of this card into** ... a variable which is later used to **set the name of the card to** ...; the statement shown above simply shows clearly the obscurity of HyperCard's approach to naming: setting an object's name to be its own name sometimes changes that name!

- When HyperCard was extended into HyperCard2, an additional property was added to cards, namely a Boolean **marked**. New commands were introduced to test and manipulate this property (e.g., **mark all cards** and **print marked cards**). One asks why only a Boolean (why not a standard variable?), and why only cards?

- It is possible to insert stacks into the inheritance path dynamically. However, a stack is not sent an initialise message when it is placed in an inheritance (*used*) path (so it can't initialise itself).[4] All handlers in a used stack come in scope, so there is no encapsulation: a used stack cannot contain hidden auxilliary handlers. Although a used stack cannot initialise itself or anything else (since it does not know when it starts being used) it does not have access to its own objects, so, apart from menu entries, there is very little it could initialise!

- It is possible for any object, including a used stack, to send messages to other handlers (hence programming a limited form of encapsulation). But the **send** primitive can only send messages to command abstractions, it cannot send messages to functions. Hence function calls cannot be encapsulated.

3.1 Data structures

In general it is not possible to construct data structures, though assuming certain restrictions (that data contains no spaces, commas or returns) it is possible to use **lines**, **words** and **items** to simulate up to three dimensional values; four dimensional arrays of bytes are possible, under the same restrictions (using the additional selector, **character**). Neither structures with named fields (as in Pascal) are provided nor are pointers. Items are always comma-separated substrings; even though some HyperTalk commands use returns and slashes for separators, it is not possible to select items separated by alternative characters. A **word** is normally a blank (space, return, tab) separated substring, unless it contains quote symbols.

Unfortunately, the variables provided by HyperTalk are limited in structure and accessibility; it often becomes necessary to store record components (*fields* in Pascal terminology) in hidden fields—involving a sleight of hand you feel should not be really necessary. Also, this trick changes the number of fields and will therefore impact on the meaning of other code. (For example, a script may want to clear all fields, but if some of these are components serving other purposes then they should not be cleared.) In short, there is no encapsulation for data structures.

3.2 Variable names

Unlike programming languages like C and Pascal, HyperTalk does not need you to declare or even initialise variables. The result is that when you accidentally miss-type a variable, everything may initially run correctly, but be incorrect. Indeed, an uninitialised variable has as its value its own name. This is a

---

[4]In contrast, stacks are sent messages like: **openstack** or **resumestack** when they are opened or resumed.

HyperTalk feature that might well be exploited by a programmer (to get default values),[5] with obvious consequences. This 'feature' results from the design decision that quote marks need not always be placed around string literals (thus "hello" and hello are equivalent, namely the strings hello, *unless* there is an initialised variable called hello). Note that this 'feature' also explains HyperCard's confusion over object names and numbers.

3.3 Generality

Not everything that the user does in HyperCard can be mirrored in Hyper-Talk. Thus there are occasions when the user will say, "I want to get that programmed" but won't be able to. Consider *dialog boxes*—where the Macintosh seizes up until the user does something (clicks on one of the few dialog box button offered). This user interaction is beyond the scope of HyperTalk even though in principle it could have been handled automatically. The result is that a number of facilities are available only to the interactive user and cannot be controlled from programs.

A specific example of a typical dialog box 'missed' by Hypertalk is the one that allows a user to interactively change the paint patterns: from within HyperTalk changed patterns cannot be detected, default patterns cannot be restored. (A user has to do each interactively.) This oversight means that program control of graphics is always unreliable. Given that a HyperCard card can be made to look exactly like a dialog box, a major simplification could have been achieved if they were treated exactly like cards (perhaps on a 'dialog box' background). This would have meant that any feature that could be controlled by the user from a dialog box could have been controlled from HyperTalk in the usual way (such as typing into fields, clicking buttons).

You can cut-and-paste most things in HyperCard (like pictures, buttons, text), but you can't cut-and-paste everything. You can't cut-and-paste backgrounds, for example, and these often contain lots of details that you therefore have to cut-and-paste one-by-one tediously. It is almost possible to write a script that cuts-and-pastes each object on the background: it fails on the graphics cut-and-paste since an attempt to cut may result in a diagnostic that there is nothing to copy (*sic*) and that one should try the background (the diagnostic obviously assumes you have tried copying (not cutting) from the card (not background) image!)

3.4 Error handling

The most severe problem of all is error handling. With some ingenuity and perseverance, the interpid programmer can overcome most problems. But errors still happen! But in HyperTalk, as soon as an error happens, the HyperTalk programmer has all control taken from him. For example, the HyperTalk program wants to copy a picture the user has drawn: but if the user has actually drawn nothing, this is an error. In HyperTalk, you can neither detect this situation to stop the error arising nor recover from it when it does happen—the *user* is given a dialog box and this takes control away from the program!

---

[5] An example is a repeat loop that tests the value of the variable flag, say, by the expression flag="flag" which is true by default until flag is assigned another value.

It would have been really easy for the HyperCard designers to arrange for each error to send a message, error "description of problem" to the object where the error occurs, to see if there is a method written to handle the error. With this approach (as used in Smalltalk) only when HyperCard itself catches the message error should it finally complain to the user. But this was not done, and the result is that any error causes catastrophe—and it is not always possible to 'program around' potential error-making traps.

3.5 Second class graphics

HyperCard has a paint model for graphics. But a HyperTalk program cannot 'see' what has been drawn; and generally the limited range of buttons available is a significant drawback (though a user, not a program, can paint new icons). Creating the effect of a controlled graphical object is difficult and requires tricks, for instance, placing the graphics under a button that can be dynamically made transparent or obscure. Using this method allows a 'one off' graphical button representation but if we want to move or copy the 'object,' then of course the separate items fall apart. Allowing graphical buttons or a whole new graphical object type would solve this major problem.

3.6 Automatic saving

A difficulty that a user (and particularly teams) must overcome is that of HyperCard's automatic saving of alterations. This feature is undoubtedly useful for the normal HyperCard user, avoiding the annoyance of an explicit save at the end of each session but it forces the programmer into the added burden of maintaining an arbitrary back-up regime.

3.7 Program structure

The main problem with HyperCard is the very thing which made it so popular with casual users—it is informal. The chatty, natural features of HyperTalk are not conducive to clear, compact, logically separated code sections and the problems with unstructured and invisible data stores aggravate the situation. The lack of rigour and plausible guidelines on where to locate methods (in the stack, on the background, cards, fields, buttons?) causes erratic, hacked solutions. One ends up with lots of global variables, and the associated difficulties of losing track of where they are initialised, and where they are used. The debugging assistance given to the programmer is minimal (and has its own bugs).

3.8 Variables and persistence

Naturally, data stored in HyperCard fields is persistent, in that it persists from one run of HyperCard to the next. Without this, of course, HyperCard's stacks could hardly function as databases! However, since field contents can be made invisible, they are a way for the programmer to implement persistent variables, whose values are maintained from one run of an application to the next.

HyperTalk provides global variables. Global variables persist during a single run of HyperCard. Thus, running a new application (stack) within the same session of HyperCard starts off with whatever global variable bindings were left by the last stack. Since there is no way for a program to determine what the names the current of global variables are, it is impossible to protect against accidental corruption of other stacks' data (stacks can be run concurrently, and therefore share the global name space).

Additionally HyperCard provides a *single* LIFO stack used for implicit transfer of control (we discuss the explicit go command below). The only operations on this shared data structure are push and pop. Since the LIFO stack is shared, one HyperCard stack can pop and go to a card pushed by another stack. It is possible to pop the top of the LIFO stack into a variable (without the side-effect of a go) to check whether it corresponds to a card in the current stack, but if it does not, push is not permitted to push a card from a different stack. Popping another stack's card is an irreversible error. Had HyperTalk provided a top function, to give the top element of the stack, it would have been possible to detect the error before taking irreversible steps.[6] In short, reliable algorithms cannot be written using push and pop: they can only make sense to the user, who like HyperCard, has a single view of all stacks running.

An obvious, conventional, but missed, solution to such extent problems is that HyperCard variables (including LIFO stacks) should have been instance variables of appropriate objects, for example individual stacks. (We describe below a similar situation, with menus, but having a more immediate impact on the user interface.)

4   HyperCard as a programming environment

HyperCard is an integrated programming environment; external interfaces (so-called *XFCN*s and *XCMD*s) notwithstanding, applications in HyperCard can be constructed entirely within the environment. HyperCard provides a text editor for editing object programs and a very simple debugger. It is also possible to monitor message sending and variable values (incidentally, the only way to determine the names of global variables).

4.1   HyperCard as a prototyping tool

It is a major selling point for Apple that all applications for the Macintosh have the same 'look and feel' through a common graphical interface [1]. Hy-perCard, however, is being used to prototype and create graphical interfaces for the Macintosh, yet does not support the standard objects that make up the Macintosh interface. It does not support a Macintosh-like style of interaction, for example, there is no mouse double-click message.

Experienced HyperCard developers may claim that these problems can eas-ily be solved by using external commands (XCMDs) and external functions (XFCNs). These are pieces of code written outside of the HyperCard environ-ment in another language such as Pascal or C, compiled and then integrated

---

[6]As well as omitting top, HyperTalk does not provide a predicate to test whether the LIFO stack is empty.

into a HyperCard application (using Resedit). This is the kind of activity that users wanted to get away from in the first place! If you have to be a 'real' programmer then nothing has been gained.

4.2 Structuring programs

HyperCard provides no browser; indeed, the basic environment does not provide facilities for finding or printing entire programs. (Utilities can, with some difficulty, be written in HyperTalk.) Since objects can be made invisible (for user interface reasons or to maintain state from one run to another) it is very easy for programmers to loose track of their systems.

When debugging, viewing hidden fields can be complicated, involving HyperTalk commands passed through the message box. If, for example, you can't remember the fields' names (or whether they're on the foreground or background) finding the required field can be very awkward. And hidden fields is only one of many tricks you get led into, trying to circumvent little restrictions that, perhaps, at first seemed to make learning more interesting.

4.3 Compilation

It is clear that many design decisions in HyperTalk mitigate against efficient compilation (e.g., the confusion of literals and names). The very varied syntax and semantics from command to command suggests that there was no systematic attempt at organising HyperTalk. It is no surprise, then, to find that HyperTalk is very slow, even in HyperCard2 which compiles scripts on demand.

4.4 Practical limits

HyperTalk permits recursion, but to a limited depth of only 95 calls (in version B1–2.1). There is no tail recursion elimination. Messages sent from handlers, even when the last thing the handler can do (e.g., using the primitive **pass**), are also very limited (24).

Suppose we have a group of cards on a common background, and we want all cards to go to the next card (perhaps invoking a visual effect, which we don't discuss here). Since HyperCard sends the message **opencard**, we can handle this in the background as follows:

```
on opencard
  -- visual effects, etc. omitted
  go to next card
end opencard
```

Such code may be conceptually simple but it is not reliable! One only needs about twenty cards before a limit is reached and the code fails catastrophically. This code, indeed, is tail recursive: there is no technical reason why, regardless of limited recursion or pending message depth, that it should be so restricted. Given that stacks can have thousands of cards, imposing such unjustifiable limits in the programming language implementation is incomprehensible.

It is possible to program around this particular problem. (One approach is to use global variables to communicate with an **idle** handler in the background.

Since HyperTalk sends the message `idle` when it is doing nothing else, it follows that `idle` will only be invoked when the recursion and message stacks are empty.) But why force programmers to be so sophisticated or devious?

5 Object orientation

We have come so far in our criticisms without mentioning object orientation. The *nice* part of HyperCard's object orientation is that objects (cards, fields, buttons) can be copied, cut and pasted as units. As such the user can operate on them with the standard select/cut/copy/paste/clear operations that are used for text editing. A copied or cut object 'carries' with it its associated program code and other properties (apart from its number and ID).

Pasting an object will generally change the message hierarchy for that object (for example, we might paste a copy of a button onto a different card, or even a different stack), so semantics are rarely preserved following a move. Furthermore, groups of related objects (for example, radio buttons[7]) that refer to each other will be compromised: there is no reliable way to refer to objects that is also unaffected by cut-and-paste operations: IDs and numbers change, and names (even if they are not changed under the normal operation of the objects themselves) may not be unique.

5.1 Graphics

Since HyperCard's graphics model is paint there are no graphical objects as such. Buttons, which are objects, have associated icons (square bitmaps of limited size), and they may be moved under program control to provide very simple animation. However, the graphical design of an icon is *not* under program control (although a program can choose an icon from a given repertoire, it cannot edit one or confirm it has changed the icon to what it expects).

5.2 Assignment

HyperTalk permits components of objects to be either the source or destination of assignments (puts). For example: in the command `put word 3 of x into word 1 of x` the component `word 3 of x` is the source, and the component `word 1 of x` is the destination. This might lead one to think that if you can write `put name of this card into x` that one could equally write `put x into name of this card`. You can't. Instead, a special syntax has to be used for certain properties of objects: as in `set name of this card to x`. In an object oriented language one would have expected operations such as setting the name of an object to have been achieved by sending messages; instead HyperTalk has a special (non-message) primitive (`set`) for this purpose. Users, then, cannot extend or adapt the properties of an object.

---

[7]A button may be highlighted when clicked. Of a group of radio buttons only one may be highlighted. Hence clicking on any button in a group must refer—by ID, name or number—to the highlighting of all other buttons in that group.

5.3 Classes

There is no concept of class; there are exactly five kinds of object (stack, background, card, field, button), not counting menus (see below). The hierarchical relationship between these objects is fixed.

HyperTalk supports a go operation, with a new twist. It is used to change the current card, but in doing so also changes the inheritance path to be through the new card and background (and possibly stack). However, the current method continues to run—meaning that its name bindings change on each go.

It is not possible to subclass objects. For example the common need for a group of mutually exclusive radio buttons has to be programmed explicitly. It would have been preferable to have a radio button class to instantiate as groups of related buttons.

5.4 Messages

Objects may send messages to other objects, either along the current inheritance path or explicitly to named objects. Two object names (*viz*, the object where the currently executing method resides and the object where the last system-generated message originated) can be obtained from primitives.

Since it is not possible to define one's own classes the utility of messages is greatly reduced, and few HyperTalk programs use messages except as procedure calls. A lost advantage of binding methods with a class of objects is that sending the same message to various objects can have a suitable effect (the classic example is sending a print message to, say, an integer or a date). In HyperTalk, if a method to handle a message is positioned in the hierarchy so that different sorts of objects inherit from it, then it will require explicit code to sort out what to do for each sort of object that is the target of the message! In a conventional object oriented language, the method to handle the message could be associated with the class of object concerned.

In HyperTalk, this means that if the programmer wants all buttons (buttons cannot be grouped into subclasses) on a card to respond to a new message cycle, say, then the method for that message must be placed in the *card's* code. Hence all fields also inherit the same message, as does the card itself. The cycle method must then use code to determine whether it was really invoked by a button.[8] Since this requires explicit programming we can hardly call HyperTalk 'object oriented': we can do similar explicit programming in other languages with no pretentions to being object oriented. And in our description of this example we have not mentioned that there are foreground and background buttons on each card, and the syntax to refer to them differs. Hence it follows that, once the method has determined to its satisfaction that it is indeed called from a button, the action it implements in response will have to be written out *twice*, once for the foreground and once for the background cases.

Such are the more easily explained semantic problems of messages. The syntax, too, of message passing is also peculiar. Although message handlers can take parameters containing commas, there is no simple way to send a message that contains parameters including commas or quotes. Thus, what

---

[8]We've already noted that the primitive required for this, the target, is bugged!

might have been written as `send cycle("a,b,c")` to button 2 has to be written: `send "cycle(" & quote & "a,b,c" & quote & ")" to button 2`. It is not possible to send function messages to other objects: `send "put f()"` to ... evaluates f in the current object regardless.[9]

Messages can also be attached to menu items, and the same problem occurs there. We discuss menus next.

5.5 Menus

Conceptually, menus are objects with a carefully prescribed user-behaviour. The user clicks on a menu and it reveals a list of choices, *menuitems*. If the user selections one of the options the corresponding action is invoked.

HyperCard implements this behaviour with *two* alternative mechanisms. The default is that a message `domenu X, Y` is sent to the current card for a menu selection X from a menu Y. The interpretation of a default menu item is under the control of the current card, background and stack (in that order). This has the advantage, perhaps, that the exact meaning of a menu item can be associated with the current context (i.e., the currently displayed card). On the other hand, if the menu really needs a fixed meaning (and not one that can be implemented by a built-in primitive of HyperCard), there is no way to implement it reliably.

The second method is to bind a *menumessage* to the menu item. Now, when the item is selected, HyperTalk will send this arbitrary message along the same path the `domenu` message would have been sent. Despite its name, the menumessage can be a command, in particular a `send` to send the required message to any desired target object.

For some reason, menumessages are restricted to a single line: unlike the code associated with all other objects. Thus it is not possible for a menumessage to check that the target object of a `send` exists, and it cannot be certain to invoke the right handler to check for it! Given that HyperCard permits many stacks to be run together, each possibly with its own menus, reliable menu programming is extraordinarily difficult.

In terms of inheritance, buttons and fields are associated with cards or backgrounds; cards are associated with backgrounds; and all with stacks. Thus, as the user moves from one card to another, if the background changes, HyperCard (naturally!) changes the current inheritance path through the new background. But menus are different. As it were, HyperCard doesn't know about menus, and the programmer has to control them explicitly. Thus it is not possible to associate a menuitem with a particular background, say, so that when the user moves from that background the menuitem disappears (or, better, is sent a suitable message so that it can decide what to do, perhaps overriding the default action).

The consequence of this is that menus and individual menuitems must be controlled explicitly by the programmer. This is a problem of considerable complexity: other stacks, running concurrently, may also alter menus and they may not adhere to any useful conventions. Menus are an object oriented disappointment.

---

[9] One problem is that send effectively applies the function value to its parameters, stopping quoted (verbatim) messages being sent.

5.6 Inheritance

If an object intercepts a message it may still want the default action to occur. HyperTalk provides no way to refer to the immediate inheritor of a message, that is the object that should implement the default behaviour (though one could program it in explicitly—which is the option for languages that are not object oriented!)

The mechanism that HyperTalk provides is **pass** which sends the *original* message on. Thus an object cannot modify the message it handles.

6 HyperCard: an object oriented disappointment

The previous part of this paper described HyperCard from the point of view of features, and served to both introduce HyperCard and to indicate various design criticisms, criticisms with respect to programming language design generally and object orientation in particular. Having provided an overview of HyperCard, then, we now briefly discuss it from the point of view of object oriented design principles.

Uncontentiously following [3], an object oriented system should provide the following functionality. We place a + before features adequately provided in HyperCard and a − before features not provided or badly provided:

− **Encapsulation.** In HyperCard, objects' state are available without restriction. Even the methods of an object may be changed by another object.

+ **Dynamic lifetime.** Objects *can* be created and destroyed as HyperCard executes. (All garbage collection is implicit.)

− **Identity.** Object naming in HyperCard is a mess; names are not unique.

+ **Substitution.** With various provisos, HyperCard objects can be substituted; indeed the cut-and-paste editing takes advantage of this potential.

− **Message.** Messages are provided, with various restrictions, both syntactic and semantic.

+ **Method.** Methods in HyperCard are termed *handlers*.

+ **Receiver and self.** HyperCard permits access to the receiver of a message and the object self, the object whose method is executing. HyperCard uses the expressions **target()** and **me** respectively—note that one is a function, the other a pseudo-variable, and that (as mentioned earlier) **target()** is unreliably implemented.

− **Class and instance.** It is not possible to draw together objects sharing common behaviour.

− **Instance variable.** The only variables provided in HyperCard are local variables (i.e., local to methods), global variables and fields (i.e., database entries). With ingenuity it is possible to use object properties (such as **name**) as an instance variable, but with severe restrictions. Instance variables (e.g., **marked** for cards) are not inherited.

+ **Inheritance.** Inheritance is provided, and is also used as the 'mechanism' to support non-HyperTalk extensions to HyperCard (XFCNs and XCMDs). If a message is not handled by a stack (in the manner described earlier), it is sent to the stack's *resources* which include the XFCNs and XCMDs, then through an ordered list of stacks (which can be dynamically configured) and their resources, then to a final stack ('Home'), to HyperCard's resources, operating system resources, then ultimately to the HyperCard system itself.

− **Multiple inheritance.** Multiple inheritance is simply not provided. A peculiar form of multiple inheritance can be simulated by using go in objects, since this changes the inheritance path, but at the cost of various side effects.

7 Summary

To conclude, HyperCard is very widely used as an application development tool, and this is because of the very real ease with which attractive graphical interfaces can be created using it. Its popularity has proven the need for such a prototying tool.

It is interesting that, even though Apple must be aware of this, they have not developed a tool specifically for this task. Have they missed the chance to exploit a user need, when at the same time they could have made their machine far more accessible as a programming platform? Or, thinking more cynically, do political considerations concerning Apple's investment in Macintosh software development and links with third party developers have a large part to play in this issue?

Apple's own HyperCard stack design guidelines [2] perhaps shows their attitude: excellent as they are for making systems look nice, they say nothing about programming in HyperTalk. And conversely, HyperCard appears designed to break Apple's own user interface design rules (e.g., not handling double mouse clicks). HyperCard systems are doomed, it seems, to look nice but feel terrible when you get down to using them. HyperCard will remain an excellent and inspiring prototyping tool, but a system that just does not go far enough for anything like serious development. Few are the HyperCard programs that you would let anyone else use. *Serious HyperTalk programming requires non-trivial compromises to be made in the user interface.*

HyperTalk is depressing: there are so many missed opportunities that it is impossible to say "HyperTalk fails such-and-such well known principle"— rather, HyperTalk fails principles wholesale. Tony Hoare once said that Algol 60 was so well designed that it was an improvement over many of its successors. Following almost three decades of research and practice, HyperTalk failed to learn anything from the Algol heritage or any other programming language developments. It would not be unfair to say that HyperTalk is a distinct step back over all its predecessors. We dispute the view expressed by Greg Kimberly (of Apple) that "HyperCard's missing features *are* a feature of HyperCard" [7]— unless he means no features are provided except by their absence.

Whatever we think of it, HyperCard *is* a success: it is free and one of the most widely used programmable systems (beating Lotus-123 and BASIC). As

Apple's CEO John Sculley has said, "With HyperCard, virtually anyone can become a software author, producing an information-based application that looks like a professionally designed Macintosh application." That is why it is successful. It is a failure because software authors can produce information-based applications that look, and only look, like professionally designed Macintosh applications.

References

[1] Apple Inc., *Human Interface Guidelines: The Apple Desktop Interface*, Addison-Wesley, 1987.

[2] Apple Inc., *HyperCard Stack Design Guidelines*, Addison-Wesley, 1989.

[3] M. C. Atkins & A. W. Brown, "Principles of Object-Oriented Systems," *Software Engineer's Reference Book*, J. A. McDermid, ed., pp39/1–39/13, Butterworth-Heinemann Ltd., 1991.

[4] Claris Corp., *HyperCard Script Language Guide*, 2nd. edition, 1990.

[5] G. F. Coulouris & H. W. Thimbleby, *HyperProgramming*, Addison-Wesley, in press.

[6] J. Gervich, "How I Learned to Stop Worrying and Love HyperCard," in B. K. Laurel, ed., The Art of Human-Computer Interface Design, pp131–133, Addison-Wesley, 1990.

[7] J. Neilsen, I. Frehr & H. O. Nymand, "The Learnability of HyperCard as an Object-Oriented Programming System," *Behaviour and Information Technology*, volume 10, number 2, pp111–120, 1991.

[8] R. D. Tennent, *Principles of Programming Languages*, Prentice-Hall, 1981.

[9] H. W. Thimbleby, *User Interface Design*, Addison-Wesley, 1990.

An Architecture for HCI in Real-time Systems

A. Burns

Real-Time Systems Group
Department of Computer Science,
University of York, UK

ABSTRACT

Although a computer system cannot ensure that a user will act in a timely manner, it is possible to build systems that will guarantee that information is presented at the correct time, and will act upon user directions within an imposed deadline. A real-time database model is presented that is used to structure all interaction between users and the real-time system. Such a database has absolute and relative temporal consistencies defined. From such a model it is possible to generate the timing requirements for a set of tasks that can be guaranteed to retain temporal consistency in the database. It is shown how the database model can be used to define an appropriate architecture for HCI in this application domain.

1 Introduction

Real-time systems are those in which the time at which events occur is as significant as the events themselves. Failure of these systems can result from a single missed deadline. This paper is concerned with systems that can lead to catastrophic failure, and that have human operations involved in at least some of the real-time activities. Typically the operator has been retained with an active role within the system because a human must be the final arbiter in issues of safety or economic performance. But as Sikorski states[1]:

> *Today, the wide use of automatic systems is radically changing the human operator's behaviour in industrial process control. Formerly, instrument monitoring and control operations were his/her main activities. Now, decision-making and creative problem-solving, especially in emergency situations, have become primary tasks. ... As a result, despite the automation and computerization of control rooms, the human operator has recently become the most unreliable component in industrial processes control.*

The design and operation of the HCI component is thus of critical importance. Dependable systems must address the separate issues of reliability, safety and security. Burns has recently[2] classified inappropriate operator interaction in these terms:

(a)   Failure to take necessary action (reliability)

(b)   Unintentionally undertaking an incorrect action (safety)

(c) Intentionally undertaking an incorrect action (security)

These issues dictate the use of an architecture that separates the HCI Components from the subsystems that are delivering the main functionality of the real-time system. This is a common structure for HCI, but is nonetheless critically important for building dependable systems. Figure 1 illustrates this simple relationship, which will be extended later.

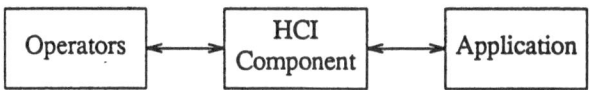

Figure 1: Basic Architectural Structure

The HCI Component can undertake input data validation and identification and authorisation of operators. Hence the Application can assume a *perfect user*[3] and be designed and implemented in a more straightforward way. A perfect user is one that inputs correct data when required and without the need of prompts (i.e. they are reliable, safe and secure). The verified *postcondition* of operator input becomes the *precondition* for the Application.

In this paper we investigate how the perfect user can also be made temporarily correct. We shall consider in the next section the additional constraints that real-time behaviour imposes. A (temporal) database model will then be proposed as the basis for a dependable architecture.

2 Temporal Constraints on HCI

Real-time systems can restrict the time that an operator has to assimilate output and to produce input. There are a number of factors that will significantly affect operator behaviour, including

- Working environment (including issues of morale and training).
- Ergonomics of interface equipment.
- Overall system architecture.

In this paper we concentrate on architectural issues. Four significant temporal interactions will be addressed.

(a) Value of user input (against time).

(b) Time attributes of system output.

(c) Asynchronous mode changes.

(d) Inaccurate or uncertain output.

Each of these issues is considered in turn below.

2.1 Value of user input

In general, events in hard real-time systems have *time-utility* functions associated with them. Figure 2 illustrates a typical case. Assume *Start-time* is the earliest time at which operator input can be delivered to the Application. The operator (process) represented in this figure has, in effect, three thresholds. The first (T1) represents "maximum utility" i.e. the time for the event to have the maximum (positive) impact on the system. The second (T2) defines the time period for at least a positive contribution, whilst the third (T3) signifies the point at which actual damage (negative utility) will be done to the system. This can be interpreted in two (application defined) ways:

- the lack of an input before T3 will cause damage; or
- the existence of an input after T3 will cause damage.

An example of the first property is that of turning on a cooling subsystem after an overheating warning of some kind. Even if the operator is slow to turn on the system it is still of benefit if they do. The second property is illustrated by a signals operator (of a railway system) that must not change the points while a train is over the them; i.e. it is better not to do the action rather than do it too late.

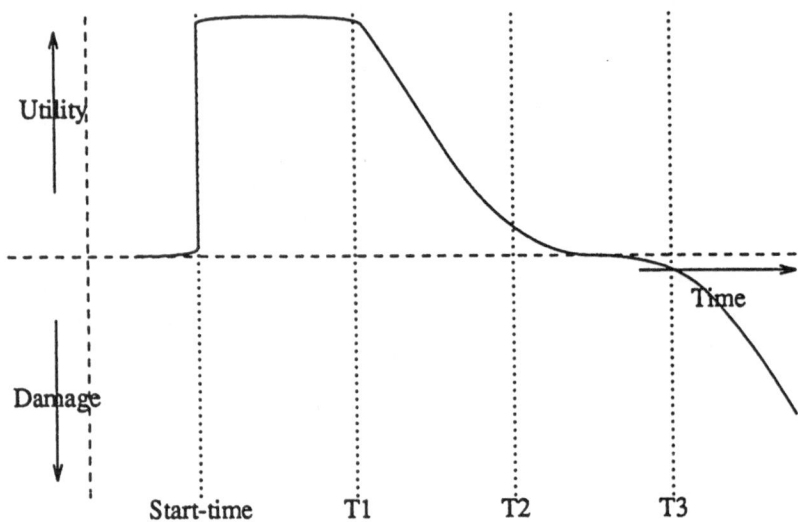

Figure 2: A Time-Utility Function

An operator's input may be associated with responding to a system output. It is important therefore to gain the attention of the user as soon as possible and to present sufficient data for the operators to respond in an appropriate and timely manner. There are a number of visual and auditory alarm techniques used to inform operators that immediate attention is needed. These must be supplemented by an appropriate architecture that allows the application software to react responsively to human instruction.

Many applications will need to take account of situations in which the operator will never respond. To give such fault tolerance, alternative actions (in the event of human silence) must be implemented. The point in time in which these alternative actions are sanctioned being derived from comparing their "utility" (and deadline) with that of the delayed operator input. The decision to switch to a default response must, of course, be communicated to the silent, though not necessarily absent, operator.

2.2 Time attributes of system output

It is generally accepted that system output (from the Application) must be used to present the operators with a sufficiently accurate model for them to understand the semantics and real-time behaviour of the application under control. As the model presented cannot be totally "up-to-date" it is important to unambiguously specify the "time" attributes of output data. For example during system specification a display may be defined to be no more than five seconds old, or not more than 3% inaccurate.

With multi-operator systems the same data must be presented to all operators. One must assume that there exists an informal communication channel between the operators; if they are not observing a consistent state then confusion may ensue. This could be made worst by a hierarchical management relationship between the operators (as exists for example between a pilot and co-pilot).

The volume of information presented to the user must also be constrained by the time period over which it must be communicated to the user. There are a number of documented incidents (e.g. Three Mile Island[4]) in which the sheer concentration of critical data presented to the operator inhibits (and at times prohibits) a constructive and timely response. An unfortunately not untypical scenario is that the controlled system becomes in some way unsafe. This condition is recognised by a number of different sensors. Each sensor produces (either directly or indirectly) alarm data for the operator. The operators' model of the system becomes compromised and a constructive response cannot be assured.

2.3 Asynchronous mode changes

In the above it was noted that system outputs must at times be constrained and that the model they present to the user is necessarily out-of-date. Where application (and therefore model) parameters change in a continuous manner then the use of time or error attributes are appropriate. There are, however, systems that are subject to discontinuous and asynchronous mode changes. Typically there are a small number of static modes in which the application operates. For these systems it is imperative that the operator is *always* made aware of the current mode. Moreover, when a mode change occurs a consistent model must be maintained at the operator interface. The user must not be able to assess old data from the previous mode simultaneously with more up-to-date information from the new mode.

Even with the above approach there will inevitably be situations (due to the asynchronous nature of mode changes) in which an operator instruction that was valid at the time it was made becomes invalid, because of the mode change, by the time the application processes it. This eventuality must be catered for at the design stage with appropriate user feedback being generated. The user must know if the instruction was acted upon before the mode change, or if the mode change invalidated it. Again with multi-operator systems a consistent view of mode is critically important.

2.4 Inaccurate or uncertain output

In addition to the inaccuracies that arise from presenting the user with an "old" view of the application it can also be the case that the data itself, even if timely, may not be precise. Due to time constraints internal to the application, computations may not have been fully completed before a timeout occurred; an approach called *imprecise computations*[5, 6]. A similar effect is possible if inconsistent (i.e. non-committed in a database model) data must be used due to the approach of a hard deadline. There is a danger in presenting information to the operator in a form that implies accuracy, if internal to the application it is known that such accuracy has not been achieved. Such information should always carry attributes of *accuracy level, confidence level* or *uncertainty value*. These attributes must be prominently displayed although care should be taken to ensure that information overload does not result (see discussion above).

Another situation that can lead the operator to mis-read the state of the application (and its environment) is to have multiple displays of a single information source. If, for example, a single sensor picks up an inappropriate temperature reading then a single display or alarm routine is an appropriate response. The operator should be able to judge whether the sensor itself is malfunctioning by considering other independent displays. But if these other displays are also presenting data from this sensor then the operator may consider that corroborating information is available when in fact it is not.

3 Meeting Timing Requirements

Most real-time systems use the concept of task (or process) to structure run-time behaviour. In the development of applications it is thus usual to map system timing requirements onto task deadlines. The issue of meeting deadlines therefore becomes one of task scheduling. As scheduling theory has improved it has become possible to define task-to-priority mappings that will guarantee run-time behaviour and give some level of flexibility during execution.

A single application will typically consist of many tasks. Each task has a single thread of control. For execution on a single processor the threads are interleaved. On a multiprocessor system there is also the issue of thread allocation.

Two distinct forms of task structure are identified in the real-time literature[7]:

- Periodic
- Sporadic

Periodic tasks, as their name implied, execute on a regular basis; they are characterised by their period (T), their deadline (D), and their required execution time (per period) (C). They would typically be used to refresh HCI displays. Sporadic tasks also have deadlines and execution time requirements but execute only when some defined event has occurred. There is a requirement for these events to be limited in their arrival (i.e. a defined maximum arrival rate). An alarm signal is often structured as a sporadic task.

To prove that a task set will meet all deadlines then it is necessary to show that the following relationship holds for all real-time tasks in all situations:

$$C + I + B \leq D$$

Where I is the interference time (the total time that other tasks are executing when the task of interest wishes to); and B is the total blocked time for the task (the time when it cannot execute because the conditions required for progress are missing). The interference factor I can be reduced by using static (distinct) priorities. Blocking is more complicated as it involves waiting for other tasks to generate required data, and delays caused by HCI issues. Clearly B must be bounded and not too pessimistic if systems are to be guaranteed. The architecture described below is aimed at ensuring that sensible blocking values are available.

4 Architectural Considerations

The earlier discussion leads to an architecture in which the HCI Components (see Figure 1) must model the *state* and *temporal behaviour* of the Application. Issues of consistency require the use of a database model; temporal concerns dictate a real-time database[8]. In this section we first consider an appropriate database model; this model is then applied to the HCI Component.

4.1 A real-time database model

Traditionally, databases are used in systems which either do not operate in real time, or where a quick response is desirable but not strictly necessary. Incorporating databases into real-time systems necessarily imposes stricter timing constraints as the failure to meet a constraint can have catastrophic consequences. Formally, the correct functioning of the system depends on timely operation as well as on functionally correct operation.

A number of algorithms have been proposed and used in order to improve the performance of conventional databases. Generally, these rely on one of two techniques.

Firstly, the consistency constraints which apply to the database, and to the views of it which can be obtained, may be weakened. Examples include *multiversion serializability*[9, 10], where older versions of data objects are maintained for read-only transactions; *semantic atomicity*[11], where the semantics of the transactions are exploited; *multilevel atomicity*[12], which is a generalisation of semantic atomicity; and *weak correctness*[13, 14], where some transactions are allowed to see the intermediate results of other transactions.

Secondly, schemes exist which take advantage of typical database access patterns, so that transactions may proceed more speedily than otherwise, on the expectation that no conflicts with other transactions will arise. If such conflicts do occur, then transactions may have to be aborted and restarted. Such a scheme is described by Kung and Robinson[15].

The above methods are characterised by the fact that the performance improvement is statistical in nature, and cannot be guaranteed.

Given the context of real-time systems it is possible to define a number of characteristics that are relevant to real-time databases:

- The number of database objects is fixed.
- Each transaction (class) accesses the same fixed subset of database objects.
- Many transactions are invoked on a regular (periodic) basis.
- There are temporal relationships between database objects.

To analyse further the requirements of a real-time database it is necessary to postulate a general model of the application needs that are satisfied by a real-time database. We are not concerned with a database that has only a peripheral or archival importance. Rather we focus on the use of a real-time database as the main structuring component of the systems architecture.

Consider an embedded (possible distributed) application that has N distinct input streams from sensors or HCI units; and M output streams to actuators (effectors) or HCI units. Timing requirements are expressed over these N+M value sets; e.g. an input must be read every n units of time, or there is an end-to-end timing requirement between a change in an input value and an associated change in an output value.

In order to calculate the correct values for the output settings, P significant intermediate values must be computed. By significant we mean a value that is passed between software components, or which may be checked by an independent component.

The database holds N+M+P primary objects. All software components interact via this database; i.e. they read a subset of objects and write to a subset. If the application is distributed then the database may not be centralised. In this case a number of primary objects will have shadow objects that notionally have the same value. A simple end-to-end timing requirement may thus involve the reading of a sensor to generate a S value in the database, the transmission of this value to a shadow S' on a different

62

machine, the calculation of some intermediate value V, the use of V to compute a new actuator setting A', the transmission of this shadow value to A, the output of this value to the system's environment, and the input of an acknowledgement flag K back into the database. An independent activity many then compare K and A (or S) to see if the system is working correctly in either the value or time domain. This is illustrated in Figure 3.

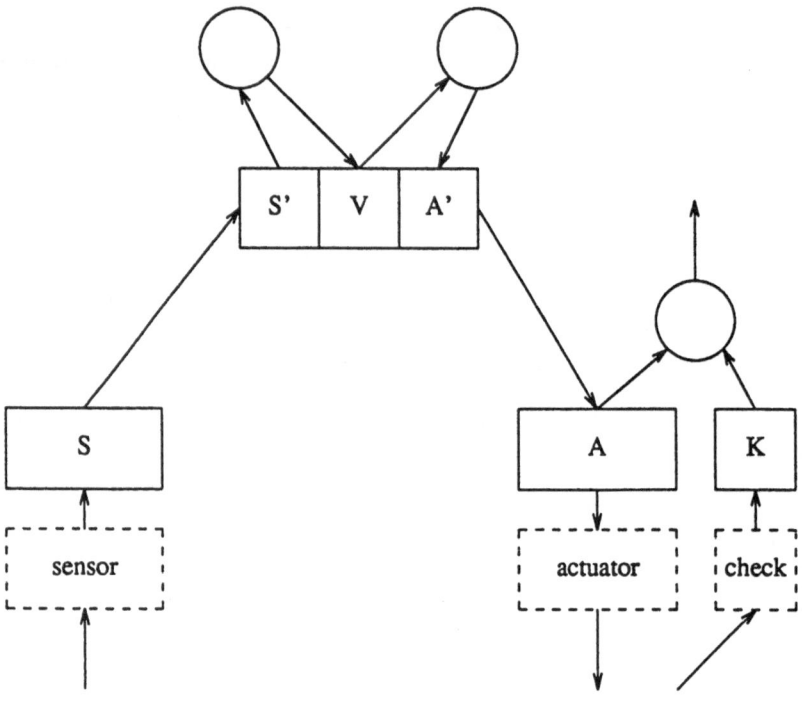

Figure 3: Database Interactions

The database is a key component of the system architecture not just because it is the repository of crucial data but it can also be used to define when activities should be invoked. A value moving outside a defined interval may initiate an error recovery activity; a real-time database should give similar support to a data object becoming too old.

4.2 Associating time and temporal consistency with data objects

In order to produce systems which maintain the required timing constraints, it is necessary to associate time with the value stored in a data object. This time will be referred to as the *time stamp* of the data object. For data objects that represent an image of some real-world quantity (the N set defined above), the time stamp represents the time at which the data object value and the real-world value coincide (within any value errors resulting from the calculation which generated the database value).

There are two notions related to the time stamp values which can be used in measures of the temporal consistency of the database. These are *absolute* and *relative* temporal consistency. The term *functional* consistency will be used to refer to value consistency, as in conventional databases.

When a transaction executes, it reads a set of data objects, performs some calculations, and writes the result to some other data object (or, possibly, set of data objects). In order for the result to be meaningful, it requires both that the values of the input data objects have values which are accurate within some error bounds, and that the time stamps associated with the input objects are sufficiently recent. The former is effectively the functional consistency of the conventional database, although in such cases the error bounds are typically zero. The latter is the requirement that the data value is sufficiently *fresh* and hence meaningful. This form of consistency will be referred to as *absolute* temporal consistency.

If a transaction reads a set of data objects, and uses the values to calculate some result, then it may be necessary that the objects all have similar time stamps. This type of consistency will be referred to as *relative* temporal consistency.

By analogy with correct transactions in a conventional database, a transaction which meets a set of temporal requirements will be called a *temporally correct* transaction. Formally, a temporally correct transaction is one which, given a temporally consistent database, will result in a modified, but still temporally consistent, database. Note that while a consistent conventional database will stay consistent if no transactions are executed, a real-time database may need transactions to execute in order to retain temporal consistency.

4.3 Reader/writer model

A conventional database has no restriction on the number of readers and writers that may access any data object. Consistency must then be retained by imposing concurrency control over the transactions. This is unfortunate for real-time transactions as the blocking time with protocols such as two-phase locking is, at best, pessimistic, and at worst, unbounded. In the model presented here it is assumed that each data object is written by a single task only. This allows certain simplifications to be made:

- Atomic, non-blocking, access to data objects can be provided using the algorithms described by Simpson[16, 17]. Briefly, these implement single processor, or multi-processor with shared memory, access to data objects, without any need for mutual exclusion mechanisms. A reading task always reads the most recent (at the time at which the read commences) completely written version of the data object.

- There is no interaction between multiple writers to a single data object. Hence, the absolute temporal consistency constraint for a data object can be mapped directly to the task which writes the data object.

- A task can update a data object, in the sense of reading its current value, modifying the value, and writing that value back, without needing to lock the object to prevent conflicting access.

Although this constraint would be extremely restrictive in the context of conventional databases, it is less so in real-time systems. New objects and transactions (tasks) can always be added to give the required single writer structure.

5 Applying the Real-Time Database Model to HCI

The HCI Component in Figure 1 is defined to consist of a real-time database plus a set of tasks that interact with the database (by running transactions) and the Operators (by changing a visual image or other output device attribute). The Application also runs tasks that can (and must) interact with the database. To model (and implement) the temporal relationships between the Operators and the Application it is necessary to define absolute and relative temporal consistencies (ATCs and RTCs) on the data objects of the database of the HCI component. This will in turn define the periods and response times of the tasks running in the Application and the HCI Component.

The database will contain all the information that could be of use to the Operators plus the images of any input data generated by the Operators. In general the database will be too large for all its values to be presented to the users at one time and hence the data must be organised so that the Operator can effectively move around the *application model*.

The real-time requirements imposed on the simple architecture of Figure 1 can be represented and implemented in a number of ways. The following details the common structures:

ATC on the application objects

A number of Application tasks will have absolute temporal consistency requirements. These will dictate the maximum age of certain database objects and hence the frequency with which the tasks must execute. This frequency will need to be guaranteed by the schedulability analysis carried out on the full Application code.

Much of the database will consist of data that is refreshed by the Application. The ATC (and hence the refresh rate) will enable the Operator to obtain a *sufficiently up-to-date* picture of the behaviour of the Application. If a database object models a real-time entity (e.g. a temperature) then the rate of change of that entity will be used (at the requirements analysis phase) to define the ATC of the object.

Note that the objects with ATC considered here are written by the Application. There is no requirement for the Operator to see all values of these objects. If the Operator (or more likely, one of the Operators) does not *view* that object then this is of no concern to the Application. All that is being guaranteed here is that if the Operator views the object its value will be sufficiently fresh.

RTC on the application objects

This requirement is best described by way of an example. Consider a dual tank fuel management system. Engines draw fuel from both tanks but the management system tries to keep the capacity of the two tanks the same by pumping fuel from one tank to another. The Operator needs to know the total amount of fuel left. Both tanks have a volume device that will give the current volume of that tank. However it is not sufficient to merely allow the Operator to view both readings; the readings must be taken close together so that the movement of fuel will not invalidate the information presented to the Operator.

The two readings may have a long absolute timing requirement but a short relative one. Whenever the Operator asks for fuel readings the database must hold values with both ATC and RTC.

ATC on the operator objects

Some safety critical systems require the Operator to periodically input an *I'm alive* signal. This is defined as ATC on an Operator object.

With both Application and Operator objects it is possible to define transactions that are invoked by the breaking of an ATC. If the Operator fails to sign-in a transaction that informs the Application will be released. Similarly an action in the HCI

Component can be used to inform the Operator that the Application is failing (at least in the temporal domain).

Transaction deadlines

In addition to temporal consistencies there are end-to-end deadlines through the database that must be guaranteed. Three classes can be identified:

- Operator Invoked
- Application Invoked
- Database Invoked

An Operator will change a database value and require that the Application has acted upon this value within a specified time (say T1 in Figure 2). Note that if the Application writes back into that database when it has accomplished this then there is a relative temporal consistency between the two objects involved.

When defining the task architecture for a system, Operator invoked transactions can be catered for in two ways. If they occur frequently then a periodic task may be appropriate. Alternatively if they occur infrequently (or irregularly) but have short deadlines then it may be better to implement the transaction as a sporadic task that is invoked by an Operator input.

An application invoked transaction will require the Operator to be made aware of some event within some specified time interval. With a multi-view (or multi-window) interface the object in question may not be in the current display. Nevertheless, the user must be informed by a visual or audible signal that the event has occurred. The Operator will usually be asked to acknowledge the event and hence there is, again, a RTC relationship between objects in the database. In other situations the Operator may need to input some data in response to the event. This may then form a further time dependent transaction.

A database is usually considered a passive entity and so the idea of it invoking transactions is not usual. The database and its support software in the HCI Component can however be considered to be a *blackboard* structure that not only is a data store but also a transaction invoker. A number of situations exist (some of which have already been mentioned) that can cause a transaction to execute:

(a) An ATC being broken

(b) A RTC being broken (between component of a transaction)

(c) A data (functional) consistency being broken

The latter allows the database itself to catch invalid data values and to initiate the appropriate error recovery action. This may involve a transaction in the Application domain or one in the HCI Component itself (or both).

The Application can therefore still assume a perfect user as long as it can cater for the scheduling of error recovery transactions.

5.1 A simple example

Some of the requirements discussed above can be visualised in a simple example taken from an existing system. This example will also illustrate how the database model can be used as a general system architecture that is easily extended into the HCI component.

The example is taken from the oil industry. A company has implemented a pipe control system to move different grades of petrol from the "end of production" to "storage". The distance involved is over half a mile (underwater) and so a single pipe is used for the bulk of the transfer. Ten different grades are accommodated by sets of tanks, pipes and valves. Grades must not be mixed more than is absolutely necessary as the result must be considered to be of the lower quality grade. Turbulence in the pipe is to be minimised to reduce mixing when a switch between grades is being made. There are also safety issues relating to maximum pressure and the early recognition of pipe breaks.

The control system is implemented as a distributed computer system with one main computer that polls remote computers that control smart actuators and sensors. Each remote computer has a small database of local variables (i.e. sensor readings, actuator settings). The main computer has an image of all the smaller databases. It also has an interface to the Operator that allows most of this database to be viewed and will allow some entries to be updated by the Operator. The main computer also executes "background" tasks that check the consistency of the database — both temporal and functional.

All routine data is polled on a regular basis and hence the main database contains data that possesses appropriate ATC. The Operators are in complete control as to what data to view on their screens. They can also choose between the presentation of numerical data (i.e. the database values) and a pictorial style showing the active pipes and rate of flow (via an associated colour scale).

Alarm data has an end-to-end deadline. A remote computer will recognise the alarm condition and the main computer must inform the Operator within a fixed time. This is achieved by fixing the polling rate over the network (for normal execution) which will define a RTC between the remote data object and its corresponding mirror on the main machine. Once the alarm condition is read a transaction is invoked that causes a visual and audible signal on the Operator console. The operator must then choose the appropriate screen and then cancel the alarm. This switch to the relevant screen can be requested by a single key action.

The main computer runs tasks to:

(a) Poll the network and keep the database temporal consistent.

(b) Execute the necessary control laws to set the actuator values.

(c) Perform all HCI work (i.e. implement the HCI Component).

(d) Undertake background consistency checking.

Much of the HCI work is not real-time but some key actions are — such as screen switching following an alarm.

Although the main computer has many different tasks to perform it can be analysed (for schedulability) because the database architecture makes all the task executions independent of each other. A typical task will read values from the database, undertake some computations, and write new values into the database. The database interactions will be non-blocking. Moreover a temporarily consistent database being subject to the timely execution of tasks will result in a temporarily consistent database. The HCI Component presents no new difficulties, it conforms to the same model.

6 Conclusion

Although a computer system cannot ensure that a user will act in a timely manner, it is possible to build systems that will guarantee that information is presented at the correct time, and will act upon user directions within an imposed deadline. Guarantees follow from applying schedulability analysis that itself restricts the architecture of the application. The use of a real-time database helps to structure the interactions between Operators and Application and enables the schedulability analysis to be carried out.

To capture real-time requirements it is necessary to both restrict and extend the traditional database model. Normal concurrency control methods ensure data consistency but lead to unsolvable scheduling problems. We have transposed all consistency requirements to be temporal ones and have then defined absolute temporal consistency on individual database objects and relative temporal consistency between database objects. In addition all objects can have at most a single writer task.

The architecture presented may be viewed as too restrictive for normal HCI. It does however appear to be appropriate for real-time dependable systems.

Acknowledgements

The work presented in this paper is due in large part to the input of colleagues; in particular P. Allen, N. Audsley, M. Richardson and A.J. Wellings.

References

[1]. M. Sikorski, "Use of Reliability Modelling for the Ergonomic Design of Industrial Process Control Systems", pp. 194-198 in *Contemporary Ergonomics*, ed. E.D. Megaw, Taylor & Francis (1989).

[2]. A. Burns, "The HCI Component of Dependable Real-Time Systems", *Software Engineering Journal (to be published)* (1991).

[3]. A. Burns, "Enhanced Input/Output On Pascal", *ACM SIGPLAN Notices* 18(11), pp. 24-33 (1983).

[4]. J. Kemeny, *Report of the President's Commission on the Accident at Three Mile Island*, Government Printing Office : Washington (1979).

[5]. J.W.S. Liu, K.J. Lin and S. Natarajan, "Scheduling Real-Time Periodic Jobs Using Imprecise Results", pp. 252-260 in *Proceedings 8th IEEE Real-Time Systems Symposium*, San Jose, California (1987).

[6]. K.J. Lin, S. Natarajan, J.W.S. Liu and T. Krauskopf, "Concord: A System of Imprecise Computations", in *Proc. IEEE Compsac, Japan* (October 1987).

[7]. A. Burns, "Scheduling Hard Real-Time Systems: A Review", *Software Engineering Journal* 6(3), pp. 116-128 (1991).

[8]. A. Burns and M. Richardson, "A Database Model for Hard Real-Time Systems", YCS.144, Department of Computer Science, University of York (1990).

[9]. C.H. Papadimitriou and P.C. Kanellakis, "On Concurrency Control by Multiple Versions", *ACM Trans. on Database Systems* (March 1984).

[10]. D. Agrawal and S. Sengupta, "Modular Synchronisation in Multiversion Databases: Version Control and Concurrency Control", *1989 ACM-SIGMOD Intl. Conf.* (1989).

[11]. W. Cellary, E. Gelenbe and T. Morzy, *Concurrency Control in Distributed Database Systems*, 1988.

[12]. N.A. Lynch, "Multi-Level Atomicity - A New Correctness Criterion for Database Concurrency Control", *ACM Transactions on Data Base Systems Vol 8 No 4*, pp. 484-502 (Dec 1983).

[13]. L. Sha, J.P. Lehoczky and E.D. Jensen, "Modular Concurrency Control and Failure Recovery", *IEEE Transactions on Computers* **37**(2), pp. 146-159 (February 1988).

[14]. L. Sha, R. Rajkumar and J.P. Lehoczky, "Concurrency Control for Distributed Real-Time Databases", *SIGMOD Record*, pp. 82-96 (Vol, 17, No. 1, March 1988).

[15]. H.T. Kung and J.T. Robinson, "On Optimistic Methods of Concurrency Control", *ACM Trans. on Database Systems*, pp. 213-226 (June 1981).

[16]. H.R. Simpson, "Four-Slot Fully Asynchronous Communication Mechanism", *IEE Proceedings on Computers and Digital Techniques* **137**(1), pp. 17-30 (January 1990).

[17]. H.R. Simpson, "Correctness Analysis for a Class of Asynchronous Communication Mechanisms", *BAe Report* (1990).

Logical Input Devices - An Outdated Concept?

D.A. Duce†, P.J.W. ten Hagen and R. van Liere‡

†Rutherford Appleton Laboratory, Chilton, Didcot, Oxon OX11 0QX, UK
‡Center for Mathematics and Computer Science (CWI), Amsterdam, The Netherlands

Abstract

This chapter gives a short history of the concept of logical input devices and the way in which the concept has evolved and is now contained in the ISO/IEC standards for computer graphics programming, GKS, GKS-3D and PHIGS. A formal description of the GKS logical input device model is given in Hoare's CSP notation, and the chapter concludes with a discussion of some of the shortcomings of the model and ways in which it can be extended.

1 Introduction

The notion of logical input devices dates back to around 1968. The early 1970's saw a flurry of activities laying the foundations for the first International Standard for computer graphics programming, the Graphical Kernel System (GKS). GKS was published as an International Standard in August 1985.[9,17] During the course of the development of GKS, an input model based on the concept of logical input devices was developed. This model has formed the basis for the input facilities in subsequently produced graphics standards (GKS-3D,[19] PHIGS[20] and CGI,[22] the device interface standard). Section 2 examines how the initial ideas of logical input devices evolved into the input model now contained in the graphics standards.

Section 3 presents a formal description of the input model expressed in Hoare's Communicating Sequential Processes notation.[8] A brief introduction to the notation is also given. The following section describes an extension to the input model which enables input devices to be composed hierarchically. The formal descriptions have been published previously.

The chapter concludes with some observations on the strengths and weaknesses of logical input devices, and ways in which the concept might be extended in the future.

2 Development of the GKS input model

2.1 Background

One of the key concerns in GKS is to abstract away from the details of specific graphical output and input device hardware and present to the application program a programming interface which is device independent, but which can be configured easily by the application program to make best use of the characteristics of the available output and input devices. For graphical output, this is achieved through the use of workstation dependent lookup tables, called bundle tables, which can be used to control the appearance of output primitives on the workstations on which they are displayed. Table entries can be set by the application program to make best use of the characteristics of the output device, for example colour might be used to differentiate the appearance of primitives of the same kind on a device with a colour capability, whilst on a monochrome device some other aspect would have to be used. The quest for equivalent concepts and control for graphical input has been more difficult, and so far, less successful.

The key idea in the GKS input model is to look at the type of input values returned by different types of physical input devices, and characterize these in terms of the uses to which they are put by application programs, for example to obtain a spatial position in some coordinate system, or to select from a set of possible alternative choices. Such an approach led to the idea of *virtual* or *logical input devices*. The essence of the idea first appeared in a paper in 1968 by Newman[11] and was developed further by Cotton,[3] Wallace and Foley[7] and Wallace.[15] The idea is that the application program has available a range of virtual input devices, the only visible aspect of which is the type of value returned. Five types, or basic classes, were identified corresponding to five commonly used functions:

- *locator* to indicate a position;
- *pick* to select a displayed entity;
- *valuator* to input a single real number;
- *keyboard* to input a character string;
- *button* to select from a set of displayed choices.

For each basic class, there is a natural type of physical device onto which to map the class, for example pick maps naturally onto a lightpen, button onto a button box. However, any of the virtual input devices can be simulated by (almost) any physical device, thus a graphics system supporting the virtual device idea can be implemented on just about any combination of available physical input devices. The application program can be moved from one physical device configuration to another, supporting the virtual devices used by the application, without changes to the structure of the application program. The drawback in this approach is that emulation of virtual devices by 'unsuitable' physical devices may lead to an interface, which though logically correct, is extremely unfriendly to use.

The logical input device model was used as the starting point for the development of GKS as it does effectively address the issue of separating the structure of the application program from the physical device hardware to be used.

2.2 GKS Version 3

The earliest version of GKS which exists in English translation is GKS Version 3.[16] Five types of logical input device were provided, corresponding to five classes of input values. The classes are essentially those of Foley et al., but with some name changes:

- LOCATOR: providing a position in user coordinates. (Version 3 user coordinates were roughly equivalent to world coordinates in the International Standard.)
- VALUATOR: providing a real number, restricted to the range [0,1].
- CHOICE: providing integer numbers specifying alternatives.
- PICK: providing names of segments (which identified one or more displayed output primitives).
- TEXT: providing a character string.

Input devices were associated with workstations and different workstations could provide devices of different classes. Input could only be obtained from the active workstation and in GKS Version 3, only one workstation could be active at a time. Only one input mode was provided, REQUEST mode. The application could request input from a specified device; the application was then suspended until the operator delivered the input.

One input function was provided per class of input devices, for example REQUEST SET OF LOCATORS, and as the name implies, all the functions returned a series of input values; rather than a single input value.

No control was provided over prompting and echoing. Low level prompting and echoing were regarded as device and implementation dependent facilities and high level prompting and echoing were regarded as the responsibility of the application program. Thus although applications would be portable between implementations providing the appropriate combination of logical input devices, the application had no way to tailor the characteristics of the logical input devices in a particular implementation to best advantage.

2.3 GSPC Core

At the same time as the GKS proposal was being developed by the German standards making body, DIN, a proposal for a 3D graphics standard, called Core, was being developed by the Graphic Standards Planning Committee in the USA. Eventually both documents were considered by the ISO working group on computer graphics and the decision was taken to process GKS as an International Standard in the first instance. The work on Core was far from wasted and has significantly influenced the development of 3D graphics standards within ISO. The influence of Core and events leading to the progression of GKS as an International Standard are discussed in some detail in Arnold and Duce.[1] It is interesting to look at the input facilities provided in Core as these influenced the later development of the GKS input model and in some areas go further than GKS in terms of functionality provided.

The Core's input facilities were based on logical input devices. Six classes were provided, which were divided into two disjoint sets; those which could only cause *events* and those which could only be *sampled*. Four of the six were event devices:

- PICK: identifies a primitive within a segment by a two-level naming structure consisting of a segment name and pick identifier
- KEYBOARD: provides a character string
- BUTTON: provides a choice between alternatives
- STROKE: provides a series of positions (in normalized device coordinates).

  The remaining two classes were sampled devices:

- LOCATOR: provides a position (in normalized device coordinates)
- VALUATOR: provides a scalar value within an application defined range.

Event devices could be used by the operator to asynchronously input values to the application. Whenever an event device caused an event, an event report was added to a single first in/ first out event queue. The application program could remove events from the event queue.

READ functions were provided to obtain input from sampled devices. These functions returned the current value of the device to the application program immediately.

It was possible to associate sampled devices with event devices, under application program control. When an event occurred, the values of the associated sampled devices were put into the event report along with the value for the event device. Associations could be many to many, so that, for example, one particular sample device could be associated with several event devices.

Functions were provided to initialize and enable individual devices and sets of devices within a specified device class. Limited control over the form of prompting and echoing for a device was provided to the application. A small number of predefined types of prompting and echoing were defined, and the application could select an appropriate one.

Core also provided synchronous (like GKS REQUEST) input. The functionality here is interesting, being based on compound input types constructed from the event devices and predefined combinations of associated sampled devices. The functions provided were:

> AWAIT-PICK
> AWAIT-KEYBOARD
> AWAIT-ANY-BUTTON
> AWAIT-STROKE-2
> AWAIT-STROKE-3
> AWAIT-ANY-BUTTON-GET-LOCATOR-2
> AWAIT-ANY-BUTTON-GET-LOCATOR-3
> AWAIT-ANY-BUTTON-GET-VALUATOR

The application was not able to construct more complex input types.

2.4 GKS (1985)

The detailed development of the GKS input model from Version 3 to the International Standard is documented in Arnold and Duce[1] and Rosenthal et al.[13] The major innovation during the development arose from the realization that there was no clear, consistent, underlying input model in the standard. This realization stemmed from the major criticisms of the input facilities in Version 6.6 of GKS:[1]

(1) the exact datatypes to be returned by the different device classes;

(2) the different levels of detail at which different kinds of input behaviour were specified;

(3) the lack of uniformity among the different logical device classes as to the details of their behaviour;

(4) the lack of a clear distinction between the concepts of:

> *Simulating* a logical device using particular types of hardware;

> *Prompting* an operator for input;

> *Echoing* an operator's actions;

> *Acknowledging* an operator's generation of events;

(5) the difficulty of relating any of these 'output' concepts to logical input devices.

The Abingdon meeting of the ISO working group responsible for GKS in October 1981 produced the input model contained in GKS in more or less its final form. The model is described in detail in the next section, but the essential features are:

(1) Logical input devices can be divided into classes according to the types of values they return. Six classes are standardized in GKS.

(2) Any logical input device can operate in any of three standardized operating modes:

REQUEST, SAMPLE and EVENT. These differ in respect of which party (operator or application program) has the initiative for input.

(3) The application program is given control over the initial value of a device, the prompting and echoing technique to be employed and the region of the display (echo area) in which echoing is to be presented.

(4) In EVENT mode, simultaneous event reports may be generated by a single operator action (this is a form of association analogous to that in Core).

There is an important distinction between the generality of the GKS input model and the restricted form in which it is presented through the functionality of GKS. There is, for example, nothing in the model to preclude the application having control over which combinations of devices should generate simultaneous events, however the GKS functionality does not support this. Similarly there is no reason in the model why the application should not be able to define its own prompting and echoing types, however GKS only allows applications to choose between predefined prompt and echo types. There are many areas in GKS where good implementations can provide rich and flexible control over input, but the standard does not mandate such facilities. This reliance upon implementation dependencies detracts rather from the elegance of the underlying model. This point has been addressed by an ISO study group on an Improved Input Model[10] and is being further addressed by the Revision of the GKS Standard which is now underway.[2]

3 The GKS input model

The GKS input model is described in the International Standard in terms of six processes:

(1) measure;

(2) trigger;

(3) prompt;

(4) echo;

(5) acknowledgement;

(6) control.

The measure of a logical input device determines the type and value of the data returned by the logical input device to the application program. The measure process maps the input values from the physical input devices which realize the logical input device, onto the values of the data type to be returned to the application. This mapping is called the *measure mapping*, and the measure process maintains the current measure value of the logical input device as the operator manipulates the physical input devices.

The trigger determines when a measure value is returned to the application program. It is only used in some of the supported input styles.

Prompt is used to indicate to the operator when the device is available for input. The echo process gives feedback to the operator of the current measure value, and the acknowledgement process indicates to the operator that a trigger has fired and a measure value has been passed to the application program. The control process controls the overall operation of the device.

GKS provides three operating modes for logical input devices:

(1) REQUEST. The application program requests an input value from a specified logical input device. The application program is suspended until the input value is delivered. Whilst the application program is suspended, the operator can

manipulate the physical input device to set the desired value of the device's measure. The device's trigger is fired to indicate when the desired value has been set.

(2) SAMPLE. When a device is operating in SAMPLE mode, the current measure value is returned whenever requested by the application program. No triggering is involved and the application program will continue immediately.

(3) EVENT. When a device is operating in EVENT mode, an event report consisting of the current measure value of the device and data identifying the device, are added to a single centralized event queue, each time the trigger for the device is activated. More than one device may be in EVENT mode at a time, and the event reports from each of the devices are collected in the queue. The application program can interrogate the queue to retrieve the events. It is possible for more than one input device to be coupled to the same trigger so that multiple event reports can be generated from a single trigger event.

Duce, ten Hagen and van Liere[4] have given a formal description of the GKS input model, using Hoare's CSP notation. Other authors have also presented formal descriptions of the input model using different notations.[6, 12, 14] In this section the CSP description is briefly presented. For fuller details refer to the original paper.[4]

CSP aims to describe the behaviour patterns of objects with each other and their environment. The first step in a CSP description is to decide what kinds of event or action will be of interest, and to give a name to each kind. Each event name describes a class of events, rather than a single occurrence of an event. There may be many occurrences of events in a class, separated in time. The set of names of events which are used to describe a particular object are called its *alphabet*. The choice of alphabet for an object focuses attention on the properties and actions of the object that are important and deliberately ignores events of lesser interest. CSP regards occurrences of events as instantaneous or atomic actions without duration. The exact timing of events is also ignored in CSP; where timing considerations are important, these are to be treated separately from the logical correctness of the design. When simultaneity of a pair of events is important (as, for example, in synchronization), it is represented as a single event occurrence; when it is not, potentially simultaneous events are allowed to be recorded in either order. The behaviour pattern of an object is termed a *process*.

In the description presented below, prompting and acknowledgement are deliberately ignored and no corresponding events are included in the specification.

Logical input devices are described in terms of an operator process, OP, a measure process, M, a trigger process, T, an echo process E and a control process LID. EVENT mode input requires an additional storage process, S. The communication structure between each of the processes for each of the operating modes is shown in Figure 1. The lines joining processes are labelled by the event name or channel name by which they communicate.

The REQUEST mode processes will be described in some detail.

Operator process, OP

In REQUEST mode, the operator can either input new physical input values from the possible set of values (denoted by the set P) or can fire the trigger (denoted by the event name *trigger*). The CSP description of the process is:

$$OP = (\prod_{p:P} m!p \rightarrow OP) \, \Pi \, (trigger \rightarrow STOP_{\alpha OP})$$

The notation:

$$R \sqcap S$$

denotes a process which behaves like R or like S. The choice between the possible behaviours is non-deterministic. The factors that would lead to one choice or the other are not modelled by the description. For the operator process, we do not model the factors that would lead to the operator to either set a new physical input value or fire the trigger. Hence the operator is modelled as a non-deterministic choice between these two alternative behaviours.

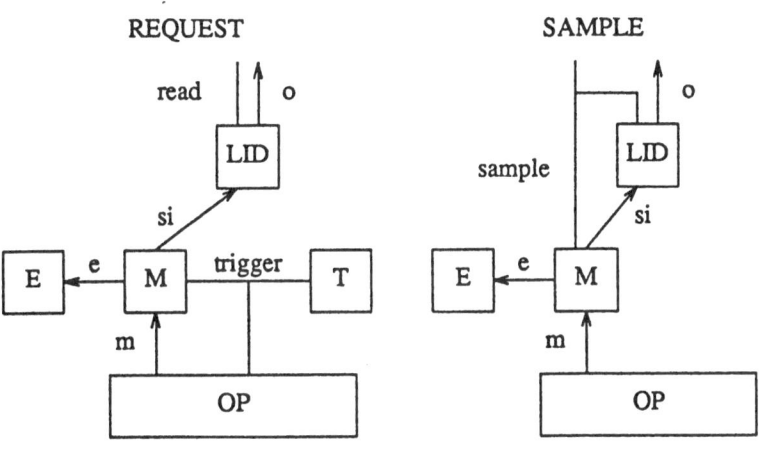

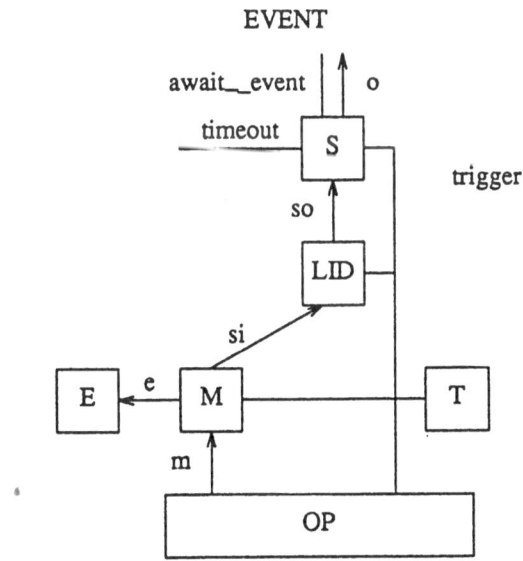

Figure 1: Process Model

The notation:

$$(\prod_{p:P} m!p \rightarrow OP)$$

denotes a process which non-deterministically chooses one of the possible values of type P and then outputs this value on the channel m ($m!p$). The process then ($\rightarrow$) behaves like the process OP. Thus the process has a recursive definition. Having selected an input value, the operator then has the choice of selecting another input value or firing the trigger.

The notation:

$$(trigger \rightarrow STOP_{\alpha OP})$$

denotes a process which engages in the event *trigger* and then engages in no further events in its alphabet ($STOP_{\alpha OP}$). The alphabet of a process R, αR, is just the set of possible events in which the process can engage. This part of the definition of the process OP says that after the operator has fired the trigger, no further interactions with the device can take place.

Measure process, M

When the operator supplies a new physical input value, the state of the measure process is updated to contain the new measure value, obtained by applying the measure mapping (denoted by the function f) to the physical input value. The measure process recording the current measure value, v, is denoted by M_v. The new measure value is communicated to the echo process over channel e. When the trigger fires, the current measure value is communicated to the control process over channel si and the process engages in no further activity. The process description is:

$$M_{v:v} = (m?p \rightarrow e!f(p) \rightarrow M_{f(p)})\,|$$
$$(trigger \rightarrow si!v \rightarrow STOP_{\alpha M})$$

The choice between the two possible behaviours is a deterministic choice (denoted by the operator |) and is determined by which of the events $m?p$ and *trigger* is presented to the process first by its environment.

Trigger process, T

When the trigger fires, this process engages in no further activity.

$$T = (trigger \rightarrow STOP_{\alpha T})$$

Echo process, E

This process echoes the values communicated on channel e. The form of the echo is not described. The state of the echo process records the value echoed.

$$E_v = (e?v\prime \rightarrow E_{v\prime})$$

The notation $e?v\prime$ denotes an event corresponding to the receipt of the value $v\prime$ from channel e.

The interaction between the echo and the display system is not described in this specification. The description of the echo process could be refined to incorporate such a description.

Control process, LID

The application program requests a value from the input device, denoted by the event *read*. The process then waits for a logical input value to be communicated on the channel *si*. This value is communicated to the application on channel *o*. The process then engages in no further actions.

$$LID = (read \rightarrow si?v \rightarrow o!v \rightarrow STOP_{\alpha LID})$$

The overall behaviour of a logical input device in REQUEST mode is described by the parallel composition of the processes defined:

$$OP \parallel M \parallel T \parallel E \parallel LID$$

The concurrent composition of processes R and S

$$R \parallel S$$

describes the way in which the two processes evolve and interact with each other. Events which are in both the alphabets of R and S require their simultaneous participation. Events in the alphabet of R and not S are of no concern to S and can occur independently of S whenever R can engage in them. Similarly events in the alphabet of S and not of R can occur independently of R.

Table 1 summarizes the alphabets of the processes defined.

Process	Alphabet
OP	m.p trigger
M	m.p e.v trigger si.v
T	trigger
E	e.v
LID	read si.v o.v

Table 1: Process Alphabets

It will be seen that the channel event $m.p$ requires the simultaneous participation of OP and M. Communication of the new logical input value to the echo process requires participation of M and E, transmission of a logical input value to the control process ($si.v$) requires participation of M and LID, and this can only occur after the trigger has fired (requiring simultaneous participation of OP, M and T).

The process descriptions for SAMPLE and EVENT mode are given in Table 2. For comparison, the REQUEST mode descriptions are included also.

	REQUEST	SAMPLE	EVENT
OP	$(\prod_{p:P} m!p \rightarrow OP)$ $\prod (trigger \rightarrow STOP_{\alpha OP})$	$(\prod_{p:P} m!p \rightarrow OP)$	$(\prod_{p:P} m!p \rightarrow OP)$ $\prod (trigger \rightarrow OP)$
M_v	$(m?p \rightarrow e!f(p) \rightarrow M_{f(p)})$ $\mid (trigger \rightarrow si!v \rightarrow STOP_{\alpha M})$	$(m?p \rightarrow e!f(p) \rightarrow M_{f(p)})$ $\mid (sample \rightarrow si!v \rightarrow M_v)$	$(m?p \rightarrow e!f(p) \rightarrow M_{f(p)})$ $\mid (trigger \rightarrow si!v \rightarrow M_v)$
T	$(trigger \rightarrow STOP_{\alpha T})$		$(trigger \rightarrow T)$
E	$(e?v \prime \rightarrow E_{v\prime})$	$(e?v \prime \rightarrow E_{v\prime})$	$(e?v \prime \rightarrow E_{v\prime})$
LID	$(read \rightarrow si?v \rightarrow o!v \rightarrow STOP_{\alpha LID})$	$(sample \rightarrow si?v \rightarrow o!v \rightarrow LID)$	$(trigger \rightarrow si?v \rightarrow so!v \rightarrow LID)$

Table 2: Process Descriptions

For EVENT mode input, there is an additional process, S, which describes the operation of the event queue. The event, *await−event*, denotes the invocation of the AWAIT EVENT function by the application program. This function returns the first event in the queue, if the queue is not empty. If the queue is empty, the process is suspended until either an event arrives, or the timeout expires in which case the special input value NONE is returned to the application program. The process description is:

$$S_{q <s>} = (\ await\_event \rightarrow o!s \rightarrow S_q)\ |\ (\ trigger \rightarrow so?s\prime \rightarrow S_{<s\prime> q <s>})$$
$$S_{<>} = (\ await\_event \rightarrow ((\ time\_out \rightarrow o!NONE \rightarrow S_{<>})$$
$$|\ (\ trigger \rightarrow so?v \rightarrow o!v \rightarrow S_{<>})))$$
$$|\ (\ trigger \rightarrow so?v \rightarrow S_{<v>})$$

The notation $<>$ denotes the empty queue, $q <s>$ denotes a queue whose first element is s, and $<s\prime> q <s>$ denotes a queue with first element s and last element $s\prime$.

In GKS, events are actually retrieved by a two stage process, in the first, the event at the front of the queue is moved to a current event report and the identification of the device which generated the event is returned by AWAIT-EVENT. In the second stage, the application can retrieve the logical input value from the current event report. This complexity is not an essential feature of the input model, rather it is a reflection of the constraints likely to be imposed by bindings of the GKS functionality to certain programming languages (for example, Fortran). Hence this complexity is not modelled here and in this specification the event report is returned directly by AWAIT EVENT.

The CSP description throws some interesting lights on the GKS input model. It will be noticed that the type of the logical input value returned is essentially a free variable in the specification: none of the process descriptions are dependent, in the sense that their behaviours change, upon the type of values to be returned. Thus other device types could easily be introduced, the behaviour model is not restricted to the six types defined in GKS. Steps are being taken in this direction in the GKS Revision activity which is introducing a composite device class. Measure values of devices of this class are tuples constructed from the six primitive classes and the construction is under the control of the application program.

Examination of the process descriptions reveals many similarities between the operating modes. REQUEST mode allows a single interaction with the device, whilst the other two modes allow an (infinite) sequence of interactions. We have not described here the mode-changing operation which terminates an interaction with devices in SAMPLE and EVENT modes. The choices available to the operator in REQUEST and EVENT modes are identical apart from the fact that multiple interactions are possible in EVENT, but not REQUEST mode.

Examination of the measure process behaviour shows that the invocation of the SAMPLE function by the application program (which corresponds to the event *sample*) has the same effect as the operator supplied *trigger* event, in returning a logical input value to the application program.

Shortcomings of the GKS realization of the input model have been identified, including lack of application control over the composition of devices, the form of prompt/echo/acknowledgement, and inability to couple input and output, for example by linking input devices directly to control the values of output transformations. These limitations are limitations in the functionality which realizes the input model in GKS. They are not intrinsic limitations of the model itself.

4 Extension to hierarchical input devices

The ideas developed in this section originated from a discussion group at the Eurographics GKS Review Workshop[18] in September 1987, which addressed the role of logical input devices in interactive applications. The model shown in Figure 2 emerged. The idea is that interaction techniques would use some form of composite devices, built up from logical input devices, which in turn are constructed from measures and triggers which map onto physical devices. Each level in the structure can have associated prompts, echos and acknowledgements, realized using the facilities provided by the graphical output part of the graphics system.

The paper by Duce, van Liere and ten Hagen[5] shows how hierarchical input devices can be described using the process descriptions already given for the basic logical input device model. An example from that paper is shown in Figure 3.

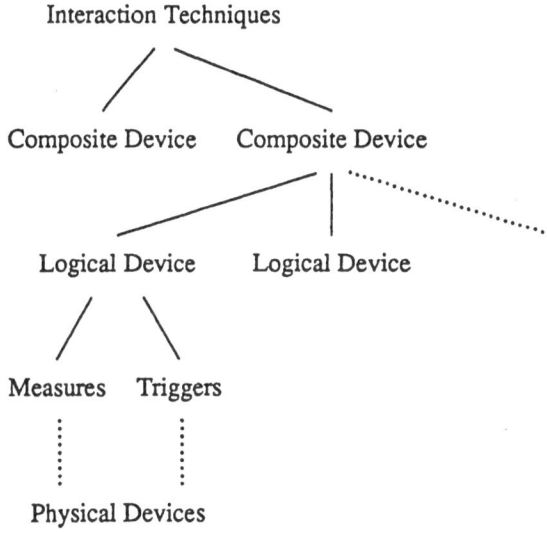

Interaction Techniques

Composite Device   Composite Device

Logical Device   Logical Device

Measures   Triggers

Physical Devices

Figure 2

The operator can manipulate the measure and trigger processes of the device at level 1 and the trigger process at level 2. The measure process at level 2 is manipulated by the level 1 device.

This style of description also turns out to be a useful way of describing some of the device classes present in GKS. The GKS STROKE device which returns a sequence of positions in world coordinates, can be modelled as a 2-level device, the first of which provides individual positions and the second assembles individual positions into a STROKE measure. The process structure of the device is illustrated in Figure 4. In GKS, the measure of the STROKE device consists of a sequence of positions in world coordinates and the number of the normalization transformation used to convert the corresponding normalized device coordinate (NDC) positions to world coordinates (WC). All the positions have to lie within the viewport of the same normalization transformation, so in fact the device is not quite as simple as a sequence of LOCATOR measures. However, this complication will not be pursued here; the structure will behave exactly as required if the LOCATOR measure process delivers values in NDC and the STROKE measure process converts the whole STROKE to WC.

The process descriptions are given below. The STROKE device is operating in EVENT mode; the description of the storage process, S, is as given previously.

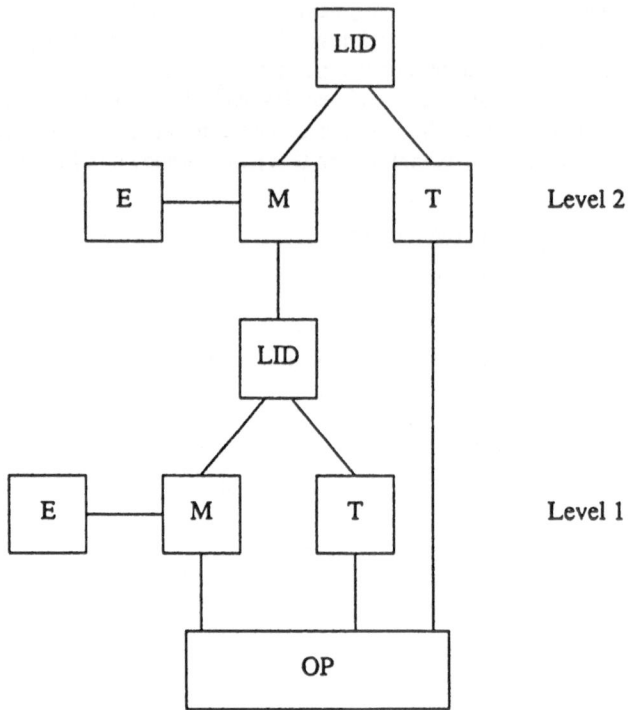

Figure 3: Example Hierarchical Input Device

$OP = (\prod_{m:M} om!m \to OP) \ \Pi \ (loctrigger \to OP) \ \Pi \ (stroketrigger \to OP)$

$MLOC_p = (om?m \to el!plm\,(m) \to MLOC_{plm\,(m)}) \mid (loctrigger \to ml!p \to MLOC_p)$

$ELOC_p = (el?p' \to ELOC_{p'})$

$TLOC = (loctrigger \to TLOC)$

$LOCATOR = (loctrigger \to ml?p \to lm!p \to LOCATOR)$

$MSTROKE_s = (lm?p \to es!sm\,(s,p) \to MSTROKE_{sm\,(s,p)})$
$\qquad\qquad \mid (stroketrigger \to ms!s \to MSTROKE_{<>})$

$ESTROKE_s = (es?s' \to ESTROKE_{s'})$

$TSTROKE = (stroketrigger \to TSTROKE)$

$STROKE = (stroketrigger \to ms?s \to so!s \to STROKE)$

The types of the variables p and s are NDCPOINT and STROKE respectively. The function plm is the measure mapping from raw physical input data (type M) to NDCPOINT, and sm is the measure mapping:

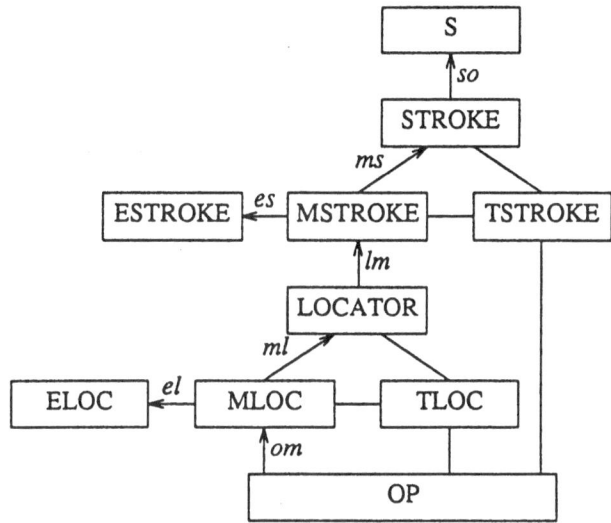

Figure 4: GKS STROKE Device

sm : STROKE × NDCPOINT → STROKE

which takes an existing STROKE, and a new NDCPOINT and delivers the new STROKE. The symbol ◇ denotes the empty STROKE.

The operator uses the LOCATOR trigger to complete the definition of individual points within a STROKE, and the STROKE trigger to complete the definition of the entire stroke. The echo processes, *ELOC* and *ESTROKE* allow the point currently being defined and the current stroke measure to be echoed differently to the operator.

The next example is also taken from GKS, the PICK logical input device. The PICK device can be modelled quite satisfactorily using the GKS input model in its simple form, with a single measure process taking inputs from the physical device by which the PICK device is realized, and mapping these to a PICK measure. A PICK measure consists of a segment name and PICK identifier, which together identify the output primitive picked. A value NOPICK can also be delivered to indicate that no primitive has been picked. In the case where a PICK device is realized by a device providing positional input, it is instructive to look at a deeper decomposition of the PICK device. The device delivers physical input values which are transformed to coordinate positions. A coordinate position is matched against the output primitives in the displayed picture to determine the primitive closest to the position. The segment name and PICK identifier of this primitive are then returned to the application program as the measure of the PICK device. The process structure corresponding to this decomposition is shown in Figure 5.

The LOCATOR process delivers positional values to the PICK measure process (*MPICK*) where they are matched agains the current picture and corresponding PICK logical input values are delivered on channel *so*. In this description, the PICK logical input device is operating in EVENT mode. The LOCATOR device is sampled by the PICK measure process. This shows how devices in different operating modes can be composed. The process descriptions are given below.

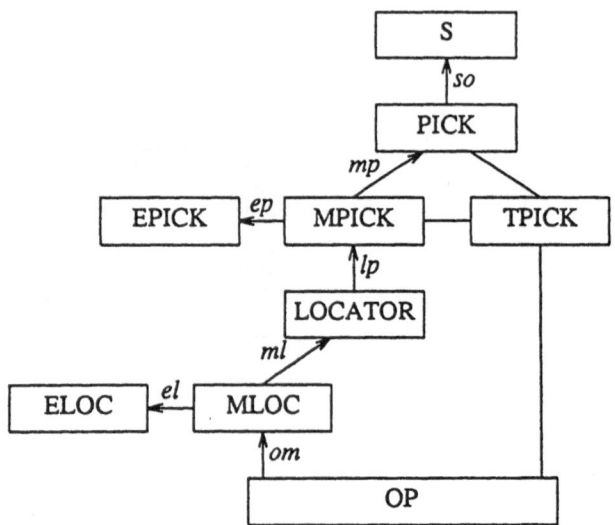

Figure 5: PICK Logical Input Device

$OP = (\prod_{m \,:\, M} om!m \to OP) \, \Pi \, (pictrigger \to OP)$

$MLOC_p = (om?m \to el!plm\,(m) \to MLOC_{plm\,(m)})$
$\qquad | \, (sampleloc \to ml!p \to MLOC_p)$

$ELOC_p = (el?p\prime \to ELOC_{p\prime})$

$LOCATOR = (sampleloc \to ml?p \to lp!p \to LOCATOR)$

$MPICK_v = (lp?p \to ep!pm\,(p) \to MPICK_{pm\,(p)})$
$\qquad | \, (pictrigger \to mp!v \to MPICK_v)$

$EPICK_v = (ep?v\prime \to EPICK_{v\prime})$

$TPICK = (pictrigger \to TPICK)$

$PICK = (pictrigger \to mp?v \to so!v \to PICK)$

The function *plm* returns the position corresponding to the raw input value *m* and *pm* returns the PICK measure corresponding to the point *p*. The description includes two echo processes. *ELOC* echoes the position of the LOCATOR device, and might take the form of a cursor which moves across the display space as the physical input device is moved by the operator. *EPICK* echoes the PICK logical input value. This might take the form of highlighting the primitive currently picked. Separation of the *MLOC* and *MPICK* processes also helps to focus attention on precisely where in the output pipeline of the graphics system picking is taking place; for example does picking take place before or after rendering? GKS itself is vague as to where picking takes place. Separation does not answer the question, but does at least cause it to be asked!

The decomposition of logical input devices into operations at different levels of abstraction, fits in nicely with the description of input contained in the Computer Graphics Reference Model, an International Standard, currently at the stage of Draft.[21]

The paper by Duce et al.[5] contains other examples of hierarchical input devices.

5 Conclusions

The logical input device concept provides a separation between the types of input values with which an application program operates and the physical devices from which such values originate. In this respect, the concept is an extremely valuable aid to writing application programs which are independent of the characteristics of the particular hardware devices used to generate the input values. The main difficulty with this concept stems from the diverse range of input hardware available and the fact that whilst a program may be movable from one set of devices to another, it is possible for one set to provide an extremely good user interface, whilst the second provides a totally unusable interface.

One approach to this problem is to provide the application program far more control over the composition of input devices and attributes such as prompt, echo and acknowledgement type than is done in the current graphics standards. The GKS Revision activity is exploring some aspects, mainly compositional aspects, of this.

The hierarchical input devices idea can help in this regard by raising the level of abstraction of the input values used by the application above the basic classes provided in GKS. If the application wants, say, a position and choice as an atomic value, this can be achieved by an appropriate hierarchical device. The application is then freed of the responsibility of constructing the value from its basic components. This ability coupled with the ability of applications to control which physical devices are used to realize the hierarchical device, gives a greater degree of independence between the application structure and device control. There is then much greater opportunity for moving the application program to a different device environment, without having to change the program structure. The work of moving the application is relegated to configuring the available physical devices in the new environment in an appropriate way.

References

1. D.B. Arnold and D.A. Duce, *ISO Standards for Computer Graphics - The First Generation,* Butterworths (1990).

2. K.W. Brodlie, D.A. Duce, and F.R.A. Hopgood, "The New Graphical Kernel System," *Computer-Aided Design* (1991).

3. I. Cotton, "Network Graphic Attention Handling," *Online 72 International Conference*, pp. 465-490, Brunel University, Uxbridge, England (1972).

4. D.A. Duce, P.J.W. ten Hagen, and R. van Liere, "Components, Frameworks and GKS Input," in *Proceedings of Eurographics '89*, ed. W. Hansmann, F.R.A. Hopgood and W. Strasser, North-Holland (1989).

5. D.A. Duce, R. van Liere, and P.J.W. ten Hagen, "An Approach to Hierarchical Input Devices," *Computer Graphics Forum* 9(1), pp. 15-26 (1990).

6. G. Faconti and F. Paterno', "Specification and Verification of Graphical I/O Objects through the Temporal Logic Formalism," CNR-Istituto CNUCE, Pisa, Italy (1991).

7. J.D. Foley and V.L. Wallace, "The Art of Natural Graphic Man-Machine Conversation," *Proceedings IEEE* 62(4), pp. 462-470 (April 1974).

8. C.A.R. Hoare, *Communicating Sequential Processes,* Prentice-Hall International, London (1985).

9. F. R. A. Hopgood, D. A. Duce, J. R. Gallop, and D. C. Sutcliffe, *Introduction to the Graphical Kernel System (GKS),* Academic Press (1986). (Second Edition)

10. ISO, "Report of the Improved Graphical Input Model Special Rapporteur Group," ISO SC24 WG1 N342, ISO Central Secretariat (1989).

11. W.M. Newman, "A System for Interactive Graphical Programming," *SJCC 1968*, pp. 47-54, Thomson Books, Washington D.C. (1968).

12. J.B. Purvis, "The use of LOTOS for the Specification of Graphics Software," B.Sc. Thesis, Department of Computer Science, Brunel University, UK (June 1990).

13. D.S.H. Rosenthal, J.C. Michener, G. Pfaff, R. Kessener, and M. Sabin, "The Detailed Semantics of Graphics Input Devices," Computer Graphics **16**(3), pp. 33-38 (July 1982).

14. D. Soede, F. Arbab, I. Herman, and P.J.W. ten Hagen, "The GKS Input Model in Manifold," CWI, Amsterdam, the Netherlands (1991).

15. V.L. Wallace, "Tbe Semantics of Graphic Input Devices," Computer Graphics **10**(1), pp. 61-65 (April 1976).

16. "Graphical Kernel System (GKS) Functional Description, Version 3," DPS 13/WG5/25 (December 1978).

17. "Information processing systems - Computer graphics - Graphical Kernel System (GKS) functional description," ISO 7942, ISO Central Secretariat (August 1985).

18. "GKS Review Workshop," *Computer Graphics Forum* **6**(4), pp. 367-369 (1987).

19. "Information processing systems - Computer graphics - Graphical Kernel System (GKS) for three dimensions (GKS-3D) functional description," ISO/IEC 8805 (1988).

20. "Information processing systems - Computer graphics - Programmer's Hierarchical Interactive Graphics System functional description," ISO/EEC 9592: 1 (1989).

21. "Information processing systems - Computer graphics - Computer Graphics Reference Model," ISO/IEC DIS 11 072, ISO Central Secretariat Geneva (1991).

22. "Information processing systems - Computer graphics - Interface techniques for dialogues with graphical devices," IS 9636, ISO Central Secretariat (1991). In press.

A Generalised Event Mechanism for Interactive Systems

Peter Rosner

Mel Slater

Allan Davison[1]

Department of Computer Science

Queen Mary and Westfield College, London

Abstract

A new generalised mechanism is described for event distribution in system architectures involving multiple threads and a hierarchy of graphical or non-graphical elements. Comparison is made with the mechanisms provided in existing windowing systems and examples are given of how the new mechanism would be used in the construction of various applications.

1   Introduction

In this paper we examine the event distribution mechanisms provided by existing windowing systems and present a more generalised mechanism that provides better support for distributed architectures in interactive systems. After presenting the mechanism, we illustrate it with the example of an office document system. We also indicate how the mechanism could be used to construct windowing systems themselves.

The work arises from the graphics research activity being carried out at Queen Mary and Westfield College London (QMW) under the ESPRIT II funded SPIRIT Workstation project.

The objective of the SPIRIT project is to design and build a high performance workstation that can perform a range of computationally demanding activities. It

---

[1] Allan Davison is now at Canon Research Centre Europe, Guildford

includes hardware and software to support advanced systems in such fields as knowledge engineering, modelling and simulation, computer-aided engineering, image processing and high performance interactive 2D and 3D graphics. Included in the SPIRIT architecture is a graphics subsystem which carries out rendering, graphical object management, and user-input; it is configurable for a range of SPIRIT (and indeed other) hardware platforms. At QMW we have designed a device-independent software layer, the *Graphics Interface Layer (GIL)* for graphical output [1] and event management to enable such device-configurability. The GIL also acts as a platform on which a variety of graphics and windowing standards, and interactive applications can be built.

Just like all other GIL facilities, the generalised event mechanism, the *GEM*, is configured and activated by the application via a set of function calls. It has been designed to take advantage of SPIRIT's multi-process and multi-thread architecture, although it is equally useful within a single-thread framework.

The GEM is based on event distribution through a tree hierarchy of nodes. These nodes can be associated with concurrent processes enabling event broadcasting amongst them. This type of architecture with a broadcasting facility is seen as increasingly appropriate for modern multi-processor and distributed systems [2], [3]. The GEM also provides extensive control by the application over the distribution space within the hierarchy, which makes it particularly suitable for use in interactive systems. Application entities such as windows in a windowing system or folders/documents in an office system can be modelled as nodes, and logical containment relationships are represented by parent-child relationships within the hierarchy.

In applications built using currently available windowing systems, it is hard to separate graphical hierarchy from logical hierarchy for the purposes of event distribution, and a node must correspond to a window. By contrast the GEM enables a separation of these hierarchies. In the office system example presented in this paper, the logical sub-hierarchy has nodes representing folders and documents. Represented separately is the graphical sub-hierarchy for rendering and hit detection. Not only can the logical hierarchy of application objects be expressed using the GEM, but also nodes can be inserted into a hierarchy that have no connection at all to an application object. For example a node for monitoring user-events can be inserted at any point in the hierarchy.

The GEM also offers a richer set of facilities to enable an application to distribute synthetic events through the node hierarchy than that provided by current windowing systems, and allows the application to control the set of nodes to which an event is sent. In fact, the mechanism can be used to construct windowing systems themselves.

As we shall see in the examples, the facility of broadcasting an event to all nodes in a particular sub-hierarchy proves to be useful for operations such as rendering a graphical hierarchy, hit detection, and setting attributes. Such control over the set of nodes to which an event is distributed can prevent potential name clashes and inefficiencies inherent in 'flat' distribution strategies of systems such as Linda [4] or NeWS [5], [7].

2   The event models of windowing systems

The event models of windowing systems such as X11 [6], [7] and NeWS [5], [7], now both included within Sun's Open Windows [7], provide mechanisms rather than policy for event distribution, but these mechanisms were designed to work in the context of a graphical output hierarchy. In practice this means that event distribution is tied to the ordering of rendering and hit-detection.

Applications are structured in 2.5D windows that act as both drawing surfaces and event-sensitive regions. The set of windows forms a hierarchical tree structure with a child occupying a space completely inside its parent. Children can overlap and the stacking order is application-settable. Typically a user event (such as a mouse action) follows a path, until it is consumed by a window, from the frontmost window in which it has occurred through its ancestors to the root window which represents the frame buffer.

Client processes or threads can express interest in a window by providing it with an event template (or interest) against which matching is to be performed. If the event matches a template, it is passed to the process or thread which then acts upon it when it is ready.

Both X11 and NeWS provide facilities whereby an event can be intercepted by a window *before* it passes through the normal leaf-to-root distribution path. The technique used is to assign special types of interests to windows. Before carrying out the leaf-to-root distribution of the event, the system carries out a root-to-leaf inspection of these special types of interest. In X11 these are *passive grabs* which, if satisfied, cause subsequent events to be directed to the client owning the grabbing window. In NeWS the special types of interest are items in a *pre-interest list* for a window.

Both X11 and NeWS also allow application-generated events. NeWS allows new event types to be defined by the application; threads can express interests in such event types and thus event broadcasting can be carried out.

In the development of applications with certain types of user-interface and application architectures, only high level toolkit components for window management, dialogue management, option selection and data entry need be used. For such architectures the limited event models provided by current windowing systems present no real problem.

However as we have indicated for more complex interactive applications, windowing systems can impose a restrictive identity between logical hierarchy on the one hand, and graphical rendering/hit detection on the other. They do not support a full enough range of event distribution strategies within the hierarchy.

Nor do they provide facilities for event broadcasting within a limited sub-hierarchy. NeWS does support broadcasting, but the event distribution space is flat, with no means of specifying a subset of threads to which an event is to be broadcast. So event broadcasting is unnecessarily inefficient, and unique names must be used for event types.

3   Outline of the GEM

In the GEM we introduce the *event-node* (or *node*), a more abstract concept than 'window' or 'graphical object'. Event-nodes are structured hierarchically in the form of a tree for purposes of event distribution. An event is distributed via a GEM function call to a specified part of the hierarchy, the distribution path being determined by the type of function and its parameters. The various types of distribution are:

- *broadcast-top-down* : to all event-nodes in a subtree below a specified event-node, in a top-down order, used for example in rendering a graphical hierarchy of objects

- *broadcast-bottom-up*: to all event-nodes in a subtree below a specified event-node, in bottom-up order, used for example in hit-detection in a graphical hierarchy of objects

- *immediate-children, immediate-children-backwards*: to the immediate children of an event-node, used for example in enabling the contents of a folder in an office system to be displayed

- *path-up, path-up-with-propagation-test*: to event-nodes in leaf-to-root order, used for example in a windowing system to implement the passage of an event from the 'hit' window back to the frame buffer

- *path-down*: to event-nodes in root-to-leaf order, used for example in a windowing system to implement the initial passage of an event from from the root window to the 'hit' window

- *single-cast*: to a single event-node, used for example to add text to a particular document in an office system

In addition to specifying the type of distribution it is possible to 'block' or 'unblock' paths between parent and children. This can further limit the distribution space.

An event-node has an associated set of *interests*. As in windowing systems, an interest contains a template against which the event is matched. Each interest can be associated with

- a *queue*, on which matching events are placed and picked up later by a thread or process

or

- an *interest-behaviour*. The term *behaviour* denotes a reference to a callback procedure that is executed immediately the interest is matched.

If an event reaches an interest in its distribution path and the event matches that interest, it can be placed on the queue (in which case it is processed later by the thread or process) or else the interest-behaviour can be executed immediately.

Apart from event distribution, the application can invoke the following:

- the creation/deletion of an event node

- the creation/deletion of a queue

- the creation/deletion of an interest and its association, in a node, with a queue or behaviour

- the positioning of an event-node within the hierarchy

- the blocking/unblocking of links between parent and child nodes. A block between a child and parent limits the distribution space for top-down and bottom-up types of broadcasting within the hierarchy

While the GEM has been designed to operate in SPIRIT's multi-process and multi-thread environment, it can equally operate in a single threaded system, where callback procedures are executed in response to matched events.

4   Detailed Description of the GEM

4.1   Nodes and interests

Figure 1 shows a sample set of nodes. Components of a node are shown in detail - each node has contents and links to a set of child nodes.

Node contents include

- the *blocked* flag which can limit the distribution space for the node and its descendants (to be described in more detail in the next section)

- the *interest-list*

- the *noPropagateOnMatch* indicator

- the *noPropagateOnFailMatch* indicator. These last two indicators control the propagation of events for the *path-up* type of distribution.

Before describing how an event is distributed amongst the nodes, we will describe the interest-list for a node and how matching is performed once an event reaches the node in its distribution path.

Each *interest* in the interest-list has

- a *field-list* of *event-fields* giving a description of how events are to be matched.

- an *exclusive* flag which specifies whether or not a matching event is to be consumed

- an *interest-behaviour* which is a reference to a callback procedure, or else is null

- a *queue* which is where matching events are to be placed, or else is null

- a *pathDownFlag* which determines whether matching against the interest is attempted for different types of event distribution. If the flag is set to true, matching against the interest is attempted for the *path-down* type of event distribution only; if it is set to false, matching is attempted for all other types of distribution

• a *priority* which determines the order of matching attempts in relation to those other interests, within the node, that have the same setting of *pathDownFlag*.

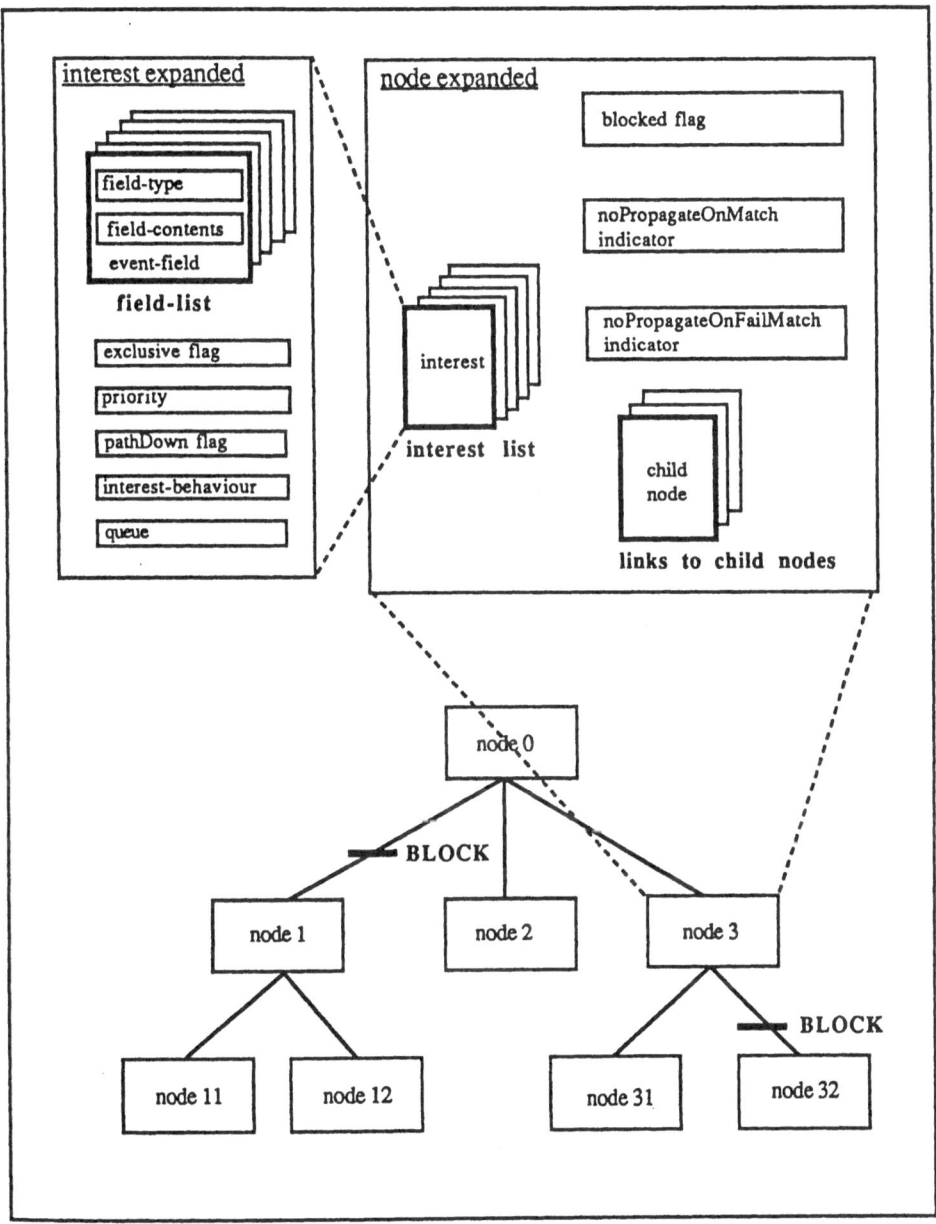

Fig 1 Expanded View of Node Structure

An event-field contains

- a *field-type*

- *field-contents*

An *event* contains

- a field-list, as in an interest

- (optionally) some data to be used by the application.

If a node is reached in the distribution path of an event, then the event is tested against interests associated with the node. For the *path-down* type of distribution, this set includes interests whose *pathDownFlag* is set to true. For all other distribution types the set includes interests whose *pathDownFlag* is set to false. The testing against interests proceeds until the subset of interests is exhausted, or else a match is encountered with an interest whose *exclusive* flag is set to true.

An event-field in an interest is tested against an event-field with the same field-type, if one exists, in the event. If no event-field of the same field-type exists in the event then matching fails. (For example if the interest contains the event-field of type 'mouse-activity', but no event-field of the 'mouse activity' type exists in the event, then matching against the interest will fail). Where field types match in the event and the interest match, further matching of the event-fields takes place as follows.

Where the field-contents of the event-field in the interest has a special wildcard value, it always successfully matches the event-field in the event. (For example, if a 'mouse-activity' type of event-field in an interest has field-contents with the wildcard value, then it will successfully match a 'mouse-activity' type of event-field in an event, irrespective of the latter's field-contents). Otherwise matching is performed by executing a *matching-behaviour*, specific to the field-type. The matching-behaviour is a boolean function that takes as parameters the field-contents of the two event-fields - the one in the interest and the one in the event. A table of field-types, with corresponding matching-behaviours, is maintained. Thus, for example, for the case of field-type 'graphical region', the field-contents of the event-field for the interest would give a reference to a graphical region, the field-contents of the event-field for the event would give a reference to a point, and the behaviour for the field-type would be 'is point in region?'.

An event matches an interest if there is a successful match for all event-fields in the interest. If this is the case and the *interest-behaviour* is null, the event gets placed on the queue given in the interest. If an interest matches the event, and the interest-behaviour is non-null, then the behaviour is executed (the queue part of the interest being ignored). If parameters denoting both interest-behaviour and queue are null, neither a behaviour is executed nor is an event placed on a queue, even though the interest and event may match.

The node's *noPropagateOnMatch* indicator and *noPropagateOnFailMatch* indicator, applicable only to the *path-up* type of distribution, are both field-lists. After the processing of the list of interests for a node, a match may or may not have been found. If a match has been found and if the *noPropagateOnMatch* field-list matches the event's field-list, then the event is not propagated to further nodes in the *path-up* distribution path. If a match has not been found and the *noPropagateOnFailMatch* field-list matches the event, propagation is similarly inhibited (this is equivalent to the *doNotPropagate* mask in X11). If both of the *noPropagate* field lists are empty, then providing an event has not been consumed (by a matching interest with *exclusive* set) within a node, then it will always propagate to the next node in the *path-up* distribution sequence.

4.2   Event Distribution

We now describe the various strategies for the propagation of events. An event is distributed via a call to one of the event distribution functions. Either the system's input event handler or an application carries out such a call. In the former case the call is always the *broadcast-top-down* type and the event is directed at the highest level node.

Depending on the interests the event encounters at a node, it may get sent on to the next node in the distribution sequence or else distribution may terminate, in which case the value returned is the handle of the terminating node.

Each distribution type can either be invoked normally or else with a block-override parameter signifying that all blocks are to be ignored. However, in the following description of the possible distribution types we assume that block-override has *not* been requested:

a)   *broadcast-top-down*

The event and the root of the required distribution space are supplied as parameters to the application call. The distribution sequence is illustrated in Figure 2 where the application or raw event handler issues a *broadcast-top-down* call with parameters *event x and node 0.* The nodes in the distribution path are shown unshaded and the order of distribution is given by the numbers in the top right hand corner of each unshaded node. The order of distribution is (recursively) left-right and top-bottom. Potentially all descendant nodes are in the event distribution space. However where a link to a child has the *blocked* flag set, the child and its descendants are excluded from the distribution space. Thus node 1 and below and node 32 are excluded. At each node event matching takes place against those interests whose *pathDownFlag* is set to false.

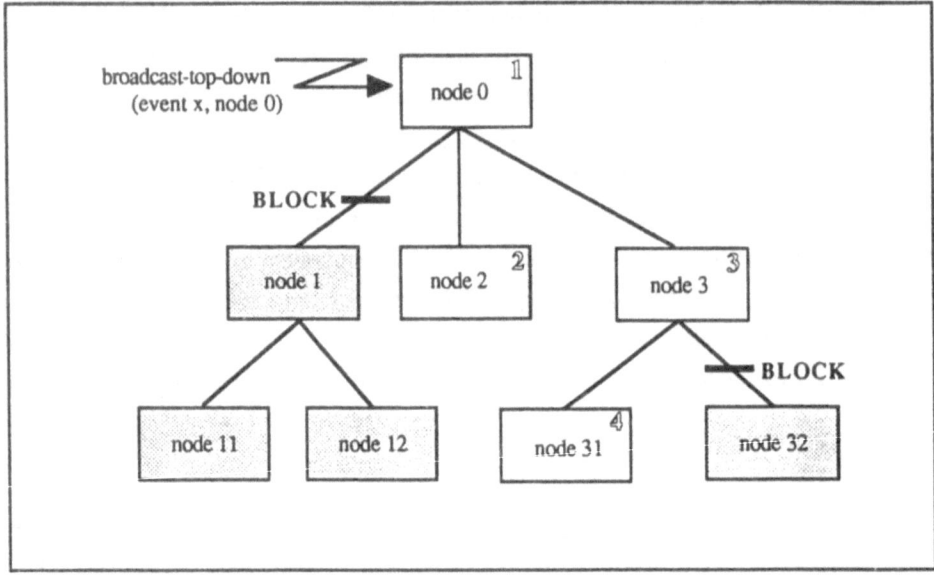

Figure 2 broadcast-top-down distribution type

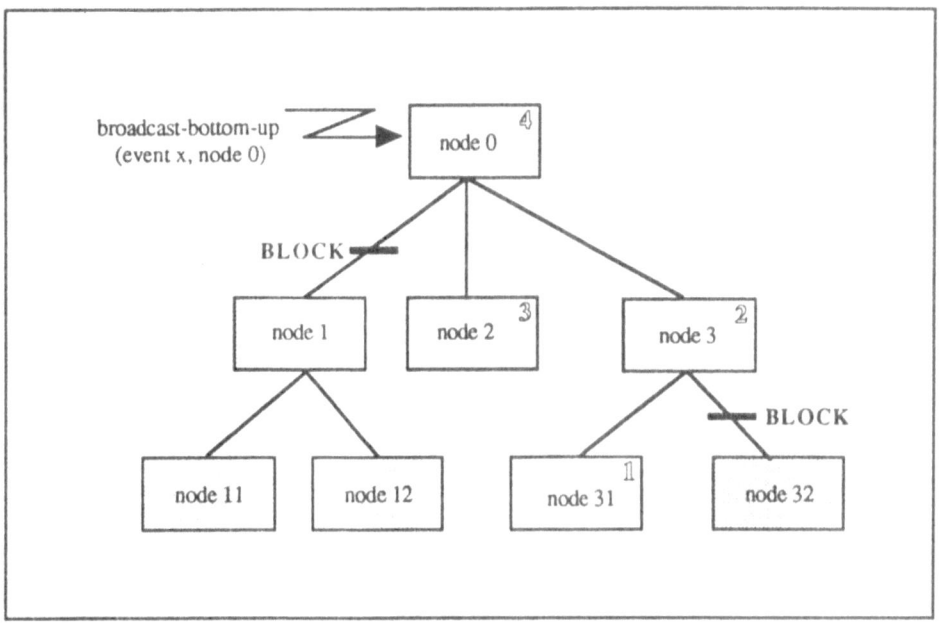

Figure 3 *broadcast-bottom-up* distribution type

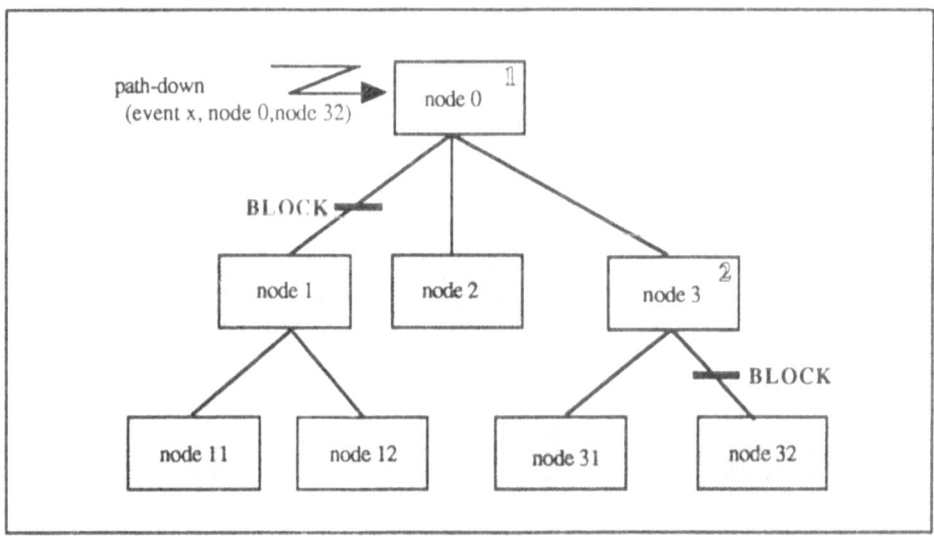

Figure 4 *path-down* distribution type

96

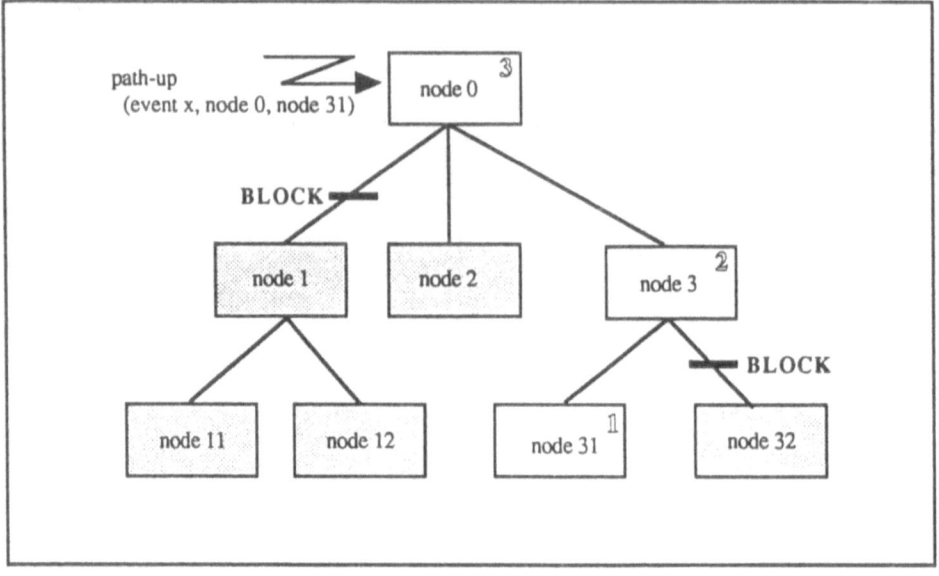

Figure 5 *path-up* distribution types

b)   *broadcast-bottom-up*

As illustrated in Figure 3, the event distribution space of *broadcast-bottom-up* is the same as for *broadcast-top-down*. However the order of distribution is (recursively) right-left and bottom-top, i.e. exactly the opposite order to *broadcast-top-down*.

c)   *path-down*

As illustrated in Figure 4, the event and two nodes are supplied as parameters to the *path-down* call. These nodes are the root node of the subtree at which the event distribution is to start and the descendant (usually a leaf node) at which it is to stop. However if there are blocks in the sequence, the distribution space excludes nodes below the block closest to the subtree root. So in Figure 4 the event is distributed only to node 0 followed by node 3. Node 32 is excluded because, despite being specified as the descendant, its block excludes it from the sequence. At each node in the sequence, matching of the event is only performed against interests whose *pathDownFlag* is set to true.

d)   *path-up*

Figure 5 illustrates cases d) and e). In both cases the event and two nodes representing subtree root and descendant are again supplied as parameters. Where there are no blocks in the sequence, event distribution starts at the descendant and proceeds upwards to the subtree root. Where there are blocks, distribution starts at the node above the block closest to the subtree root and proceeds to the subtree root. At each node in the sequence, matching is carried out against those interests whose *pathDownFlag* is set to false.

e) *path-up-with-propagation-test*

This is the same as case d) except that propagation to the next node in the sequence depends upon not only on the fate of the matching at the current node, but also on tests against the node's *noPropagateOnMatch* and *noPropagateOnFailMatch* interests described earlier.

f) *immediate-children*

As illustrated in Figure 6, two parameters are supplied: the event and the handle to a node. Distribution of the event proceeds to all immediate children, without passing to their descendants. Where a child node is blocked, it is excluded from the distribution. Matching takes place against interests whose *pathDownFlag* is set to false.

g) *immediate-children-backwards*

This is the same as case h) except that the distribution is carried out from the last to the first of the immediate children.

h) *single-cast*

As illustrated in Figure 7, two parameters are supplied: the event and a handle to a node. The event is matched against interests with *pathDownFlag* set to false, but not passed on to any other nodes. A block on a node does not prevent an event being *single-cast* to it.

98

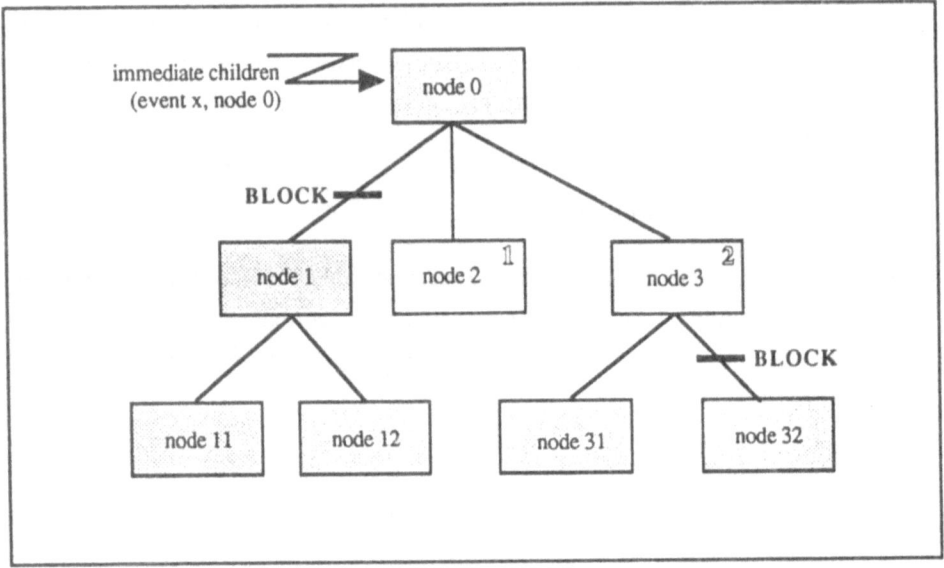

Fig 6 *immediate-children* distribution type

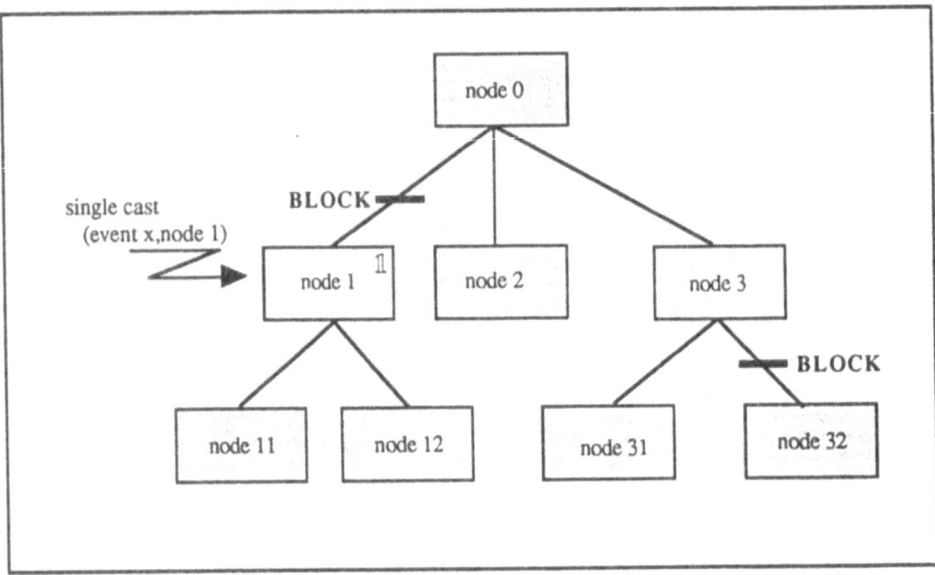

Fig 7 single-cast distribution type

4.3   Redistribution

In addition to the different types of distribution, there is also the facility for an application to *redistribute* an event once it has been consumed by matching an interest whose *exclusive* flag is set. Redistribution would proceed at the point at which propagation was last terminated in the distribution sequence. To enable this, an event contains extra fields to store the type of distribution, the node parameters for the distribution, the latest node and the last interest matched.

5   A direct manipulation office system

Imagine a direct manipulation desk-top document system in which a folder contains either documents or folders. There is a logical relationship between a folder and the document or folder it contains. This relationship is dynamic: a document, for example, may move from one folder to another. However this relationship should not necessarily determine or constrain the graphical structure when displayed. For instance the documents could be stacked, laid out in a grid or spread across different desktops.

This separation of logical and graphical hierarchies can be reflected in the GEM structure as shown in Figure 8, where the document system hierarchy contains two sub-hierarchies, one to represent the logical structure and one representing the front-to-back ordering of the documents and folders on the display. The important difference between this system and a windowing system is that whilst the logical hierarchy initially determines the order of rendering and hit detection for the office entities, the user may alter the rendering and hit detection ordering without altering the logical hierarchy. Each folder or document, has a single associated node in each of the hierarchies.

If an entity is not currently being displayed, the *blocked* flag is set in the link between the corresponding node in the rendering hierarchy and its parent. Figure 8 shows that only the top level master document is currently being displayed. For an entity to be brought to the top of the rendering hierarchy, it is made the first child of *rendering hierarchy*.

We describe here a way of using the GEM to carry out various operations within the office system. These are selecting a document or folder by bringing it to the front of the display, opening a folder so that its contents also appear on the desktop, and specifying the security level of a folder and its contents.

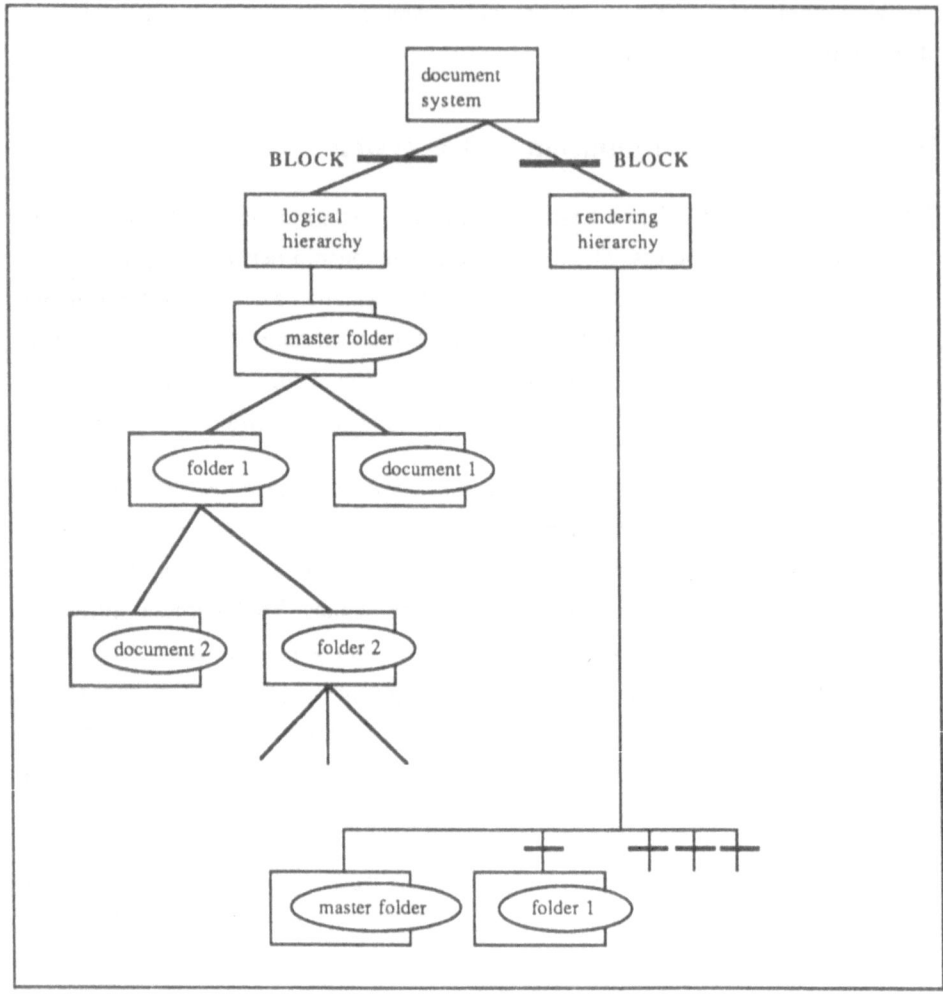

Figure 8 Document system hierarchy

5.1 Selecting a folder or document

Selecting an office entity involves access to the rendering hierarchy only. All raw input events are broadcast to the top level *document system* node. Suppose the user executes an action (for example a mouse click) to select a folder or document that is currently partially obscured.

In response to this type of event the *document system* performs hit detection behaviour by issuing a *broadcast-bottom-up* call with two parameters: the event *select* (with mouse coordinates), and the node *rendering hierarchy*. Each child node of *rendering hierarchy* has been set up by the application with an interest whose interest-fields include the *select* event and a field-behaviour to test for the region occupied by the document or folder. However the event will only be broadcast to nodes corresponding to visible entities in the rendering hierarchy, since an invisible entity has the links to its parent blocked.

If a match is found, then the corresponding behaviour at the 'hit' node places that node as the first child of *rendering hierarchy* and a *broadcast down* call is performed with parameters: the *render* event and the *rendering hierarchy* node. The document or folder will thus appear at the front on the display.

5.2   Opening a folder

Opening a folder involves accessing both the logical hierarchy and the rendering hierarchy. Suppose the user executes an action (for example a mouse double click) to indicate the opening of a folder. A behaviour corresponding to this event type at the *document system* node issues a *broadcast-bottom-up* call with parameters: the event (e.g. *double-click*) and the node *rendering hierarchy*.

At the node where a hit is detected, another behaviour causes the event *emerge* to be sent to the immediate children of its corresponding node in the logical hierarchy. Thus for example if the user had indicated the opening of the folder *master folder*, then the *emerge* event would be sent to *document 1* and *folder 1*. Interest-behaviours activated by successful matching of the event at these nodes then move the corresponding nodes in the rendering hierarchy to be the first children of the *rendering hierarchy* node and their blocks to their parent are removed. The 'hit' node is then placed as the first child of the *rendering hierarchy* node. Finally the event *render* is *broadcast-top-down* from the node *rendering hierarchy*.

As a result the folder and its contents now appear at the front of the display.

5.3   Changing Security Level

Changing security level requires accessing the logical hierarchy only. (The security level might determine access by different levels of user.) Suppose the user wishes to alter the security level of all documents that are descendants of a particular folder. This is achieved by issuing a *broadcast-top-down* call with parameters: the event *securityLevel* (with the new value of the level) and the node for the folder. Only nodes associated with documents (as opposed to folders) would have an interest in this type of event and therefore only their associated behaviours would be carried out to change the security levels.

5.4 Adding nodes to carry out monitoring

Suppose that we wish to monitor all raw input events from the user, to be stored for later replay. This could be done by adding another child, with no block, to the *document system* node. Attached to this new node would be an interest that enabled all types of input event to be detected and a queue which would allow an asynchronous thread to collect together these raw events and store them.

This is an example of a node that bears no relation at all to entities in the application, yet nevertheless can be inserted into the node hierarchy. This node could be inserted to perform input event monitoring in any type of system, with minimum disruption.

6 GEM and the construction of windowing systems

GEM not only supports the construction of interactive applications such as the one outlined in the last section, it also provides the basic building blocks for the construction of windowing systems themselves.

Because a window is both logically and graphically contained in its parent, only a single event distribution hierarchy is needed, each node of which corresponds to a window. In a similar fashion to the office system example, the *broadcast-bottom-up* type of distribution of the raw event enables hit detection to be carried out. Once the 'hit' node has been established, the *path-up* and *path-down* distribution types are used to implement the passage of an event along a single path in the tree as outlined in section 2 of this paper. Finally the *broadcast-top-down* type of distribution is used to implement rendering of windows.

7 Further Work

The GEM is currently being developed for the SPIRIT project. We are also looking into further applications, besides those given in this paper, where the GEM may prove useful. This includes scene modelling and interaction in 3D graphical applications.

8 Conclusions

We have outlined a generalised event mechanism that supports the construction of interactive applications which can be modelled using a distribution hierarchy for events. GEM has greater flexibility than the event models provided by windowing systems in that it gives the facility for the graphical and logical hierarchies within an application to be separated. It also enables greater control by applications of event distribution and enables selective distribution to localised parts of the hierarchy. Finally, it can be used for the construction of windowing systems themselves.

References

[1] Slater M., Miranda E., Davison A., Drake K., Kordakis E.: *The Graphics Subsystem of the Spirit Workstation*, Procedings Graphics and Interaction In ESPRIT Sessions, Eurographics 89, Hamburg FRG

[2] Tanenbaum A.S., Renesse, R. van, Staveren H. van, Sharp G.J., Mullender J., Jansen J., Rossum G. van: *Experiences with the Amoeba Distributed Operating System*, Communications of the ACM, December, 1990, Vol 33 No 12

[3] Rozier, M. and Martins, L.: *The Chorus distributed operating system: some design issues*, Distributed Operating Systems - Theory and Practice (ed Y. Paker et al.), NATO ASI Series, vol F28, Springer-Verlag, pp 261-87

[4] Carriero N., Gelernter D.: *The S/Net's Linda Kernel* ACM Transactions on Computer Systems Vol. 4 No. 2, May 1986

[5] *NeWS 2.1 Programmers Guide*, Sun Microsystems

[6] Scheiffler R.W., Gettys J.: *The X Window System*, ACM Transactions on Graphics, April 1986, Vol. 5 No 2 pp 79-109

[7] Davison A., Drake K., Roberts W., Slater M.: *Distributed Window Systems, a Practical Guide to X11 and OpenWindows*, 1992, Addison-Wesley

Acknowledgements

We would like to thank Kieron Drake and Eliot Miranda for the initial proposals of the generalised event mechanism we have described and the early discussions on the topic. We would also like to thank other members of the Advanced Computing Environment Laboratory at the Computer Science Department at Queen Mary and Westfield College, in particular Mark Brown and Morten Ronseth, for useful feedback and comments in writing this paper.

Generalising MVC to ERID : orthogonalising entities, representations, and input dispatching to interaction classes

Ramzan Mohamed*

Institute of Educational Technology

Open University

Walton Hall

Milton Keynes MK7 6AA, U.K.

Stephen W. Draper

GIST (Glasgow Interactive Systems cenTre)

University of Glasgow

Glasgow, U.K.

Abstract

Limitations of Smalltalk's Model-View-Controller (MVC) paradigm are discussed. A novel approach to generalising MVC is described. Our approach based on application Entities, visual Representations and Input Dispatching (ERID) decouples the conventional interdependence of MVC's View and Controller subclass hierarchies. Instead we have generalised the user interface capability of visible entities by allowing each entity to handle its own user interaction through the incorporation of a generic input dispatcher. The interface is easily configured by the use of a variety of generic interface controllers.

1   Introduction

In many ways Smalltalk is currently the best environment for building experimental programs with a high HCI (human computer interface) component to their design, partly because of its support for rapidly modifying prototype versions. A large project in which

---

* Now with Object Designers Limited, Glebe House, Great Hallingbury, Bishop's Stortford, Hertfordshire U.K. CM22 7TY

we participated[†] [1,2] consequently selected Smalltalk-80 as the platform. We built a program, Direct Manipulation of Mechanics Microworlds (DM^3), which presented simulations of moving objects in order to aid in teaching Newton's laws of motion. While the outline of the underlying functional requirements (e.g. for the simulation engine) were clear from fairly early on, many aspects of its presentation to the end users (school children) went on evolving throughout the project in response to pilot testing on children. Smalltalk supported most of these changes well, but in one respect we were led to improve its ability: we often needed to change the interactive response of some screen object to user input (for instance to make it respond to grabbing). The possible set of interactive responses was relatively fixed, yet each new combination of screen object and behaviour required new code to be written as long as only the basic Smalltalk MVC mechanism was available. We were led to generalise this (into a software model we call ERID for Entities, Representations, Input Dispatchers) so that any new combination of existing behaviours with existing screen objects could be accomplished by sending a single simple message.

2   Smalltalk MVC

The basic MVC (Model-View-Controller) paradigm [3,4] in Smalltalk allows multiple visual representations of a single conceptual entity to be coordinated (generally within a single application window). There is a single underlying application entity ("model") (for instance, an entire simulation in our case), which holds the variables and domain contents (e.g. objects, forces and meters). It may be represented in any number of windows (views); for each such window, it has a corresponding matching controller (figure 1). The view is responsible for specifying the screen appearance; the controller handles user input events. Whenever the application entity ("model") changes, all screen representations ("views") are, typically, automatically notified. User input in any window may interact via the controller (for that screen representation of that entity instance) associated with the view; and may result in sending a message to the underlying application entity; if so, then other screen representations (views) may well be updated too. This update mechanism is normally via Smalltalk's dependency mechanism (dashed arrows in figure 1).

[†] Conceptual Change in Science - a three year ESRC funded multi-disiplinary project comprising R. Driver, R. Hartley, C. Mallen and D. Twigger (Leeds University); S. Hennessy, T.M.M. O'Shea and E. Scanlon (Open University); C. O'Malley (Nottingham University) and the authors.

The advantages are that screen representations, e.g. icons, may be changed by assigning a different graphic image to a variable in the "view" (screen representation object instance); and input behaviour associated with a screen representation may be changed by installing a different controller class or more infrequently by editing a method in the "controller" instance associated with the view. This flexibility is enough for the familiar approach (cf. the Macintosh tool box), where all user interaction is via a few standard types of objects: buttons, icons, check boxes etc. Here interactive behaviour (e.g. clicking, dragging) is uniformly associated with a class of screen representation. This close association between Views and Controllers is reflected in the similarity of the Smalltalk class hierarchies for the View and Controller classes. The closeness between views and their associated controller's classes is also illustrated when we realise that the addition of a totally new type of view is not complete until both the new view and new controller classes have been created.

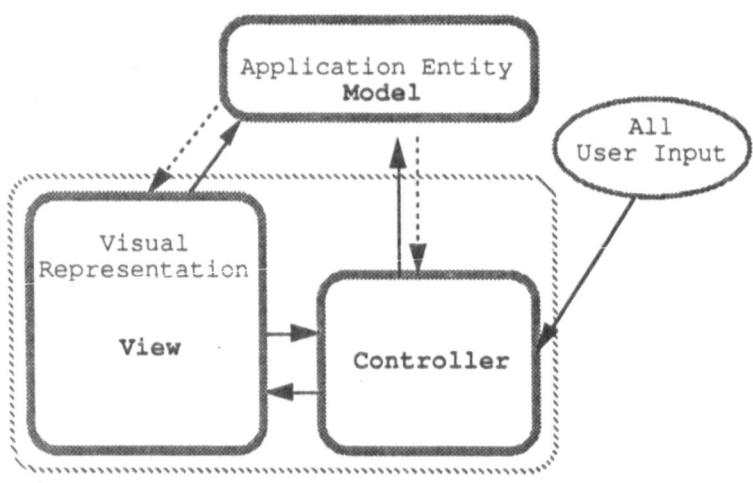

Figure 1 Smalltalk Model-View-Controller Relationships

However in our project we were interested in a more thorough-going interpretation of direct manipulation, inspired by Randall Smith's ARK [5]. Here, user interaction should be "directly" associated with all objects, not just a few standardised control objects like buttons or sliders. For instance balls not only bounced, but could be grabbed, lifted, thrown by users. Consequently we were constantly trying out alternative behaviours and combinations of behaviours from a relatively fixed set (pointing, dragging, etc.) on each of our simulated objects: balls, skaters, speedboats, cardboard boxes etc. It was obviously wasteful to be rewriting controllers manually for each new combination of object shape and behaviour (either singly or in combination).

3   An Alternative Approach

3.1   User Interactivity

An examination of the basic nature of human computer interaction reveals that it is essentially a combination of two elements, a visual focus and an interaction (e.g. Smalltalk controllers). We can see that the visual focus is useful in "guiding" the user to a particular area of the screen. In addition, the visual nature of the focus can give the user valuable cues as to the interaction style they may encounter there, e.g. labelled (rounded) boxes may imply a button style of interaction, while an array of (externally labelled) circles may imply a "radio-button" style of interaction.

The interactive element essentially gathers the user's input, and through the use of appropriate feedback mechanisms (e.g. highlighting or key clicks, etc.) registers with the user the current state of the interaction. Ultimately the result of a particular interaction is communicated back to the underlying application.

In most conventional user interfaces the link between the visual focus and the interaction is a direct one, e.g. when adding a radio button to a dialogue box, the programmer adds the button as a single entity, the visual appearance (focus) and interactivity are combined. While this linkage is useful in many situations, there are situations where the user interface builder would like to decouple the visual appearance from the underlying interactivity. It is a useful feature of a flexible user interface system for this direct linkage to be broken.

3.2   ERID

Our requirement was to be able to write the code to do with each separate behaviour (e.g. dragging) just once, via a generic controller for each type of behaviour, but without any significant coding to create any combination of screen representation, behaviours, and sensitivity to subareas of the screen graphic associated with an object.

In effect we have generalised the MVC approach to a four component approach we call ERID. Slightly different from the MVC, an individual underlying Entity corresponds to the "model", where its screen Representation is controlled by a Smalltalk object instance corresponding to the "view". The "controller" for this entity is in effect split into an Input Dispatcher and zero or more generic interaction objects (controllers), see figure 2.

In line with our conclusion in the previous section, we have split the direct link between an entity's (screen object) representation and its interactivity. The representation, in the present implementation of ERID, is an attribute of the entity and as such may be changed throughout the life of the entity. Indeed, entities from the same class (type) may possess different representations from their default representations.

The generic input dispatcher receives user input events from the window controller if the mouse is over the active boundary of the screen object (thick rectangle), and consults a table specific to that screen object in order to decide how that particular event is to be handled. The table consists of triples (implemented as composite objects), one triple per behaviour to which that screen object is sensitive. Each triple specifies the type of input event, the subarea of the screen representation (e.g. which part of an icon) which is to be sensitive, and the generic interaction controller (e.g. dragging or clicking) to which control is to be handed. When the interaction is terminated, control is handed back to the window controller.

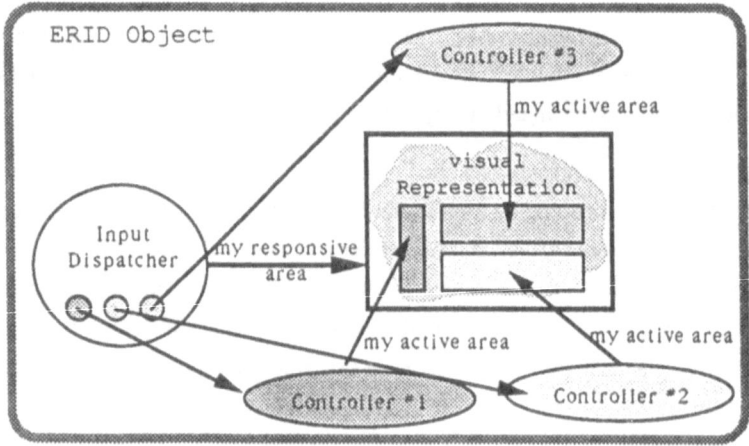

figure 2 ERID component Relationships

Figure 2 illustrates a situation where a screen object possesses three different types of interactivity (denoted by controllers #1 to #3), with each controller active over a small subarea of the screen object's representation (the three filled rectangles). If an appropriate input event matches that of one of the three triples in the input dispatcher's internal table, then control will pass from the input dispatcher to that controller.

In the present implementation the subareas are held in normalised form, with reference to their screen object's representational dimensions. This means that if a representation is expanded or shrunk, then the active subareas will still occupy the same relative areas of the representation, and no repositioning of subareas is needed.

The present design of the ERID input dispatcher just relies on a combination of event type and active subarea to determine whether the associated generic controller will be given control. The generic input dispatcher may be made more sophisticated by the inclusion of addition constraint parameters. Indeed the design will support a number of different "generic" input dispatchers. With our current input dispatcher there is no restriction on the number or types of interactions that an entity may possess. The active areas may be separate as in figure 2, or they may overlap (figure 3). In the latter case, the first triple in the input dispatcher's dispatch table that responds to the event type will be given control - this heuristic may of course be changed.

3.3   Interface Customisation

Making a given screen object sensitive to a new (or another) behaviour now requires only the addition of a new entry (triple) to its input dispatcher's dispatch table. Figure 3 shows the same ERID input dispatcher as in figure 2, but now with another triple added to its dispatch table. The net result is that the ERID entity now possesses another degree of interactivity. The ERID approach enables us to customise any screen object's user interface to a large degree using our (currently small) set of generic interface controllers, event types and visual representations in an orthogonal way.

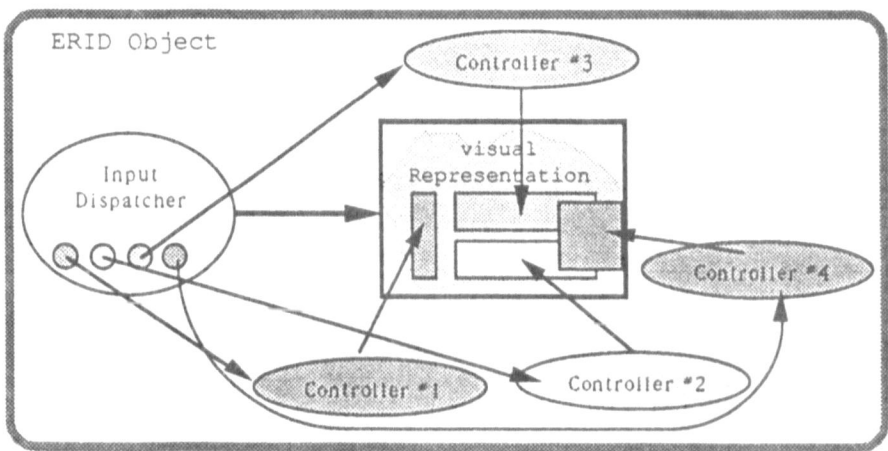

Figure 3 Adding more interactivity

Adding a new kind of interactive behaviour to the system (e.g. rotating the icon) simply requires implementing a new subclass of generic controller specialised to handle this particular behaviour. Once added, however, it can be immediately used by any or all screen objects, simply by adding an appropriate entry to each screen object's input dispatcher table. Figure 4, below, illustrates this by showing how we can use this new interactivity to make our example screen object rotatable about diagonally opposite corners (controllers #3 and #4). We could easily have made it rotatable about any corner by simply adding two more entries into this entity's input dispatcher table with active areas over the other two corners.

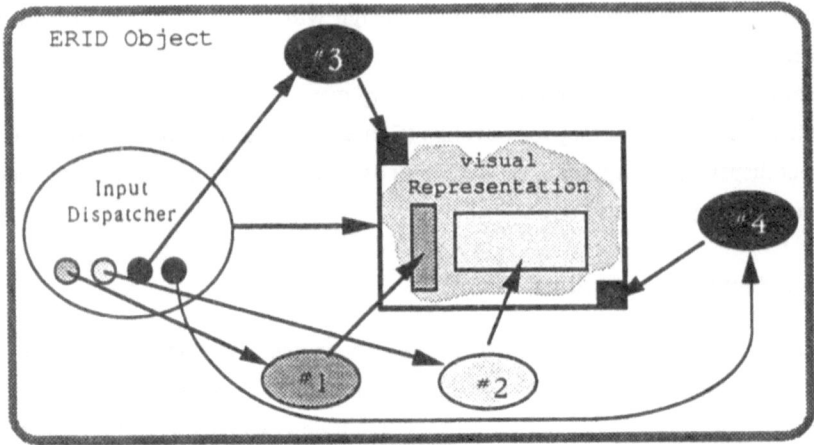

Figure 4 Adding a new interaction style

3.4 ERID Controllers

In our current design the generic controllers that support the interactivity of ERID objects incorporate forms of both interactive feedback and semantics. Each class of generic controller is responsible for providing its own feedback mechanisms, either visual and/or acoustic, to the user. The type of feedback used depends entirely on the style of interaction of the controller. In DM^3, a number of feedback mechanisms were trialled. Each trial necessitated some recoding of the controller.

The semantics of the ERID controllers fall under two groupings, fixed and flexible. The majority of controllers have a fixed notion of semantics (e.g. dragging, grabbing, etc.) where the interaction has a single meaning in the context of the ERID object.

An example of an ERID controller with flexible semantics is our button controller. This generic controller mimics the interactivity of button presses. When the button controller takes over, it provides feedback, and initiates the consequences of the user's action (pressing a button). However the semantics of the action will vary. We have chosen to model this variability by providing the button controller with the ability to handle a list of consequent actions rather than limiting it to a single action. These actions are defined in terms of Smalltalk message expressions, i.e. we can specify an action by specifying a message and the object that will receive that message. In this way we can allow a single button to trigger a complex sequence of actions programmed *a priori* and initiated by the user. This scheme has worked well in the context of DM^3 to the extent that our colleagues were able to synthesise radio buttons by simply allowing each individual button tell its neighbouring buttons to disable themselves. The action list associated with each button instance can be dynamically configured by an external agent. The actions in the list will be performed (only) when the user presses the button.

3.5 Extending ERID across multiple windows

So far we have discussed ERID within the context of a single application window. As the ERID architecture stands it can accommodate the support of ERID objects across multiple windows by simply changing a single attribute of the ERID object's input dispatcher that describes its environment (window). However the ERID object will appear identical, visually and behaviourally, across all windows.

We have extended the flexibility of the ERID architecture by endowing ERID objects with the ability to support a range of representations and input dispatcher tables at one time (see figure 5). Applying these two features orthogonally in association with a particular window will create an ERID object that possesses a complex mosaic of representations and behaviours spanning a multitude of application windows.

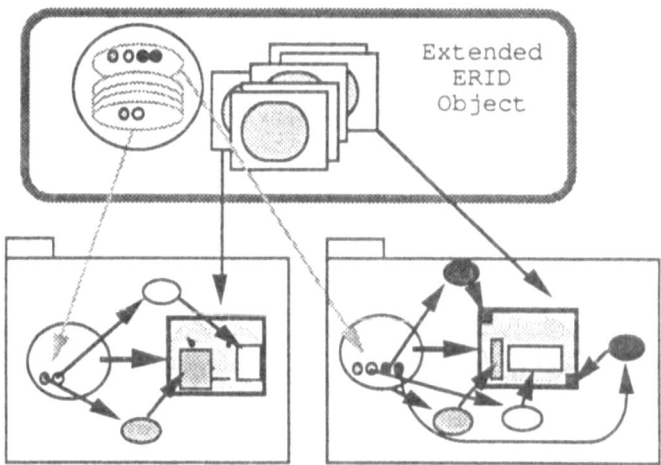

Figure 5 ERID Support for Multiple windows

3.6 Summary

In this approach there is one generic controller type per interactive behaviour, shared by all screen objects that use this style of interaction (e.g. dragging, clicking). It is represented by its own subclass, one of a number of generic controller classes. As before, each screen representation of an entity (possibly several, each in a different window) has its own screen graphic as one of its essential properties. Associated with each such screen representation is an input dispatcher. These have individual dispatch tables for each representation instance, but usually share a generic mechanism for interpreting the tables to dispatch events. Table entries contain references to one of the generic controllers specifying a type of interactive behaviour. Underlying application entities in effect contain lists of pairs consisting of a screen representation and an input dispatcher, one pair per window in which a representation of the object appears. Combining visual representation and interactivity independently not only increases the reusability of components but also provides a very potent tool for graphical user interface experimentation.

4   Discussion

User interfaces bring out the need to combine several aspects in one item: underlying application semantics, screen appearance, and interactive behaviour. Each of these may usefully be drawn from its own inheritance hierarchy. Conceivably multiple inheritance might be used for this. However this would still require the creation, by programming, of a new subclass for each combination used or tried. More importantly, several instances of each kind of thing may be required e.g. several simultaneous screen representations of the same entity. This could never be done by an inheritance mechanism alone. The obvious approach is to use variables to point to the properties required. The MVC approach did this for linking multiple views to one entity, and for changing the graphical appearance of one view. The ERID approach extends this to the methods defining interactive behaviour, and copes with the need for combining several such behaviours in association with a single screen representation.

A comparable approach is described as part of the Lisp-based Garnet system [6,7,8]. In Garnet, generic "interactors" each embody a piece of interactive behaviour. These are associated with (visible, screen) objects typically through a scripted specification drawn up by the application programmer. The specification is passed to the Jade tool which produces a graphical dialogue which can then be tailored by a graphics designer through a direct manipulation tool (Lapidary).

Like ERID, Garnet possesses a small number of generic interactors and can support several interactors per screen object. The division of events to the interactors is handled by making changes to a number of the interactors' parameters, thus no separate dispatcher object is involved. (Thus it might be a little more difficult to review the set of behaviours currently applying to a particular instance i.e. screen representation.) In order to create a new combination it is just necessary to create a new instance of the appropriate interactor and edit its parameters. This approach has the advantage of not requiring editing of the interactor's code in order to customise a particular interactor's behaviour. Both systems provide similar improvements to the Smalltalk MVC.

The advantages of decoupling and orthogonalising representations and interactions are also described by Shan [9]. Shan's user interface management system, Mode Development Environment (MoDE) outwardly resembles the approach taken by ERID. MoDE is based around the notion of a mode, an object that possesses three attributes; appearance, interaction and semantics. A mode is equivalent to an ERID object, as both possess the three attributes stated earlier.

There are a number of differences in the two approaches. In MoDE, the semantics are encapsulated by a separate entity, while in ERID the generic controller is responsible for both interactivity and semantics (in the sense of the set of consequent actions: messages sent to other objects as a result of the user action). A mode is composed of single instances of each type of component (appearance, interaction and semantics), in ERID multiple instances of representations and interactions are supported.

The Iconographer program [10, 11] has also achieved this separation. Here generic input controllers called "devices" (cf. Garnet's "interactors") can be bound into novel combinations with screen representations (created by "icon generators") in "editor instances", which are created by a few menu selections in a control panel. The separation of screen representations ("icon generators") from application entities is done at the "switchboard" that is Iconographer's central feature. However since Iconographer deals with sets of objects sharing a common type, an editor instance specifies one of a set of interaction methods that apply uniformly to all icon instances of a given type. Thus to customise an individual icon's behaviour, as in ERID, it would have to be given a type of its own.

The ERID model could probably be implemented in X windows, but the basic architecture does not support the model. For instance X windows dispatch tables have a place only for events, not for the subregion of an icon ("widget"). Furthermore, the actions in the dispatch tables may not have parameters; thus you must code a new procedure per widget even if all it does is call a generic controller with a parameter pointing to the specific widget.

5   Conclusion

ERID provides an effective vehicle for exploring novel user interfaces for visible objects in DM^3 microworlds. The decoupling of interface elements has proved crucial to its effectiveness. We are sure that ERID's generality will prove useful for interface design in other domains.

6 Acknowledgements

The research supported here has been funded by the Economic and Social Research Council's InTER programme (Grant number X/203/25/2005).

References

[1] Driver R., Scanlon E. Conceptual Change in Science. Journal of Computer Assisted Learning 1988; 5:25-36.

[2] Twigger D., Byard M., Draper S., *et. al.* The 'Conceptual Change In Science' Project. Journal of Computer Assisted Learning 1991; 7:144-155.

[3] Adams SS. MetaMethods: The MVC Paradigm. HOOPLA! 1988; 1(4).

[4] Krasner GE., Pope TS. A Cookbook for using the Model-View-Controller User Interface Paradigm in Smalltalk-80. Journal of Object Oriented Programming 1988; 1(3): 26-49.

[5] Smith RB.(1987). The Alternative Reality Kit: an example of the tension between literalism and magic. Proceeding of the Conference on Human Factors in Computing Systems and GI 1987: 61-67 (ACM Press).

[6] Myers, B.A. (1990) "A new model of handling input" ACM trans. on information systems vol.8 pp.289-320.

[7] Myers BA. Encapsulating interactive behaviours. Proceeding of the Conference on Human Factors in Computing Systems 1989: 319-324. (ACM Press).

[8] Myers BA., Giuse GA. *et. al.* Garnet: Comprehensive Support for Graphical, Highly Interactive User Interfaces. Computer 1990; 23(11): 71-85.

[9] Shan Y. MoDE: A UIMS for Smalltalk. Proceeding of ACM Conference on Object-Oriented Programming, Systems, Languages, and Applications in SIGPlan Notices 1990; 25(10): 258-268

[10] Waite, K.W. & Draper, S.W., (1991) "User input to Iconographer" in HCI'91 People and Computers VI: Usability Now! (eds.) D.Diaper & N.Hammond pp.187-198 (Cambridge University Press: Cambridge).

[11] Waite, K.W. Draper, S.W., & Gray, P.D. (199?) "Iconographer: a tool for rapidly configuring interactive iconic representations" submitted to ACM trans. on information systems

Constructing front-ends to existing software systems

E.A. Edmonds*, I. Reid, S.P. Heggie*, D J Cornali

*LUTCHI Research Centre
Loughborough University of Technology
Loughborough
Leicestershire, LE11 3TU
UK
(Telephone: +44 509 263171 - Email: e.a.edmonds/s.p.heggie@uk.ac.lut)

Numerical Algorithms Group (NAG) Limited
Wilkinson House
Jordan Hill Road
Oxford, OX2 8DR
UK
(Telephone +44 865 511245 - Email: ianr/del@uk.co.nag)

1 Introduction

The FOCUS project is concerned with the development of tools and methods to aid in the construction of knowledge-based front-ends to existing software systems. The purpose is to extend the life and usability of valuable code that could be more widely used. An architecture and some associated tools have been developed. Following an evaluation in which complete systems were built in industrial environments, the architecture has been revised and extended. The extensions will help to cope with the complexities of large systems by automating some of the HCI design work and by dealing with some of those issues dynamically as unpredicted events occur. The lead partner, NAG Ltd, have already identified certain exploitation paths for some of the interim results.

2 Background

2.1 The Problem

The development of libraries of numerical software, which began in earnest in the sixties, did much to ease the burden of scientific computer users. Prior to this, it was necessary for those users to develop or obtain their own solutions, the many disadvantages of which are clear. Well designed libraries encapsulate problem solving algorithms in a portable, reliable and reusable form, saving much time and effort for users. However, although these software components were welcomed, frustration amongst scientists soon grew because of the need to use programming languages rather than abstract scientific concepts. The result was a growing gulf between the needs of users and the manner in which solutions were presented.

Early attempts to bridge this gulf centred around software packages aimed at particular communities. The statistics community developed several packages aimed at both general and specific areas of their field. These packages aimed to provide an environment in which the problem solving needs of the user in that particular domain could be met. For example, graphical output capabilities were often incorporated, and for the more sophisticated packages, graphical interaction.

This approach is still in use today, but while it frees the user from computer languages, most packages have inherent limitations. Amongst the most notable limitations are: having to learn a new command language; restrictions on the algorithmic solutions available and inter-package incompatibility.

To compound the problem, the working environment of the scientist is changing rapidly. Workstations and PCs are in abundance and windowing systems are becoming the norm rather than the exception. This speed of change makes the task of the package builder, in keeping user-interfaces etc. up to date, almost impossible.

It is abundantly clear that the software available in libraries and packages is necessary, and in some cases still sufficient, to allow the scientists to solve the problems. This software has been tried and tested over many years, and the expertise contained therein is so great that it would be foolhardy to discard it. However, it is equally clear that scientists should not have to struggle with general purpose programming and command languages, often needing to learn to use several software systems in order to solve one problem.

The answer is to provide support for the use of these systems and, where appropriate, to develop tailored, bespoke systems for scientists' needs. This often means providing knowledge of how to use the system, because much of the specialist software is based on deep knowledge. Hence, these specialist systems are only available to an equally specialised base of end-users.

2.2 The Solution: Front-Ends

User interfaces, or front-ends, which provide knowledge about the system are termed intelligent, or knowledge-based, front-ends (KBFEs) and are intended to make this specialist software available to a wider community of end-users whilst providing them with the routine procedures and guarding them from making elementary mistakes [1]. There are obvious advantages from a commercial aspect, since a larger audience generally means more sales. In addition, from the stand-point of end-user companies, they can use more junior personnel to carry out the expert's more mundane tasks, whilst freeing the expert's time to do the more challenging activities.

Earlier experience with a KBFE for statistical analysis was valuable [10]. In particular, it was found that much of the work conducted in pursuit of a separable user interface was applicable to this problem [3].

It is clearly important that these systems, whether more usable front-ends or full KBFEs, be produced in such a way that they can be extended algorithmically. They must also allow the user interface to be amended to reflect current standards/trends where appropriate. As ever, portability across machine ranges is important, but in addition it is also becoming necessary to produce distributed software systems; that is, systems in which major software components can be resident on more than one host. In short, a generic strategy is needed, providing a methodology and tools capable of providing solutions for a large class of real-world applications.

2.3 The FOCUS Project

FOCUS is and acronym for Front-ends for Open and Closed User Systems. The distinction between open (e.g. libraries) and closed (e.g. packages) user systems is no longer thought to be an important one, however, the acronym remains!

The project began in December 1988 and is due to run for four years. It is budgeted to consume 56 person years of effort at a cost of 8 million ECUs, and the consortium for the third and fourth years is:

NAG (prime contractor), Oxford, UK
InDeCon, Athens, Greece
Imperial College, London, UK
LUTCHI, Loughborough, UK
Solvay, Bruxelles, Belgium
Universitat Politecnica de Catalunya (UPC), Barcelona, Spain

Westfälische Wilhelms Universität (WWU), Münster, Germany

FOCUS aims to provide tools, techniques and methodologies for the development of front-ends. It is worth noting that the front-ends developed within the project have tended to be knowledge-based, and also that the application software, or back-ends, need not be numerical.

The first version of the FOCUS architecture is shown in figure 1. It was described in Edmonds and McDaid [5]. Briefly, the Seeheim user interface model [6] was extended in a number of specific ways. The basic Seeheim model is here incorporated within the component known as the Harness.

Surprisingly little attention has been given to the linkage between an interface and the functional code [4]. It is a major issue, however, for front-ending. The Back-End Manager is the Focus solution to the problem.

Firstly, the concept of a Back-End Manager was introduced. This component is responsible for handling the details of the interactions between the front-end and each back-end system, of which there may be many. Its main tasks are, therefore, to map between system-independent specifications of the task and ones that can be used in practice to run the existing systems and, conversely, to extract the required data from the systems' output [9].

Secondly, a set of knowledge-based modules are added in order to provide the help and support that the user needs. Whereas the back-end manager contains specific information about how to run the back ends, a knowledge-based module will contain, for example, knowledge about which back-end to run in order to solve which problem.

This structure enabled a third innovation, which is the use of standard message structures for the passing of information between the KBFE components. A major use of the messages is for KBM's to create or modify end-user interaction objects. The project is, therefore, developing an abstract notation in which to describe logical interactions independent of their physical realisation.

3 The Architecture Evaluated and Extended

Version 1 of the architecture and the associated prototype tools has been used to build a number of knowledge-based front ends with direct industrial value [8]. In evaluating and reviewing the architecture a number of new points have become clear. Two specific issues are the provision of graphics, which was largely omitted from the first prototype, and the need to support knowledge based front end developers in 'programming' the Harness. The graphics requirements and the associated implementation issues are discussed by Branki et. al. [2]. The need to 'program' the Harness has been a significant factor in the development of an architecture for the Front End Harness Version 2.

The requirement for a Harness programming environment has resulted in an important change of emphasis in considering the overall architecture. In the Prototype Harness the most critical entity, in terms of end user interaction, has been the 'message'. Message types have defined the functional boundaries of such interaction and the realisation of messages as concrete, on-screen interaction objects has been a one-stage process, performed by in-line code. If knowledge based front end developers needed to extend the function of the Harness they had to change or extend code *within* the Harness. The architecture for Harness Version 2 introduces the new concept of 'abstract interaction objects'. An abstract interaction object is defined as a prototype interaction object in which the presentation details are not specified. Each available prototype is defined in a knowledge base and the definition consists of a logical description of the contents and attributes the object may have. In Harness Version 2, abstract interaction object prototypes replace messages as the critical entities in end user interaction. They can be created and edited by knowledge based front end developers without affecting Harness code, and the introduction of a new prototype constitutes an extension of Harness functionality in a manner equivalent to the introduction of a new 'message type' to the Prototype Harness architecture. This approach provides the basis for a Harness programming environment which will support rapid and safe extension of functionality without involving changes to Harness code.

In addition to a harness programming environment, the requirement for two additional components has been identified. These are:
(i) Dynamic Presentation Manager
(ii) Dynamic Dialogue Manager
These components handle the dynamically changing needs for interface design and control. The Dynamic Presentation Manager deals with presentation design as, for example, messages of unforeseen length need to be displayed, rather in the manner of Mackinlay [7]. The Dynamic Dialogue Manager makes dialogue control decisions based, for example, upon the need to keep the cognitive load on the user within reasonable bounds. This is made necessary by the potentially large number of components interacting with the user through the Harness.

A bonus of the evaluation process has been that it has become clear that a number of exploitation paths exist for interim results from the FOCUS project.

4 Version 2 Architecture

The revised architecture of the Front End Harness component is shown in Figure 2. The principal changes from the Prototype Harness architecture involve the introduction of new components and the distribution of functions between these components. The syntax of communications messages has also been changed to reflect the revised architecture and the introduction of Abstract Interaction Objects.

4.1   Components and Functions

The principal changes from the version 1 architecture are:

(i) The refinement of the KBM/application interface through the introduction of the Communications Manager. The Communications Manager is responsible for establishing and monitoring all logical and physical communications and for message routing.

(ii) The extension of the concept of the Dialogue Control component to the Dynamic Dialogue Manager. The Dynamic Dialogue Manager is responsible for the logical management of all communication with the end user, for negotiating conflict resolution at the interface and for maintaining the logical link between the state of the KBFE and the state of the interface.

(iii) The division of the Presentation function between the Dynamic Presentation Manager, which is independent of any software environment, and the Physical Presentation Layer, which may contain material which is specific to an operating system, window manager or widget set. The Dynamic Presentation Manager is responsible for the creation, modification, destruction and management of interaction objects. The Physical Presentation Layer is responsible for directly mapping interaction objects to a particular window management system and/or widget set.

(iv) In order to support a Harness Programming Environment which is separate from Harness code, information about abstract interaction object prototypes is stored separately and declaratively in a Presentation Knowledge Base. This may be modified and/or extended via an Interaction Object Editor.

Each component of the revised architecture is discussed in more detail in the following sections.

4.2 Presentation

The Presentation function is controlled by the Dynamic Presentation Manager, which is independent of any operating system, window management software or widget set, and the Physical Presentation Layer, which may contain software dependent material. A Presentation Knowledge Base contains definitions of all available interaction object prototypes, and the Dynamic Presentation Manager instantiates these prototype definitions using the contents of messages. The Physical Presentation Layer is responsible for directly mapping instantiated interaction objects to a particular window management system and/or widget set.

4.2.1 Dynamic Presentation Manager

The Dynamic Presentation Manager manages all messages sent to the end user and 'passed' for realisation by the Dynamic Dialogue Manager. It is responsible for the creation, modification, destruction and management of abstract interaction objects.

A message may also request the destruction of one or more abstract interaction objects. The destruction of an abstract interaction object will cause the destruction of all sub-objects contained within it.

A message containing the Id of an abstract interaction object which has already been realised is automatically treated as an 'update' message. It may:

(i)   Add one or more new sub-objects to an existing object

(ii)   Change the contents of one or more objects

(iii)   Change any of the attributes of an object, including controls

Return messages to the KBM can be activated in three ways:

(i)   Event: when some pre-specified event occurs - e.g. the user activates a control

(ii)   Request: when a KBM issues a request for the state of an abstract interaction object to be returned

(iii)   Sample: when the Harness repeatedly returns the state of an abstract interaction object at specified intervals.

The default mode is 'event', as in version 1.

4.2.2 Physical Presentation Layer

The Physical Presentation Layer is responsible for mapping instantiated abstract interaction object prototypes to physical interaction objects supported by a particular window management system and/or widget set, and for realising the physical objects on screen.

The Physical Presentation Layer also realises any changes to on-screen objects required by 'update' messages and handles the removal of objects when interaction is complete.

Since all interaction with the windowing system is handled by the Physical Presentation Layer, only this component need be modified in order to use different window managers.

4.3 Dynamic Dialogue Manager

The Dynamic Dialogue Manager is responsible for the logical control of all dialogues which involve the end user and for conflict resolution in end user interaction. It maintains knowledge which includes:

(i) The number of abstract interaction objects currently active on screen
(ii) The complexity of new abstract interaction objects, which dictates the cost, in time and resources, of realising them
(iii) The cognitive load on the end user.

This knowledge may be used to monitor and control an appropriate level of complexity at the end user interface and to negotiate with KBMs when necessary.

The Dynamic Dialogue Manager is informed by the Communications Manager of the instigation and termination of all application processes. It informs the Dynamic Presentation Manager of process termination in order that any associated on-screen interaction objects may be destroyed.

4.4 Communications Manager

The Communications Manager is responsible for all communication within the KBFE. The Communications Manager supports three categories of application:

Networked: The KBM or application process runs on a different machine from the Harness and is connected to the Harness via a local area network or a packet-switched network. The file server for the remote application may not be mounted with the Harness.

Same Processor: The KBM or application runs on the same machine as the Harness, but in a different process.

Same Process: The KBM or application runs in the same process as the Harness. It is not necessarily the case that all of a KBFE's applications would be in this category.

The category of an application, as well as the underlying communications necessary to support that category, is transparent to the application.

4.5 Interface Model

The various components of the FOCUS architecture use the Communications Manager to pass messages. Messages destined for the end user are passed to the Physical presentation Layer via the Dynamic Dialogue Manager and the Dynamic Presentation Manager. The basic unit of end user interaction is the abstract interaction object. Prototypes of abstract interaction objects are defined in the Presntation Knowledge Base. Each definition specifies the permissible contents and attributes of the object, together with information about their mapping to interaction primitives.

When the Dynamic Dialogue Manager receives a message for the end user, it must decide whether or not to pass it on for immediate realisation. If the message is not to be passed immediately - eg. because the screen is full or the user is already interacting with a complex object - it may be queued for later processing or discarded. The originating component may specify, within the message, which action should be taken and whether or not the originator should be informed.

The Dynamic Presentation Manger receives the message and checks whether or not the abstract interaction objects referenced in it have already been displayed as physical, on-screen objects. If so, the current state of the objects is modified to reflect the contents of the message - eg. an attribute may change or the contents of a displayed field may be modified. If an abstract interaction object has not already been displayed, the Dynamic Presentation Manager extracts the relevant prototype definition from the Presentation Knowledge Base. The prototype definition always contains default values for all attributes of the object. These are replaced by any values contained within the message - ie. the message need only specify variations from the default. The prototype definition may also specify the contents of an abstract interaction object - eg. a frequently used text string. In this case, the contents parameter of the calling message may be empty. However, if it is not empty then it overrides the contents contained in the prototype definition. In general, the contents of an abstract interaction object will not be contained within the prototype definition and will be taken from the calling message.

When the prototype has been completed and/or modified using the contents of the message, it is passed to the Physical Presentation Layer for realisation.

Initial releases of Harness Version 2 provide a small number of 'ready made' abstract interaction object prototypes. These include selection, question, query, panel, inform and hypertext objects. The range of prototype objects will be extendfed throughout the development period, using input from KBFE developers in the project who have built new objects for their own purposes.

5. Conclusion

The FOCUS project has developed an architecture and a set of prototype tools for the construction of KBFE's. A number of systems have been implemented as part of an evaluation exercise and, as a result, the architecture has been revised and extended. This has led to a number of interesting innovations involving the dynamic management of user-computer interaction. In addition, the evaluation process has helped the consortium to identify preliminary exploitation routes for some interim results.

Acknowledgements

The work described was partly funded by the ESPRIT project 2620. An earlier versionof this paper was distributed at the ESPRIT Conference 1991 in ESPRIT: Information Processing Systems, Results and Progress of Selected Projects.

References

1. Bundy, A. (1984) *Intelligent front ends*. DAI Research Paper 227. Edinburgh University, UK.

2. Branki, N.E., Edmonds, E.A., Dutron, Y., Govearts, B. and Cryer, C. (1991). *KBFE developers' requirements for graphics*. FOCUS Document FOCUS/LUTCHI/8/4.3-C.

3. Edmonds, E.A. (1990) The emergence of the separable user interface. *ICL Technical Journal*. 7,1. pp 54-65.

4. Edmonds, E.A. and McDaid, E. (1990). An architecture for knowledge-based front ends. *Knowledge Based Systems*. 3, 4. pp221-224.

5. Edmonds, E.A. (editor). (1992). The Separable User Interface. Academic Press.

6. Green, M. (1985) Report on dialogue specification tools. In Pfaff, G. (ed) *User Interface Management Systems*. Springer Verlag. pp 21-29.

7. Mackinlay, J. (1986) automating the design of graphical presentations of relational information. *ACM Transactions on Graphics*. 5, 2. pp 110-141.

8. Murray, B. S., Edmonds, E. A. and Govaerts, B. (1991) *An experimental knowledge-based front end developed using the FOCUS architecture*. Internal report. LUTCHI Research Centre, Loughborough University of Technology, UK.

9. Prat, A., Lores, J., Fletcher, P. and Catot, J. M. (1990) The back-end manager: an interface between a knowledge based front end and its application subsystems. *Knowledge Based Systems*. 3, 4. pp225-229.

10. Wolstenholme, D. E., O'Brien, C. M. and Nelder, J. A. (1988) GLIMPSE: a knowledge-based front end for statistical analysis. *Knowledge Based Systems*. 1, 3. pp 173-178.

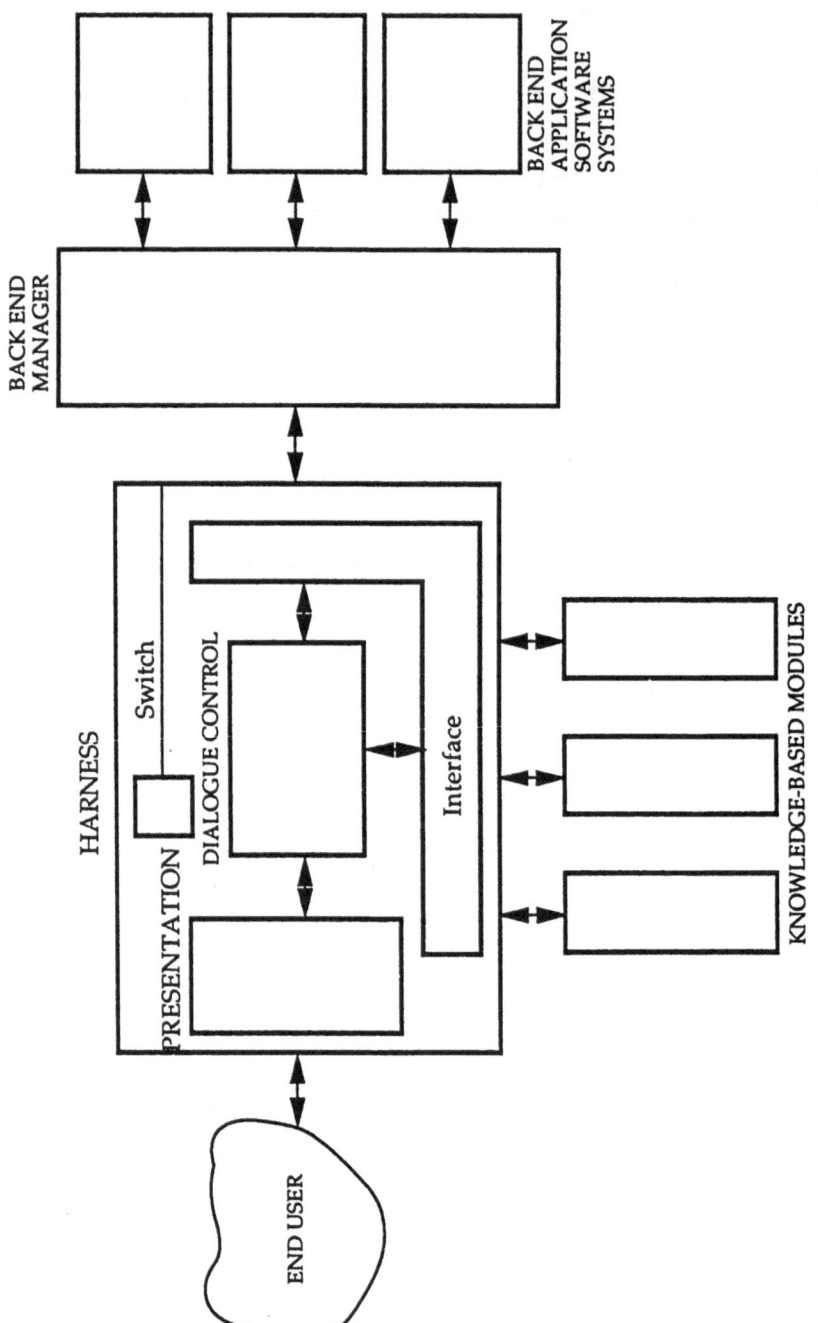

Figure 1. The version 1 KBFE architecture

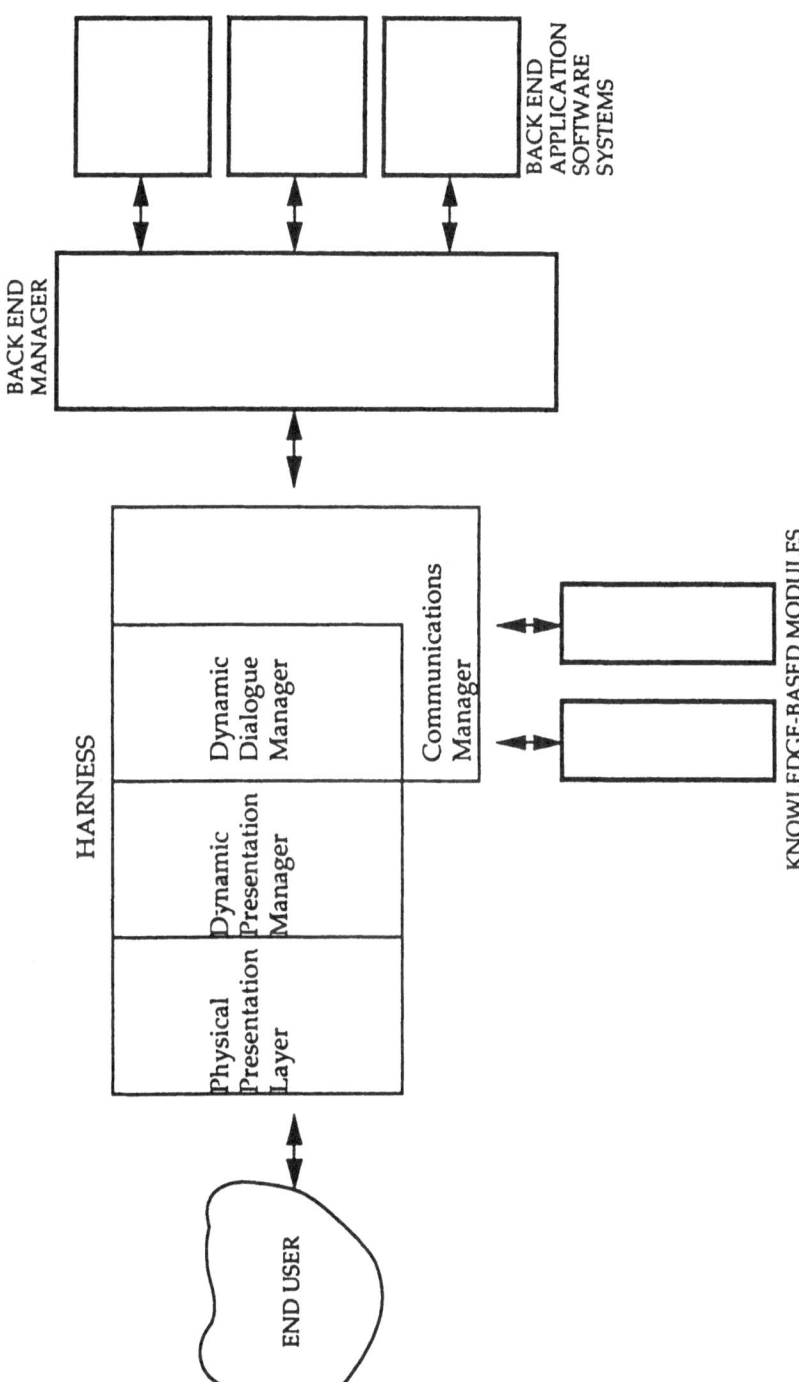

Figure 2. The version 2 KBFE architecture

II Tools

The previous section of this volume was devoted to the abstract, to presenting useful software structures for the construction of interactive systems. This section, on the other hand, is firmly rooted in the concrete; every paper describes programs – software tools – which assist in the process of constructing the user interfaces to interactive systems. Apart from this similarity, the tools presented are very different from one another and represent a wide range of ways in which the complex tasks involved in designing and implementing user interfaces can be computer-assisted.

The notion of tool used here must be distinguished from that of a user interface toolkit, such as the Macintosh Toolbox or the X widget toolkits. The latter are interaction libraries offering subroutines which create, configutre and activate a wide variety interaction objects such as windows, menus, editable text objects, dialgogue boxes and so on. While powerful, such toolkits demand that the user interface constructor be familiar with the structure and allowable parameters of these objects, as well as being a skilled programmer in some general-purpose programming language, such as C or Object Pascal, capable of ordering the subroutine calls correctly, adding the correct header files and supplying the necessary arguments in the proper form. Even the most trivial change in the interface specification requires changing the source code and hence recompiliation, necessitating a lengthy rebuilding process to generate the change in the working system.

The tools described here, however, provide a higher level of assistance to the constructor by:
- minimising the information the constructor must supply,
- lessening the knowledge the constructor must have of the implementation system,
- employing direct manipulation and visual programming techniques for specification, and
- allowing changes to be reflected immediately without time-consuming recompilation.

The particular mixture of these features, and the techniques by which they are offered, vary from one tool to another, and are dictated by the job the tool is intended to do. At one extreme, we may identify tools designed for non-programmers, usually to create prototypes for user-based evaluation; such tools are likely to emphasise design-time support, in the form of specification by supplying parameters or selecting from sets of alternative components or by visual programming, plus dynamic reconfigurability of the tool's product. The price for such support is paid for in limited alternatives (i.e., the "design space" may be restricted) and in lowered performance of the product system. At the other extreme are tools for generating fully-functioning, deliverable interactive systems, rather than just prototypes. These are tools designed mainly for programmers and no apologies are made for the fact that, at some point, the tool user will have to write code in some high-level programming language. The focus is on support for implementation, particularly by means of pre-existing collections of re-usable interactive object classes which are amenable to specialisation, facilities for defining new interactive objects or classes of such objects and for specifying the relationships among such objects. Although this distinction between design-heavy and implementation-heavy support is useful as a starting point in considering construction tools, actual tools seldom fall at either extreme. The tools described in this section all have features of both, with some systems like HyperNeWS providing a range of levels of support.

The paper by Gray describes a system called Iconographer which enables a wide variety of iconic representations of computer-based data to be created using visual programming techniques. Support for the constructor is offered in several ways. First, the information required by the Iconographer system is designed to match closely the task of describing the representation, thus reducing the transformations necessary from a design-oriented to an implementation-oriented specification of the representation. Second, alternative representations are selectable from a set of "packaged" alternatives, thus focussing the specification on linking, by direct manipulation, of relevant pictorial attributes to the attributes of application data which are to be represented. Finally, the tool presents a visualisation of the top-level architecture of the run-time system, thus presenting the constructional task as one of "visually building the run-time system".

The Iconographer system is able to reduce radically what the constructor must know and do to produce a working system by limiting the range of alternatives to combinations from fixed sets. Where the alternatives do not supply what is required, new alternatives must be programmed in the base implementation language, Smalltalk. The HyperNeWS system, described in the paper by Waite, deals with this trade-off between specification freedom and implementational cost by offering a number of *levels of abstraction*, each instantiated in the HyperNeWS system by pre-defined but configurable objects. The objects at each level are defined in terms of those at the next lower level. A user interface constructor need only work at the lowest level necessary for the desired degree of specificational freedom. Objects to be incorporated in the final system are copied from pre-existing objects in other HyperNeWS applications and then configured by means of built-in interactive tools for modifying the location, size, appearance and other presentational and behavioural attributes. Where necessary, additional behavioural specialisation may be carried out by modifying or creating code in a specially designed scripting language.

The system discussed by Hopkins and Wallis was designed by enable CBT courseware authors to build simulation-based training systems. It avoids the need for conventional programming skills by a judicious choice of pre-existing interactive objects called gadgets. Like HyperNeWS's objects, gadgets may be added to the target system by graphical manipulation and attributes may be defined via selection from supplied alternative functions. The Hopkins and Wallis paper also provides an illuminating account of the results of testing a prototype version of the tool.

XDesigner, like Iconographer and, to some extent, the Hopkins and Wallis system, visualises the underlying structure of the target run-time system (in this case an X widget-based interface) and uses this visualisation as the locus for specification, rather than using the appearance of the target system. Alistair George argues that such an architecture-centred specification provides advantages, particularly in terms of easy access to otherwise "invisible" aspects of the interface structure.

The Sirius system described by Windsor is actually a framework for buiding object-oriented interactive systems. In this case constructor assistance is afforded by the flexibility of the framework architecture rather than by any special-purpose configuration tools. The issues discussed in the paper address several of the themes in the Architectures section of this volume, such as separability of interface and application, inter-object communication mechanisms and flexible class hierarchies for interactive objects. Nevertheless, the value of the Sirius framework is exemplified in the Windsor paper by its use in building prototype interfaces to a demanding and distinctive application area, viz., air traffic control displays and consequently provides an illustration of the way in which a powerful and flexible architecture may itself be viewed as a tool for user interface construction in that the ease of configuration of the run-time system offers considerable constructional assistance. It should be noted that this paper is considerably longer and more detailed than the other contributions in this volume; it was the opinion of the editors that the comprehensive description of the Sirius system offers the reader the rare opportunity to examine the fine details of a complex, object-oriented interactive system.

Correspondence between Specification and Run-Time Architecture in a Design Support Tool

Philip Gray

Department of Computing Science

University of Glasgow

Abstract

The Iconographer system is a tool for rapidly creating a wide variety of pictorial representations of computer-based data. It is intended to provide an environment in which designers of such representations may explore a variety of alternative design solutions. Its architecture, based on four basic structured components, may be viewed as corresponding to a designer-oriented view of the specification of representations. Furthermore, the design tools which Iconographer provides offer a visualisation of this architecture by means of which the design-oriented specification may be instantiated as a run-time system. These correspondences between specification and architecture offer a means of reducing the gulf between the designer's conception and the end-product which instantiates it.

1   Introduction

The Iconographer system, developed by the Innovative Iconic Interfaces Project at the University of Glasgow, is a visual programming system for the specification and instantiation of interactive visual representations of sets of computer-based data. Iconographer's users are, by intent, creators - *designers* - of iconic representations. The system has been variously described as an iconic interface prototyping tool [13], a data visualisation system [3], and a data modelling tool, but whatever its particular application, Iconographer offers its users the ability to build and modify descriptions – *specifications* – of visual representations en route to instantiating them.

Iconographer's architecture (its modularisation into components with specific functional roles) is, like the architecture of any system, the result of a diverse collection of system requirements, including functionality, usability, and performance. But central to the architecture are the demands placed upon the system by the nature of the tasks its users will perform. Iconographer's architecture corresponds closely to a characterisation of the task of describing a representation. For each identifiable part of the specification of the design, there exists a component in the architecture which implements it. That is, the architecture of the system is homomorphic with a model of design of the products of that system. This similarity offers important advantages to a designer of representations. First, it minimises the "distance" from the designer's conceptualisation, or abstract description, of the artefact to the system-significant description required for a specification. Second, each component in the system architecture provides *a locus of configuration*; design-time tools can be developed which are associated with each run-time component, allowing a designer to select from alternative components or to supply parameters to an existing component. The support offered to the designer by such tools is made much simpler to implement by the match between subtasks in the design task process and components in the architecture.

Iconographer is not entirely alone in displaying this relationship between specification and architecture. In general, design tools, and the run-time systems which they produce, can be measured with respect to the degrees of correspondence which exist between the conceptualisations of designers, the specification language as expressed by the tools, and the run-time architecture. In Section 2, the correspondence between architecture and specification will be examined in more detail. Section 3 presents Iconographer's architecture from a designer's point of view, identifying a novel component which has been added to the Iconographer architecture for reasons of design support. Finally, Section 4 considers the visual programming facilities we have added to the components as a further aid to design.

2   The Gulfs of Design and Implementation

To discuss the relationship of system architecture to designer support in user interface or data visualisation construction tools, there are several features of such systems which must be identified. The ultimate *product* of the use of such tools is definable in terms of system output, viewed in the broadest sense. An Iconographer user aims to produce perceivable representations of computer-based data, i.e., perceivable system output, perhaps persistent and perhaps changing over time. In the case of user interface construction tools, the tool product must also include reference to system behaviour as a result of user-generated input.

Although the product as defined above is abstract, it entails the production of an artifact, a *run-time system* which is capable of generating the product. The product may be thought of as the primary aim of the tool user, while creating the run-time system is the secondary aim.

For both product and run-time system one can identify descriptions, or specifications, which serve as the source and/or justification of actions on the part of the tool user. A *design-oriented specification* is a description of the product; it may be capable of being satisfied by a number of different run-time systems. It is often the way the designer conceives of the run-time system. The *implementational specification* consists of the information required to be passed to the construction tool(s) in order to produce the run-time system; it determines the way the run-time system must be specified in order to be implemented.

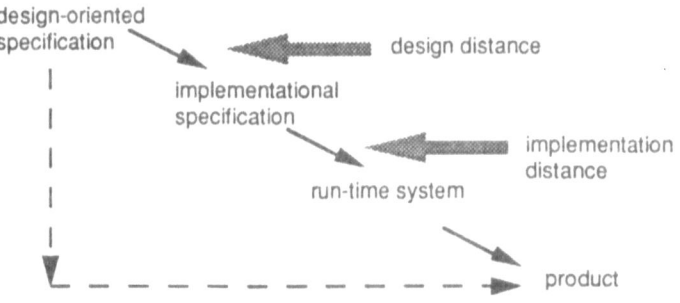

Figure 1 Design and Implementation Gaps

The relationship among user aims and types of specification is shown in figure 1. Given that a successfully produced run-time system produces the desired product by definition, **the important issue for a construction tool is the way it lessens the gaps between (i) the two types of specification and (ii) the implementational specification and the run-time system.** These gaps are instances of semantic and articulatory distances [5] as applied to system design and implementation. The design distance refers to the transformations necessary to change a design-oriented specification (e.g., "a pop-up menu with three items arranged vertically") into an implementational specification (e.g., "a form widget containing three command widgets, with appropriate layout constraints"). The implementation distance refers to the user actions necessary to generate the run-time system from the implementational specification (e.g., writing some C code using X toolkit functions or perhaps using an X widget builder).

2.1 The Relationship of System Architecture to the Gulf of Design

One way of reducing the design distance is to derive the architecture of the run-time system from the structure of the design-oriented specification of the product. The architecture of a system is a description of that system in terms of the separate components which comprise it, the functions of those components and the relationships among them. An implementational specification can be (indeed usually is) homomorphic with the system architecture, thus, if there is a similarity between the design-oriented specification and the system architecture, the gulf of design will be reduced since no structural transformation is needed from the designer's description to the implementational specification.

2.2 Design-Architecture Correspondence in the Seeheim Model

A good example of such a correspondence between design-oriented specification and architecture is provided by the Seeheim model of interactive systems [10]. The Seeheim model, one of the earliest attempts at an abstract model of interactive system architecture, identified three basic user interface components (a fourth component, the bypass pipeline, will be discussed below):

- the *presentation system*, which handles the capture of input from physical input devices and the generation of (graphical) output on physical output devices,

- the *dialogue control system*, which handles the recognition of system-significant sequences of user actions (i.e., commands), and

- the *application interface model*, which provides an abstraction of the application functionality in terms of a set of commands and their parameters (or objects and actions).

According to the Seeheim model, these components are connected to allow a single (possibly two-way) data-flow as shown in figure 2.

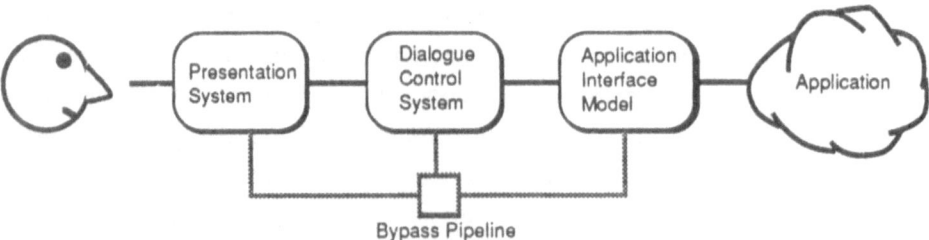

Figure 2 The Seeheim Model

The Seeheim architecture corresponds to a linguistic model of user-computer interaction [2]. According to this model, a user-computer interface can be viewed as a language via which users communicate commands to the application and the application communicates task-relevant information to the user. It follows that the outcome of a user interface design, then, is a language.

From this view of interaction follows both *a structure for design-oriented specification and a logical model of design*. The logical design model is a simple design task analysis, identifying the categories of design decision which must be taken when specifying a user interface and the relationships among and constraints upon those decisions. The features of this model of design are based on the methods of design and implementation of formal languages already exploited in a number of computing domains. According to this model, designers of user interfaces must decide on the semantics, syntax and lexical properties of the interface, in that order [8]. Furthermore, decisions at one level are taken to be independent of decisions at a lower level. The design model establishes the design space in which user interface design takes place and provides a structure for that space.

The close correspondence between the linguistic model of user interfaces, and interface design, on the one hand, and the Seeheim UI model on the other, lies in the identification of each of the three Seeheim components with one of the three components of a (formal) language specifying the interface, and with one of the three phases of language design. The run-time system is an interpreter for this language of interaction. User interface design tools are then based on language-generation tools, such as compiler-compilers for automatic interface construction and syntax diagram editors for graphical specification of dialogue control. The success of the Seeheim architecture, and its continuing life well beyond its "sell-by date", lies in the power of the linguistic model of interaction within its restricted domain of application and the existence of well-understood techniques for the design and implementation of formal languages.[1]

---

[1]   It may be conjectured that the Seeheim model also retains its currency simply because it identifies three general categories of design decision which must be taken in specifying an interface: appearance, behaviour and application semantics. Viewed in this most general way, the Seeheim model is universally applicable, but uninformative about how the decisions are related or how an architecture can be constructed to support them.

The main problem, of course, is that while suitable for simple, command language-based interfaces, the linguistic model does not capture in a simple and intuitive way important characteristics of modern highly-interactive graphical user interfaces such as the persistent nature of graphical objects (the lexical tokens) and the existence of interleaved dialogues and fine-grained semantic feedback [2]. It also fails to acknowledge relationships among design decisions which demand a degree of bottom-up design [1]. Naturally, the Seeheim model has been accused, rightly, of suffering from the same (or equivalent) defects [11].

As was mentioned above, a fourth component, a data bypass pipeline, existed in early descriptions of the model, to allow for the application to communicate directly with the presentation system, for example, to allow for real-time updating of the display with minimum performance costs. This component has been the source of considerable controversy and confusion [4, 15]. Often it does not appear explicitly in some versions the model at all [6]. Given that its existence is due to performance considerations, it is clearly not part of a design-oriented specification and thus is required to be added when transforming the design to the implementational specification. It appears likely that the added distance between design and implementational specification which it introduces has made it, and the architecture which includes it, less acceptable than the simplified three-component Seeheim model.[2]

It is not my aim to argue for, or against, the linguistic model of interaction or the Seeheim architectural model. It is important to note, however, that the defects described above do not arise because of a mismatch between the model of design and the architecture. As we have noted, the match between design and implementation is quite close. For certain classes of interface - command-languages especially as well as certain highly sequential menu and form-based interfaces - Seeheim-based user interface management systems perform well. The problem lies in the applicability of the model and hence the usefulness of the architecture.

---

[2]   A modified four-component model based on the original Seeheim model re-introduces the pipeline, but with a different function [4]. This architecture appears not to widen the design gulf, but rather increases the usefulness of the basic Seeheim model for a wider class of products.

2.3 The Relationship of System Architecture to the Gulf of Implementation

The implementational specification (see section 2.1) refers to what must be specified in order to produce a run-time system. Under this interpretation, an implementational specification is to be distinguished from a full description of the run-time system. What must be specified depends upon the construction tools being used. Thus, many tools supply default values for a number of system properties. Others undertake inferences from user-supplied input to generate parts of the specification automatically.

Thus, although there is likely to be a correspondence between run-time architecture and the implementational specification, the nature and degree of the relationship may vary considerably from one system and construction tool to another. Tools for building early UIMSs [7, 14] often provide a tool or set of tools focused on the specification of the dialogue control, with interactive graphical construction of the transition network representing dialogue control structure. One architectural component, the dialogue control system, is treated as central to the specification, with specification of presentation and application functionality treated as part of the task of specifying control (viz., labelling arcs with input events and application functions to be called when traversing the arc).

A second specification technique, in which presentation is central, is to work with a representation of the product itself, rather than a representation of the run-time system architecture. Examples are Hypercard™, NeXT™ Interface Builder, and most X Window System widget builders and systems like Garnet which employ rule-based inference to generate a specification from examples supplied by the user. Construction proceeds by selecting template interactive objects and placing them in the window which stands for the product of the final run-time system. Further specification of these objects is carried out by supplying parameters for configuring appearance and behaviour or even by writing code. Run-time system architecture is visible in these systems in that the objects on the tool's display (the objects which the user manipulates) stand for components in the run-time system.

3 A Design-Centred View of Iconographer

As mentioned above, Iconographer is a visual programming system for the specification and instantiation of interactive visual representations of sets of computer-based data. In this section I shall consider the relationships among design-oriented specification of representations, the creation of such representations in Iconographer and Iconographer's architecture.

For a fuller description of the Iconographer system, the reader is referred to [13].

3.1 Designing Representations in Iconographer

An iconic display in Iconographer may be thought of as the result of a function taking as arguments an application universe, an iconic universe and a set of functionally defined links between application attributes and iconic attributes. Thus, creating an iconic display consists of specifying:

- an application universe
- an iconic universe
- a set of application attribute - iconic attribute links, and
- a display medium.

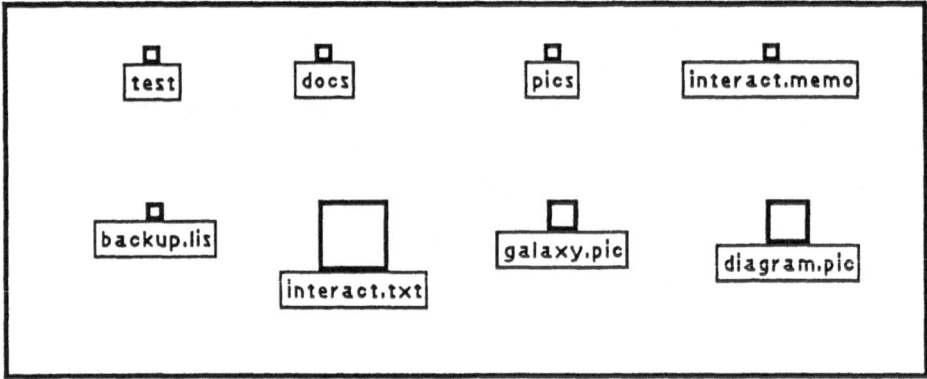

Figure 3 A typical Iconographer display

Figure 3 shows a typical Iconographer-generated display, in this case a representation of the contents of a file directory. The display has been specified such that:

- each icon is labelled by the name of the directory or file it represents and
- the size of the icon corresponds to the size of the represented file.

The display medium in this case is a bitmapped screen. The application universe consists of a set of files, each possessing a name attribute and a size attribute, perhaps along with other attributes such as read-write permissions, creation date, and so on, not currently indicated by the icons. The iconic universe consists of a set of entities each possessing a label attribute and a size attribute. The links are quite simple: file names are mapped onto the strings defining icon labels and file size is mapped onto icon size using a simple arithmetic conversion function. Icons are a privileged set of entities in that, when presented to a display surface, they are capable of being rendered on the display such that visible properties of the rendered images correspond to the (abstract) attributes of the icons.

From the point of view of a designer using Iconographer, then, the task of creating a representation consists of four major subtasks. Specifying an application universe and specifying an iconic universe are independent of one another, but both tasks clearly must be completed before the inter-universe links can be created. Furthermore, the choice of a display surface affects the choices which may be made in the iconic universe, since different display media are capable of displaying different types of iconic entity. The entire task may be thought of as *creating the run-time system* which generates the representation.

3.2 Iconographer's Architecture

Iconographer has a four-component architecture. Each of the components corresponds to one of the representation specification subtasks discussed in the previous section. Figure 4 shows this overall architecture.

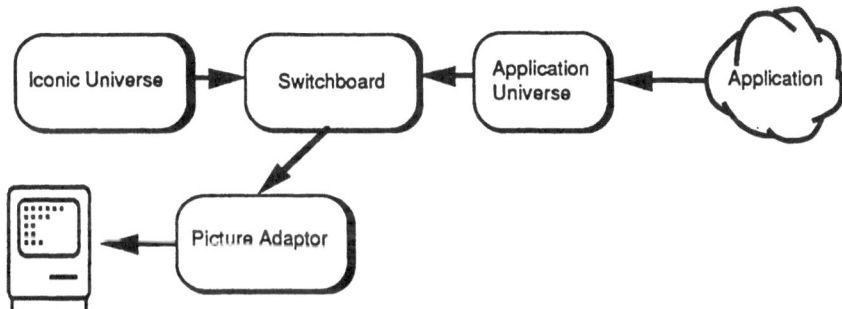

Figure 4 Overall Iconographer Architecture

The application universe corresponds to the Seeheim's application interface model and presents an abstract description of the application. Presentation and behaviour are combined in the iconic universe component, similar to interactive object architectures such as the widget architecture of the X window system, although low-level device dependencies are separated out into the separate picture adaptor component. Finally, the switchboard handles inter-universe linkage.

In the remainder of this section, each component will be examined in greater detail, focusing on the method of specification supported. The correspondence between designer-oriented specification and architecture is reflected in the nature of an implementational specification, thus reducing the gulf of design.

3.2.1 Specifying the Application Universe

Application universe specification is performed by selecting one of a set of pre-defined *object adaptors,* as shown in figure 5. These produce a representation of the application data as a set of tuples of attributes, where each attribute is a named Iconographer data-type. For example, the file named 'interact.txt' would be represented by:

< name='interact.txt', size=76, type=file, readable?=true, writeable?=true >

Primitive attributes include textual, discrete (enumerated set) and continuous types. Thus, 'name' in the above example is a textual attribute. Further user-defined attributes may be defined from these by the use of compositional operations.

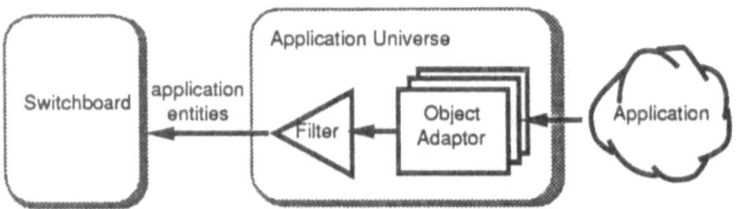

Figure 5 The Application Universe

Once selected, an application universe can be modified by additional operations, including:

- a filter (shown in figure 5), which enables objects to be removed from the final universe, based on expressions over application attributes, and (not shown in figure 5)
- a merger, which allows two universes to be combined, and
- a summary operator, which generates a new universe with a single object possessing quantitative information about the original universe.

3.2.2 Specifying the Iconic Universe

The iconic universe, shown in figure 6, is specified by selecting:
- an icon type, called an icon generator,
- a spatial layout policy, called a compositor, and
- one or more relationship handlers.

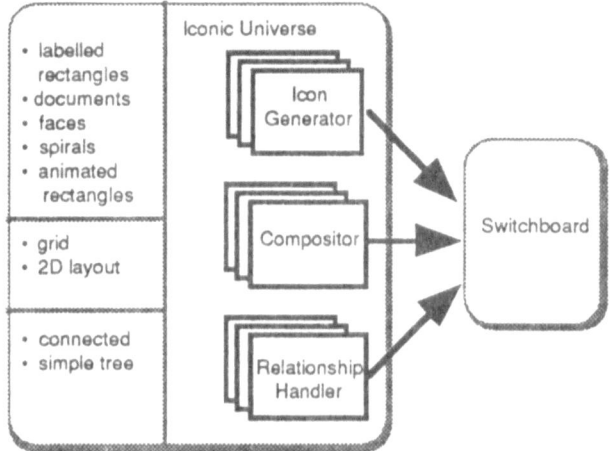

Figure 6 The Iconic Universe

This triple defines the set of attributes which all icons will possess and, given a display medium, determines the effect of attribute values on display generation. A number of icon generators and compositors have been produced. Currently implemented icon generators include:

- a simple rectangular icon (shown in figure 3) with textual label, height, width, internal and border colour attributes and
- a face icon with eye direction, hair colour, lip configuration as attributes
- a stationery icon, in which the internal image stands for the document type, depth (thickness) indicates size and colour represents age.

Compositors available include:
- a simple gridded layout (used in figure 3),
- a 2D Cartesian coordinate system,
- a tree layout.

Of these, the grid layout automatically places icons in a pre-selected position in a tabular format on the display, while the 2D layout allows position on the X and/or Y axes to be determined by the value of some attribute of a related application entity.

The task model underlying this structure is one of "select from list". We have found this to be suitable for the specification of a wide range of presentations, although it is clearly not universal. First, compared to other systems, the primitives (viz., the icon generator, the compositor and the relationship handler) offer only coarse control over the specification. Second, the assumption of independence of selections cannot be sustained. Choosing layout based on containment, for example, will have ramifications for the selection of an icon generator, viz., it must be one which supports containment.

However, we have intentionally kept this design task simple (and the component which corresponds to that design task) in order to focus on the next (sub)task, that of linking the application and iconic universes.

3.2.3 Creating a Representation: Connecting the Universes

Finally, links between the two universes are held in a component called a Switchboard. These links enable attribute values of icons to be generated as a function of application entity attributes. Each link has its own function, which may be supplied by the designer, if desired, although a default function is supplied when a link is created. Where the application and icon attributes are of different types, type conversion must take place; default functions carry out such type coercion automatically.

3.2.4   Viewing the Display

Once complete, a representation may be viewed via one of a set of picture adaptors. Each of these serves to render the (abstract) set of icons onto the display. The selection of a picture adaptor can affect the types of icon available, since some icon types can only be displayed by appropriate picture adaptors.

3.3   The Switchboard: Promoting an Interface to a Component

In other interactive system architectures, the connection between the application (or application interface model if one is present) and the rest of the user interface is not a separate component. The routines which handle communication of data between the components reside *in* one of the components. This means that to change the mapping requires a change to one or the other of the communicating components. Given a presentation and/or structure and an application model, the designer cannot change the mapping from one to the other without making a change to them. In many cases, this is not a problem, but where *the mapping itself is (one of) the primary areas of design decision*, then there is good reason to promote the interface between the two components into a separate component. This is the policy taken in the Iconographer system.

In the Seeheim architecture, the feature which corresponds to the switchboard's role is the interface between the Application Interface Model and the Dialogue Control component, represented in Seeheim as a connecting line (an interface) rather than as a box (a component). By promoting this interface to a component, (as shown in figure 7) Iconographer acknowledges that the interface between the Application Interface Model and the rest of the system must be configurable. One wants a designer to be able to attach different views onto the same application model and, indeed, to try out representationally similar presentations of different application data. The switchboard makes these associations explicit so that they may be described abstractly.

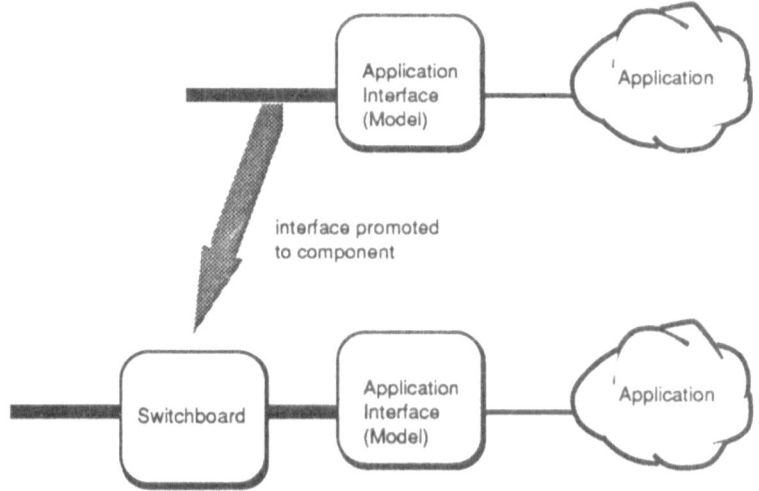

Figure 7 Promoting the Application Model interface to component status

4   Iconographer: Visualising the Run-Time System

Iconographer is a fully integrated design and run-time system. That is, the interactive tools by which an implementational specification can be input are part of the same system which generates the iconic representations which are the ultimate product of the system. For each of the four components of the run-time system architecture, there exists one or more tools by which those components may be specified. The generative principle underlying the design of these tools is that *an Iconographer user is building the run-time system by means of a visual representation of the architecture*.

The simplest expression of this principle occurs in the specification of the object adaptor and the subcomponents of the iconic universe. In all these cases, the user selects a pre-exiting component from a menu of available alternatives. The selected component becomes part of the run-time system. This technique has worked reasonably well for a wide variety of applications and representations. However, research is currently underway to expand the degree of freedom the user has in creating these components via more flexible visual programming techniques. More novel is the way in which Iconographer's architecture is exploited in the top level representation and in the switchboard configuration.

4.1 The Top-Level View

The fact that the output of a specification task is a component of the architecture means that one can represent the specification task visually by means of a diagram of the architecture itself. Not only is specifying the system a matter of building the system; this interactively specifiable architectural diagram lets one *see* that it is.

The top-level view in the Iconographer designer's interface is a window in which the run-time system is built. Each architectural component is represented by an icon and may be selected from a "warehouse" of components. Once placed in the central window, these icons may be connected together via lines which represent the legal dataflows in the system.

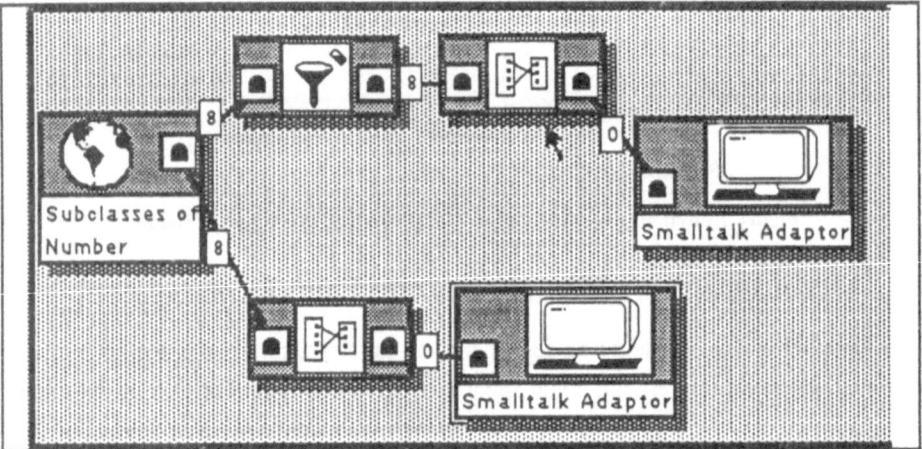

Figure 8 An Iconographer Top Level View

Figure 8 shows a typical result of such building. On the left-hand side of the display is an icon representing an object adaptor. It is linked to a filter and to a switchboard. The filter component is itself attached to another switchboard. Each switchboard is in turn connected to a bitmap display picture adaptor. Links between components are labelled with the number of entities, application or iconic, which flow to the destination component. Selection of the filter and switchboard icons will open visual programming tools which allow the components to be configured. The picture adaptor icon can be selected to open up a window in which the iconic representation is displayed.

Note that there may be multiple instances of the components, allowing multiple views onto an application model or even iconic representations of the model at several points in its development. Furthermore, the fundamental interaction techniques presented in this top-level view - selection and connection - are employed throughout the tools, thus providing a consistency of style.

There are, however, two respects in which this top-level view does not correspond to the architectural model presented earlier. First, there is no representation of a single application universe component. Given the data flow model of the application, it is reasonable to consider the output from any object adaptor, filter or merger as a legal application model. There is no single application model (as is typical with many user interface management systems) but potentially as many as the designer wishes to select/program, each available for viewing by attaching a switchboard onto the output of any appropriate component.

Second, there is no representation at all of the Iconic Universe component. As we shall see when examining the switchboard's visual representation, the Iconic Universe specification tools are attached to a switchboard. The reasons for this approach are discussed in the next section.

4.2   The Switchboard: Visualising the Inter-Universe Links

The switchboard construction tool is the means by which the links from application attributes to iconic attributes are specified. Since the switchboard will automatically generate a function which maps from the source to the destination attribute, the user's basic task is to identify an application attribute to be represented and an iconic attribute which will do the representing. The switchboard specification tool visualises this task in terms of drawing physical links between representations of the attributes.

In the switchboard shown in figure 9, the labelled rectangles on the left-hand side stand for the attributes of entities in the application universe (in this case information about machines in a local area network) while the rectangles on the right-hand side represent the attributes of icons (faces have been specified).[3] Where the types of attribute on both sides of the switchboard are the same, the link is shown as a single uninterrupted line and is created by dragging a rubber-band line from an attribute icon to one on the other side. Where a type conversion is necessary, Iconographer will automatically add it,

---

[3]   In all diagrams of Iconographer architecture shown up to this point, the application universe is shown on the right and the iconic universe on the left, to allow comparison with the Seeheim architecture. However, the switchboard visualisation employed in the actual software uses the reverse arrangement.

signalling this fact by placing an additional rectangle, labeled with the function name, on the attribute link. Function editors are available by which the Iconographer-generated functions can be modified by the user. Additionally, new attributes may be created via an attribute building tool.

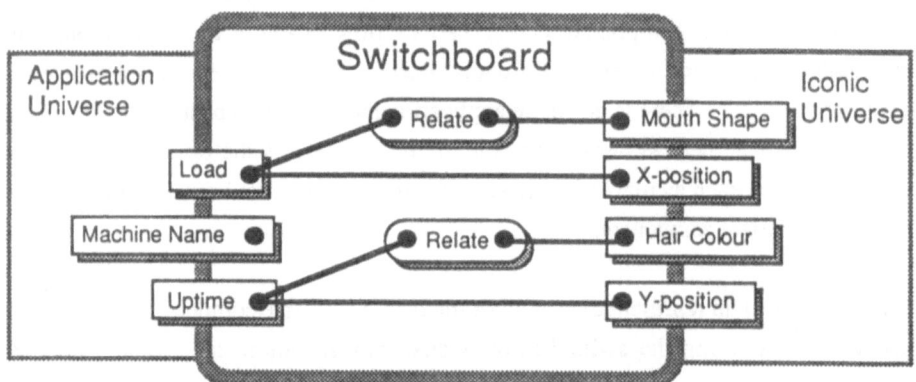

Figure 9 The Visualisation of the Switchboard

As mentioned in the previous section, the iconic universe is specified by selecting from lists of pre-existing icon generators, compositors and relationship handlers, much as the object adaptor is specified. However, rather than being performed at the top level, these lists are attached as menus to the switchboard window. This asymmetry between the way the application universe and the iconic universe are treated has arisen for reasons of expediency in design. That is, our first attempt at a visual representation of the implementational specification treated choice of iconic universe as part of the same overall task of which switchboard configuration was a part. However, an alternative approach is being explored which will decouple iconic universe specification from the switchboard and treat it symmetrically with application universe specification.

5   Conclusion

Iconographer illustrates two ways in which the architecture of the run-time system can be related to the specification process. First, the architecture itself corresponds closely to the structure of the task of producing a design-oriented description of the final product of the system. Second, implementational specification takes place via a visualisation of the architecture. I believe this combination of correspondences leads to a considerable diminution of the design and specification gulfs. And since the tools are fully integrated with the run-time system itself, the result is a representation construction tool by which radically different iconic representations can be produced in a matter of seconds.

The Iconographer system is still under development. Recently, Iconographer's icons have been made sensitive to user input, allowing a user to interact with the end-product iconic display in order to communicate with the application [12]. Also, the application universe is being modified to allow more expressive application models to be incorporated. Both of these developments will necessitate changes to the architecture and new visual programming tools to be produced. In both cases, however, the specification-architecture-tool correspondences will remain an underlying design principle of the system.

Acknowledgements

The Innovative Iconic Interfaces Project, which has produced the Iconographer system, is funded by SERC grant GR/F 67129. I wish to thank my colleagues in the Innovative Iconic Interfaces project, Dr. Kevin Waite and Dr. Steve Draper. Kevin and Steve are responsible for many of the design ideas discussed in this paper and Kevin is solely responsible for Iconographer's implementation. I also wish to thank Steve, Kevin, Dr. David England and Dr. Roger Took for their many many constructive comments on an earlier draft of this paper.

References

[1]   William Buxton. *Lexical and Pragmatic Considerations of Input Structures.* ACM Computer Graphics (January '83). pp. 31-36.

[2]   J. Coutaz. *Architectural Models for Interactive Software: Failures and Trends.* In G. Cockton, ed., Engineering for Human-Computer Interaction, North-Holland, 1990. pp. 137-151.

[3]   S.W. Draper and K.W. Waite. *Iconographer as a visual programming system.* In D. Diaper and N. Hammond, eds., People and Computers VI, Cambridge University Press, 1991. pp. 171-185.

[4]   E. Edmonds and Hagiwara, N. *An Experiment in Interactive Architectures.* In Proceedings of Interact '90, North-Holland, 1990. pp. 601-606.

[5]   Edwin L. Hutchins, James D. Hollan, and Donald A. Norman. *Direct Manipulaton Interfaces*. In Norman & Draper, eds., User Centered System Design, Lawrence Erlbaum, 1986. pp. 87-124.

[6]   Scott Hudson. UIMS *Support for Direct Manipulation Interfaces*. ACM Computer Graphics 21,2 (April '87). pp. 120-124.

[7]   Robert J.K. Jacob. *A state transition diagram language for visual programming*. IEEE Computer (August '85), pp. 51-59.

[8]   Tom Moran. *The Command Language Grammar: A Representation of the User Interface of Interactive Computer Systems*. IJMMS 15 (1981), pp. 30-50.

[9]   Brad A. Myers, Dario A. Giuse, Roger B. Cannenberg, Brad Vander Zanden, David S. Kosbie, Edward Pervin, Andrew Mickish, and Philippe Marchal. *Garnet: Comprehensive Support for Graphical, Highly Interactive User Interfaces*. IEEE Computer (November '90). pp. 71-85.

[10]   Gunther Pfaff, ed. *Proc. of the Workshop on User Interface Management Systems*. Seeheim, Nov. 1983. Springer-Verlag, 1985.

[11]   Roger Took. *The Active Medium: A Conceptual and Practical Architecture for Direct Manipulation*. In D. Diaper and N. Hammond, eds., People and Computers VI, Cambridge University Press, 1991. pp. 249-264.

[12]   Kevin Waite and Stephen Draper. *User Input to Iconographer*. In D. Diaper and N. Hammond, eds., People and Computers VI, Cambridge University Press, 1991. pp. 187-198.

[13]   K.W. Waite, S.W. Draper and P.D. Gray. *Iconographer: A Tool for Rapidly Configuring Interactive Iconic Representations*. Submitted to ACM Transactions on Information Systems, October, 1991.

[14]   Anthony I. Wasserman. *Extending State Transition Diagrams for the Specification of Human-Computer Interaction*. IEEE Trans. Software Engineering 11,8 (1985). pp. 699-713.

[15]   Catherine A Wood and Philip D. Gray. *User Interface–Application Communication in the Chimera UIMS*. Software: Practice & Experience, 1992, to appear.

Incorporating an Incremental Learning Model in the Design of HyperNeWS2.0

Cathy Waite

The Turing Institute

36 North Hanover Street

Glasgow, Scotland

Abstract

One of the main aims for environments which support the design and execution of graphical interfaces is to support the specification of interfaces without having to resort to low-level programming. However, it is also desirable to be able to support a wide range of interfaces, which requires a general, powerful specification technique such as the use of programming languages. This paper discusses an attempt to address this contradiction in the design of HyperNeWS 2.0, an object-oriented environment which supports rapid-prototyping of graphical user interfaces.

1 Introduction

HyperNeWS is an object-oriented environment which supports interactive rapid prototyping of graphical user interfaces. It can be used both for the design and implementation of user interfaces, allowing links to applications written in C, Lisp, Prolog or PostScript. HyperNeWS runs under OpenWindows on Sun workstations using the NeWS server, and is written in PostScript, a powerful page description language. Interfaces are designed within HyperNeWS by copying existing objects, and then specialising their presentation and behaviours by changing pre-defined attributes, or adding new ones by defining small programs called scripts.

As part of a collaborative research project with Sun Microsystems, Hyper-NeWS is currently being redesigned. The design for HyperNeWS 2.0 is almost complete, and has been partly implemented. An important goal of the new design was to provide an incremental learning model, that would ease users into employing the full power of HyperNeWS. To achieve this, and to improve the structure of interfaces designed using HyperNeWS, the architecture of objects within HyperNeWS had to be re-structured. This paper will discuss how, by focusing on the implementation and presentation of objects within Hyper-NeWS, many improvements have been made to the architecture of HyperNeWS – generalising the control structures, and thus increasing the range of interfaces possible – while at the same time improving the interface to HyperNeWS itself, thereby making it easier to use.

1.1 Requirements of the Design

A preliminary design document set out the requirements for HyperNeWS 2.0 [13]. These requirements are summarised below. The first aim was to maintain the essential features of HyperNeWS 1.4 [7, 8], these were identified as:

- reduce the learning curve,

- support a wide range of interfaces, and

  - the integration of graphics into the user interface by the provision of an on-line graphical editor;
  - direct manipulation of user interface components;
  - separation of the user interface and application;
  - persistence of user interface;
  - the ability to program the dialogue.

In addition, HyperNeWS 2.0 has been extended to support:

- OPENLOOK compliant user interfaces [5, 6] by integration with the Sun's NeWS toolkit that provides OPENLOOK components (TNT);

- a generalised container hierarchy, providing improved control structures;

- dynamic control over object attributes through the use of scope variables;

- use of a C-like scripting language, PdB.

The two requirements, reducing the learning curve and supporting a wide range of interfaces, could be seen as being contradictory. Attempts to reduce the learning curve for interface specification usually result in a high level specification technique being adopted, which although is easier to use, generally results in a smaller ranger of interfaces (or design space) which can be specified using that technique. In an attempt to address this contradiction, the design for HyperNeWS 2.0 [1] incorporated several specification techniques, ranging from high-level direct manipulation to low-level programming. Although the design space at the higher levels is restricted, the lower levels provide for a diversity of interfaces. The result is an easy to use interface design environment, which provides the flexibility to construct a wide range of interfaces. This paper will briefly cover the structure of the objects, and then will concentrate on the learning model such a structure affords.

2 The Structure of HyperNeWS Objects

Interfaces constructed using HyperNeWS are built from communicating objects. The representation of these objects defines what the interface looks like, whilst their behaviour defines the dynamic aspects of the interface. A full discussion of HyperNeWS objects can be found in Niblett [9]. Every object within HyperNeWS is a kind of *container*. A container is an object which may contain

---

[1] From now on all references in this paper to HyperNeWS will refer to HyperNeWS 2.0

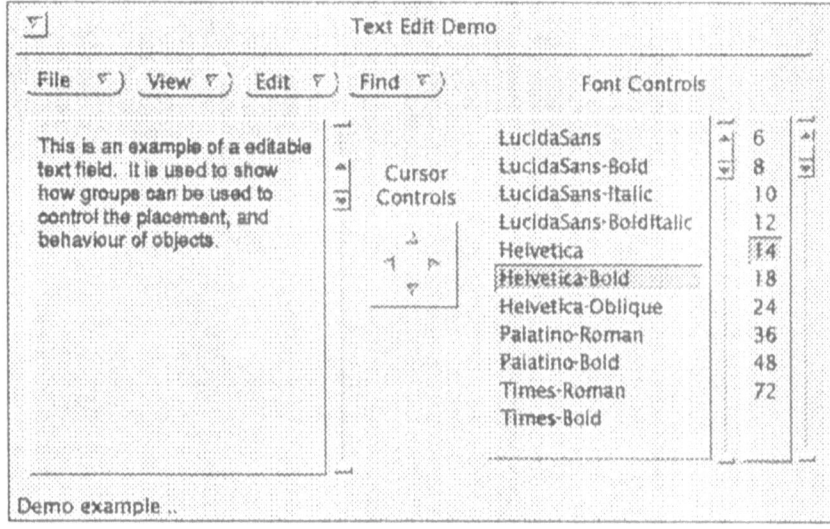

Figure 1: An Example HyperNeWS 2.0 Interface

other objects, its *members*. As each container can also be a member of another container (its *parent*), a container hierarchy is formed, which determines the run-time structure of HyperNeWS interfaces. Although powerful, the container model is very abstract, and thus difficult for new users to understand and use effectively. To provide a more concrete model, several specialised containers have been provided which can be used to simulate the stack/background/card model used by earlier versions of HyperNeWS and also by HyperCard [1]. Using these pre-defined containers it is also possible to create OPENLOOK complaint interfaces (see Figure 1). These pre-defined containers are provided as concrete examples only; using them as templates it is possible to implement a wide variety of interfaces, perhaps conforming to other interface standards, such as Motif [10].

The pre-defined containers include *windows* (which will always be at the root of the container hierarchy) which have *layouts* as their members. Layouts are analogous to cards. Only one layout is visible at a time, with the window controlling which one it is. There is also a special layout called the *window layout*. This is always visible behind the other layouts (analogous to backgrounds), and is used to hold controls which must always be visible, such as *Quit* buttons. The pre-defined class hierarchy is shown in Figure 2.

The layouts can have groups or controls as their members. Controls are the main objects with which the user interacts and include buttons, sliders, textfields, scrollable choices, menus etc. The groups can be used to display related components together, using placement policies to dictate how the members should be arranged within the group (e.g. left-to-right, or top-to-bottom).

These placement policies ensure that if the group is resized (or if the group's parent is resized), the members of the group will maintain the correct relative position. Groups can also be used to form a focus of control over related objects by adding new behaviour to the group which controls the members of the group. For example, to implement radio buttons, a group would be created with the

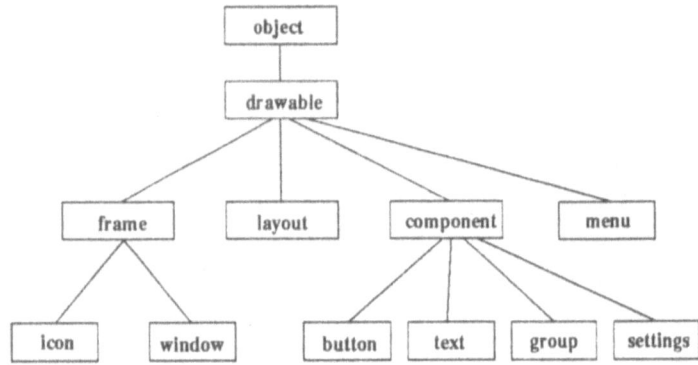

Figure 2: The HyperNeWS Template Class Hierarchy

radio buttons themselves as the members of the group. The behaviour of the group would then be specialised to control the radio buttons, ensuring only one radio button is selected at a time. This specialisation results in a new class, a *radio button group* class.

The interface in Figure 1 has been expanded to show its container hierarchy in Figure 3. Previous versions of HyperNeWS (together with other common user interface design environments) had a fixed run-time hierarchy, the basic groups being stacks, backgrounds, cards. This means that all controls (i.e. buttons, textfields), have to be members of a card or a background. There is no grouping of related objects. If the text editor example (Figure 1) was implemented in a fixed, two level hierarchy (like HyperNeWS 1.4), then its structure would look like Figure 4. This is obviously a poorer control structure as there is no way of grouping objects together and ensuring they stay together, or imposing some locus of control over a set of objects (such as a group of radio buttons). A flat structure results, with all behaviour written into the card. If a second group or radio-buttons were to be added, the same behaviour would need to be written into the card a second time, rather than just add another instance of the *radio-button group* class.

2.1 Message Passing

The container hierarchy also defines the way messages are passed between objects in an interface. It is possible to send messages to explicitly named objects. However, if a message is sent to an object such as a button, and the button cannot handle it, the message is passed on to the button's parent in the container hierarchy, who may in turn pass the message on to its parent (see Figure 5). Thus by inserting groups in the hierarchy it is possible to change the perceived behaviour of members of the groups, by intercepting messages as they pass up the hierarchy.

HyperNeWS supports the notion of *unreliable* messages. When an unreliable message is used, if the message is not handled, no error is raised. This allows for a form of incomplete specification. An object may send messages to another object not yet implemented, and these messages will be ignored. The message passing in HyperNeWS affords a degree of anonymity. Objects do not know who eventually handles the messages they send.

This anonymity allows for flexibility when prototyping applications, as is discussed below.

2.2 Interface–Application Communication and Separation

An optional client, or application, can be inserted at any point in the message hierarchy.

As well as sending messages between HyperNeWS objects, it is possible

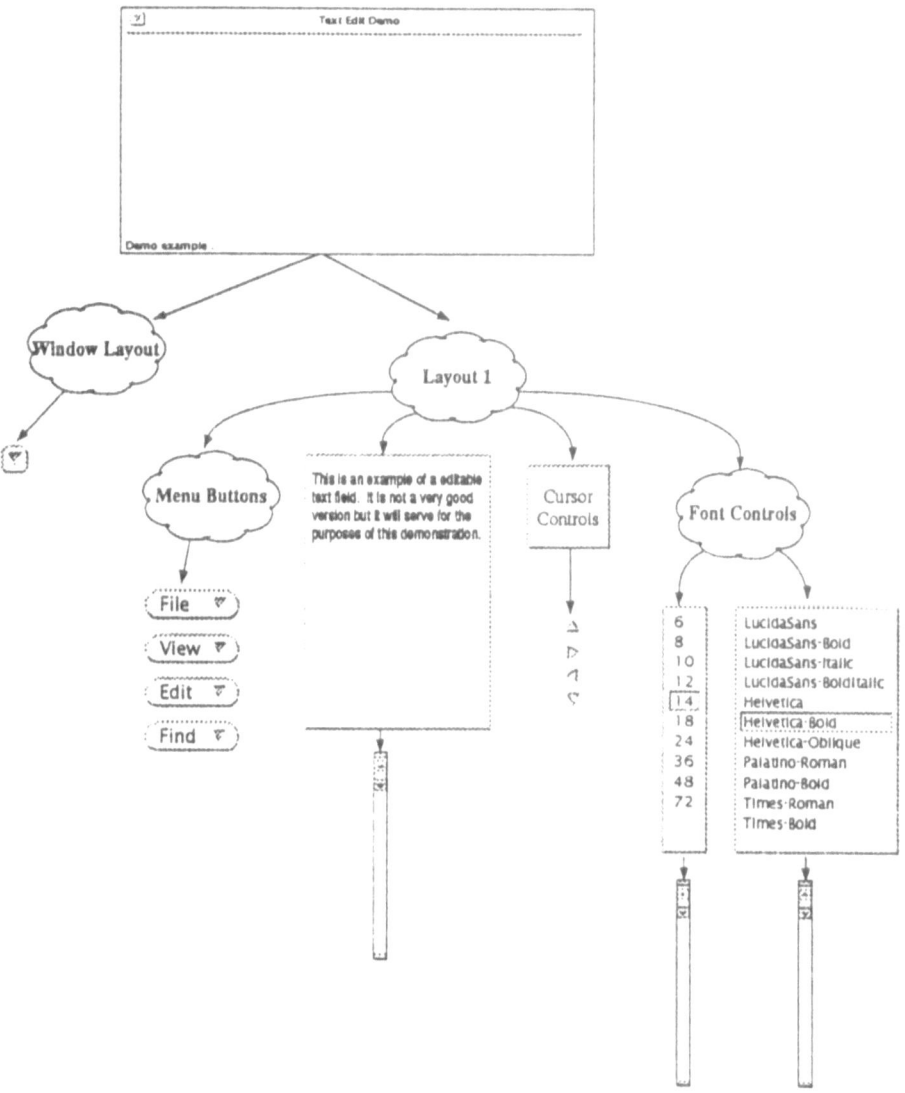

Figure 3: The Container Hierarchy for Figure 1

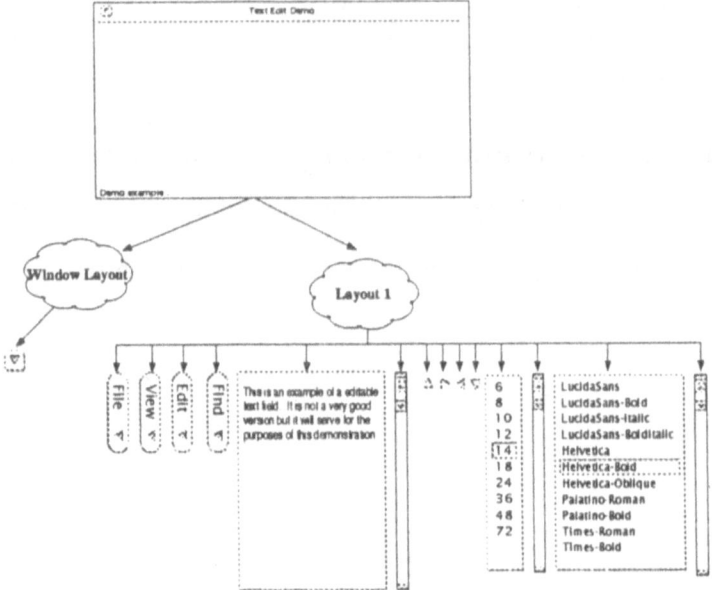

Figure 4: The Flat Hierarchy for Figure 1

for each HyperNeWS object to communicate with an application, or *client*. This communication takes place via a high-level interface. The clients can be separate processes implemented in C, Prolog or Lisp, running on the same or other (networked) machines, a PostScript process running in the NeWS sever, or another HyperNeWS object. HyperNeWS objects communicate with their clients by sending messages to them. Clients are notionally inserted in the container hierarchy between the object and its parent. So any messages the object does not understand will be sent to the client for processing. If the client does not handle it, the message is passed up the container hierarchy as usual,

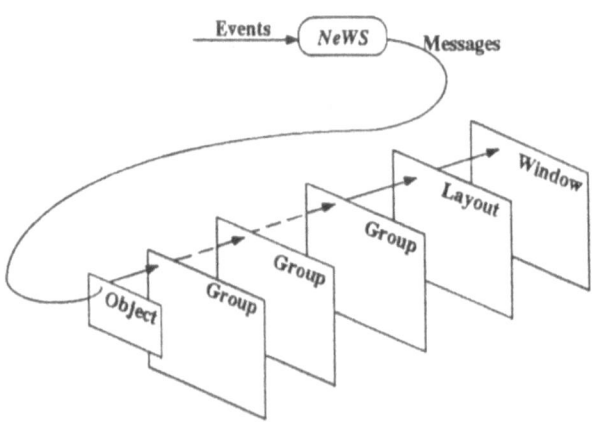

Figure 5: Message Passing in HyperNeWS

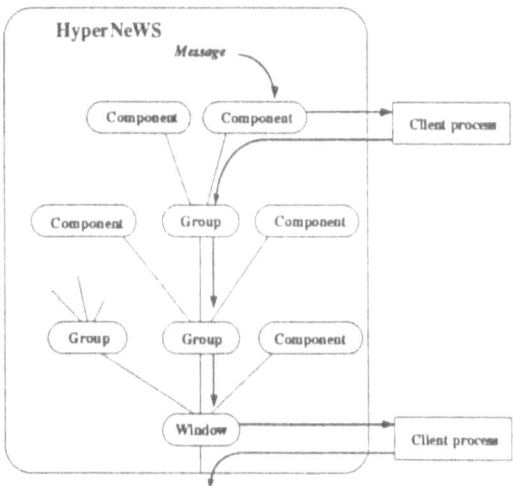

Figure 6: Message Passing between objects and clients

see Figure 6.

As all communication is carried out via message passing with the sender having no knowledge of the receiver, it is easy to prototype the interface using another HyperNeWS object (or even the user) to simulate the application, and then link up to the real application at a later date. In the early stages of design a HyperNeWS object (generally the window) can be used to simulate the application functionality. This functionality will be accessed via message sends from other HyperNeWS objects. When the interface is ready to be connected to the actual application the simulation methods can be removed from the window, and messages will automatically be passed on to the application (or client). The client–interface communication is at the level of message sends. The clients can use provided methods to create references to HyperNeWS objects, and send messages to these. In addition the client can register which messages it expects to receive from which HyperNeWS objects, and define call backs to be invoked when these messages are caught.

There are several architectures described in the literature for interface–application communication, ranging from the Seeheim model [4], with a monolithic application communicating with a monolithic dialogue component, to the PAC model [3], where each object in the interface contains a part of the application. HyperNeWS is flexible enough to model this entire spectrum. The window can communicate with a monolithic application (as in the Seeheim model), or each individual HyperNeWS component can communicate with its own client (as in PAC), or any combination of these.

The different ways of communicating between the client and the interface also provides different levels of separability. It is possible to have the whole application functionality defined within HyperNeWS, which gives you a low degree of separability, but a high degree of interactivity as required by some applications (such as drawing packages like *HyperDraw* discussed later). At the other end of the spectrum, the application functionality can be provided by several independent UNIX process, giving a high degree of separability.

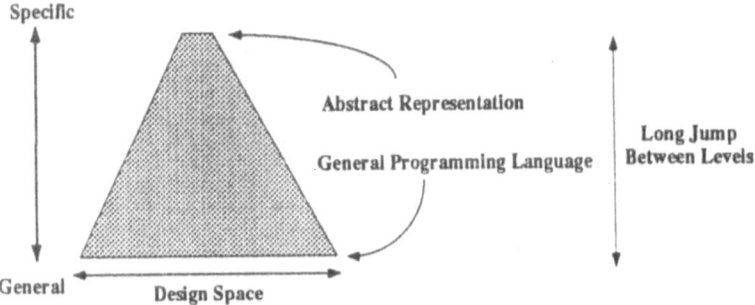

Figure 7: The Design Pyramid for two levels

2.3 Scoped Variables

HyperNeWS objects inherit attributes from their parent classes via the class hierarchy. However these attributes are statically inherited when the object is first created. It is often useful to have a dynamic inheritance mechanism which passes attributes down the *container* hierarchy at run-time. This is necessary, for example, when constructing an OPENLOOK compliant interface, where the 3-D effect can only be maintained if consistent colour schemes are used. OPENLOOK defines variables used when defining the colours of the OPENLOOK components, including colours for the background, stroke, highlight and shading. Problems arise when a component is copied from another window, which may have a different colour scheme, causing the correct 3-D effect to be lost.

HyperNeWS provides scoped variables to allow dynamic inheritance of certain attributes of components (such as colours, fonts etc) from their parents in the container hierarchy. Each member of a group automatically inherits the values of its parent's scoped variables. Thus when a button is copied into a window, if it uses the OPENLOOK naming scheme for its colours, it will dynamically inherit the colours of the window (which in turn inherits them from the user's environment). This also means that if the user develops a HyperNeWS interface in an environment which is set up to be based on pinks, when another user starts up that interface in their own environment (based on blues), the HyperNeWS interface will automatically adopt the colour scheme of the second user's environment (i.e. blue).

This section has briefly covered the structure of HyperNeWS objects. The remainder of this paper will concentrate on how these objects are used to construct graphical interfaces.

3 Defining HyperNeWS Objects

Make the simple things easy ... and the difficult things almost as easy. (Adapted from the original attributed to Alan Kay)

The main goal of HyperNeWS was to aim for an incremental learning model which initially protects the user from the internal details of the components,

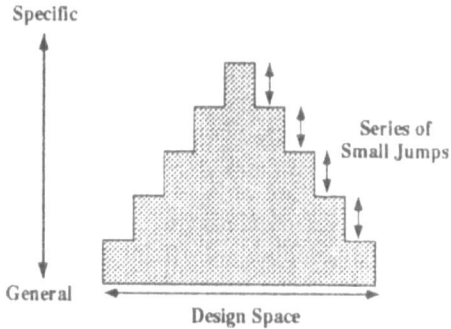

Figure 8: The Design Pyramid for HyperNeWS

and progressively reveals the details as the user becomes more confident and demanding. It is common for user interface design environments to support a high level of abstraction used to define the interface. Although these abstractions (or specification techniques) tend to be easy to use, it is usually the case that they are not general enough to allow the specification of all the required facets of the interface. To get round this problem *trapdoors* are often included which give access to a lower level programming language which is used to implement the higher level abstractions, and which is general enough to allow all aspects of the interface to be defined. These low level languages are difficult to use, and it is a long jump for designers from the high level abstractions to the low level languages. This is shown by the design pyramid in Figure 7. The width of the pyramid represents the design space support at that level. At the top level, although interfaces are easy to generated, the designer is limited to a narrow design space. In contrast, at the base of the pyramid, the specification language is more general, and the design space is correspondingly wider. The sharp edge of the pyramid shows the long drop from the high level to the general language. This drop can often prove intimidating for designers, and certainly involves a steep learning curve.

In HyperNeWS an attempt has been made to provide several levels between the two extremes. These levels are supported in the HyperNeWS interface by providing several ways of accessing and updating the internal structure of the objects which constitute the interface. The levels range from easy to use, with a restricted design space; to a more general, un-restricted design space which requires programming. Our claim is that the smaller the step between the levels, the easier it is for designers to move between them. The design pyramid with multiple levels in shown in Figure 8.

The levels are implemented as different ways of creating and manipulating a single universe of objects. Any changes made to an object at a higher level, will be accessible at the lower levels in a different representation. Thus the designer can learn about the different representations by making changes in higher levels, moving to lower ones, seeing the effects and if required, refining them. This is illustrated in the following sections.

Interfaces are usually constructed in HyperNeWS by copying existing objects from previously designed, or system provided, interfaces. These components are then specialised. The idea of using a small set of pre-defined objects which can be configured is common in current user interface development systems, such as HyperCard or Guide [11]. However, these systems tend to allow flexible specialisation in terms of behaviour only. In most user interface design environments it is possible to specialise objects by augmenting their behaviour, either by defining callbacks for fixed events (as in Guide), or by adding new methods through scripts (as in HyperCard). Configuring the appearance of the objects is possible, but only by setting fixed attributes. As HyperNeWS is built on top of PostScript it has added power through the flexibility of the PostScript graphics model. It is possible to change the presentation of buttons and windows to any graphics representation. A lot of the power and extensibility of HyperNeWS stems from the fact that the levels of configurability apply both to the presentation and behaviour of objects. Although the user would usually mix the definition of presentation and behaviour, they are discussed separately below.

3.1 Levels of Presentation

Unlike systems such as HyperCard or SunView, where there are fixed parameters which can be changed to configure the representations of objects, Hyper-NeWS harnesses the full power of PostScript in the definition of the presentation of objects. There are various ways in which the presentations of objects can be configured.

Level 1: The attributes of an object easiest to change are its position and size. Using the mouse it is possible to position objects where required, and scale them to the correct size. Each container provides an edit context, in which it is possible to edit the members of the container. If any of the members are themselves containers, they can be selected as the new edit context. So it is possible to move up and down the container hierarchy editing the contents of each group (see Figure 9). Objects can be copied from an existing interface or the *Object Warehouse* and pasted into the window being developed. Figure 10 shows the layout for the Object Warehouse, which contains template OPENLOOK objects. The user can add his own sets of objects to the Object Warehouse, or tailor those already on it.

Level 2: Each object has associated properties which can be edited via a properties window (see Figure 11). Attributes such as text font, text size, labels, colours etc may be changed by editing the properties window. In addition, those attributes which can be changed by direct manipulation at level one (such as position and size) can also be changed at level 2. This allows for exact control over an object's position which may have been roughly positioned by direct manipulation. This illustrates the idea of having all information set at higher levels visible at lower levels.

Level 3: The representation of any object (including windows) may be changed to a drawing created using the drawing tool, HyperDraw (see Figure 12). This tool can be used to design pictures from scratch, or as a means of

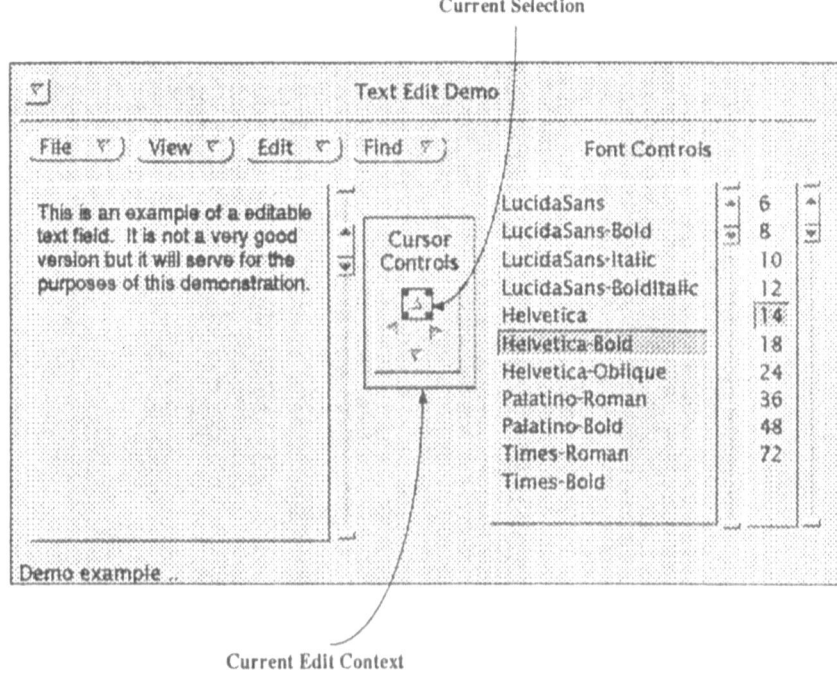

Figure 9: The edit context for the cursor controls

importing graphics created using other tools, such as images or Encapsulated PostScript. As the drawings are based on PostScript it is possible to have any representation, size or shape (see Figure 13). Any drawings created in HyperDraw can be used for the window representation, or for a button representation.

Level 4: When a HyperDraw drawing is pasted into an object, the *Draw* method for that object is replaced with the PostScript required to draw the new representation. It is possible to change the representation by editing the *Draw* method by hand. Each object has an associated *script* which the user can edit to update existing methods, or add new ones. Scripting will be discussed more fully later. For example, there are some pre-defined methods such as *Path* (which defines the shape of the objects), *Draw* which paints the object. By changing the *Path* method (for example) it is possible to create arbitrary shaped objects, such as triangular or cloud shaped buttons. The buttons shown in Figure 14 were created by changing the scripts shown to the right of the buttons. In all aspects, except shape, these buttons are the same.

Level 5: Extending level 4, it is possible to introduce totally new drawing procedures via the script of an object, which may add new attributes to an object. Taking the slider as an example, it is possible to make it look like a dial, just by changing the drawing routines in the script (see Figure 15). To work properly, this new object needs added behaviour.

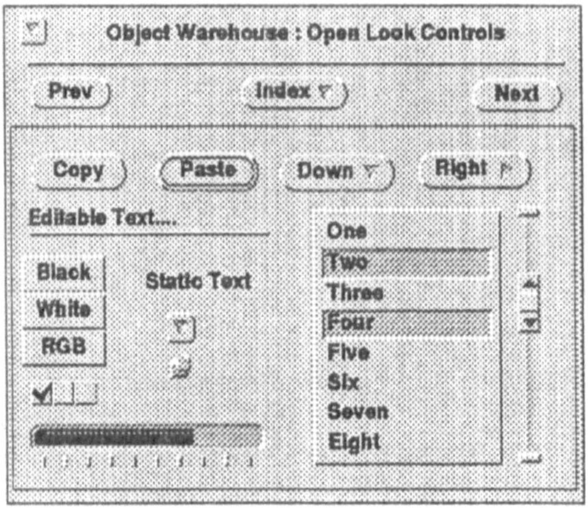

Figure 10: The Object Warehouse

Techniques for changing the behaviour of objects are discussed in the next section.

When new attributes are added to an object, it is generally the case that a new Properties window is created. This can be done by copying the existing Properties window, and adding objects to manipulate the new attributes. At this point, there is a complete revolution, where the new attributes which are added via scripts, can henceforth be manipulated using the Properties window (i.e. level 2 above).

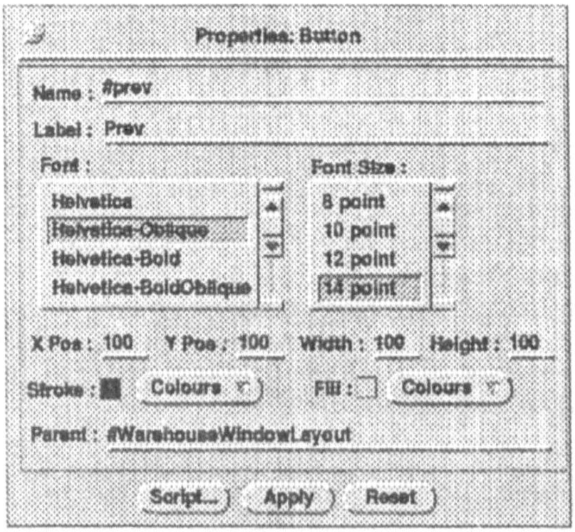

Figure 11: The Properties Window for Button Objects

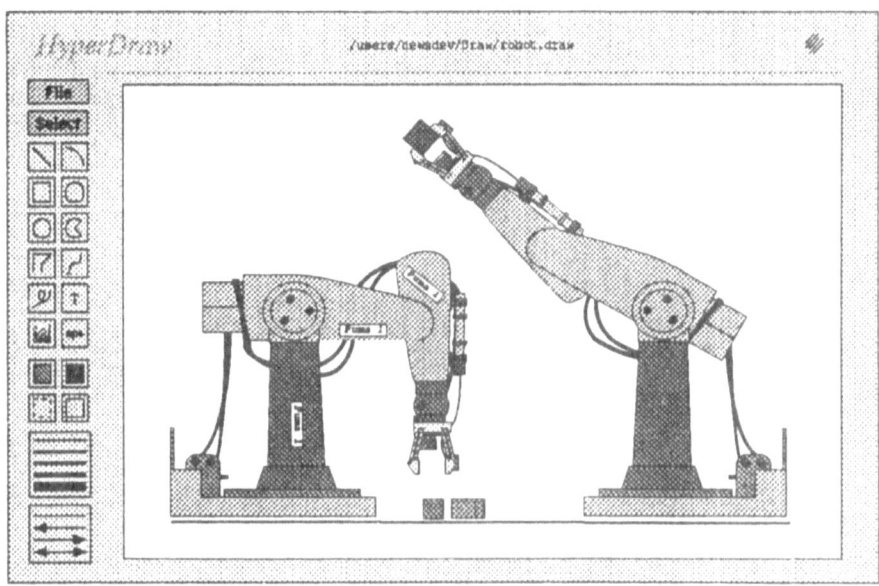

Figure 12: The HyperDraw Graphics Tool

3.2 Levels of Behaviour

The behaviour of the objects can also be configured in a variety of ways. Each technique requires more programming and a greater knowledge of HyperNeWS, but at the same time provides greater flexibility. The actual levels to be used in HyperNeWS have not been fixed yet but the following are ideas of what the levels may look like. Further analysis is required to identify some standard behaviours that are common enough to all interfaces that it is worth while adding support for them at the higher levels. So far, the only behaviour supported at higher levels is that of linking objects to layouts, to support HyperText or HyperMedia applications.

Level 1: The properties window for objects, as well as containing presentational attributes, also contains attributes which may affect the object's behaviour, such as whether or not a text field is scrollable, the maximum or minimum value of a slider etc.

Level 2: The second level allows linking of objects to other layouts either on the same or other windows. This linking can also be done via the properties window, by filling in a field *Link To....* The name of the target layout can be entered directly, or found by using the menu option *Name of ...* to find the name of the layout, which can then be pasted into the link field.

Level 3: The third level provides ease of use for programmers. It does not require programming in HyperNeWS, but it does require programming of the application. The user can specify the behaviour of an object by registering a client procedure name with a predefined method for an interface

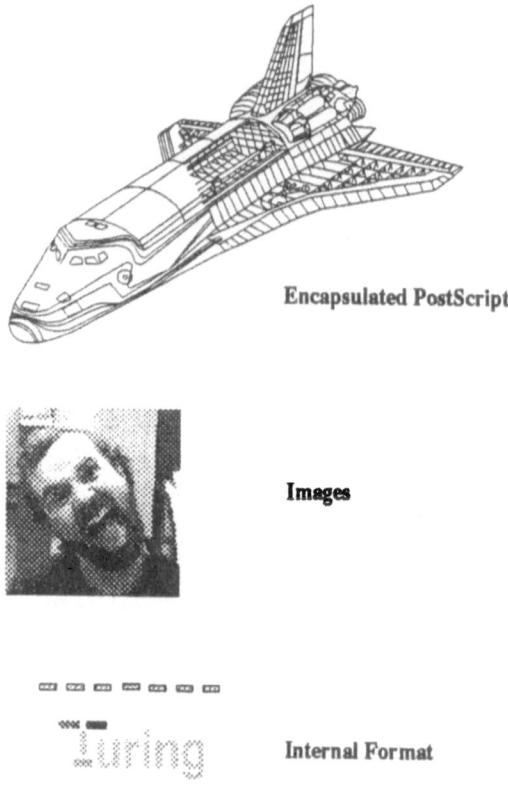

Encapsulated PostScript

Images

Internal Format

Figure 13: The Integrated Drawing Formats available in HyperDraw

object. For example, when selected a button gets sent the message *Action*. The user can register any client procedure with the button message *Action* which will be called when the button is selected.

It is possible to define the application completely using this technique. Many projects (for example Optimist [2]) have used HyperNeWS to build highly interactive interaces for applications without any scripting at all. These projects depend on the message hierarchy to pass all messages from objects to the client. Thus the application programmer can define all interface and application behaviour in the same language.

Level 4: In the previous levels the actions taken by the user will cause scripts to be generated automatically, although the user need not be aware of this. However, users will soon learn of the scripts, and the HyperNeWS generated code will serve as examples of simple scripts. Thus the user need never start from scratch. In previous version of HyperNeWS, the scripting language used was PostScript. This introduced new complexity to the system as few users were familiar with PostScript, which is a fairly low-level language. In an attempt to improve the accessibility of the scripting facilities within HyperNeWS, but still keep the flexibility and power of PostScript, a C-like language, PdB, was implemented. PdB has C data structures and syntax, but PostScript semantics. Scripts written

```
          void Path()
          {
              int rounding = min(Round,min(Height,Width)/2));
              rrectpath(rounding,0,1,Width-1,Height-1)
          }
```

```
          void Path()
          {
              moveto(0,0);
              lineto(Width,0);
              lineto(Width/2,Height);
              closepath;
          }
```

```
          void Path()
          {
              int angle = 40;
              int iterate = 360;
              gsave();
                  scale(Width,Height);
                  translate(0.5,0.5);
                  while(iterate > 0)
                  {
                      iterate--;
                      rotate(angle);
                      arc(.2,.2,.2,-10,-100);
                  }
                  closepath();
              grestore();
          }
```

Figure 14: The effects of changing the Path script for buttons

in PdB are compiled into highly optimised PostScript.

Through scripting, the user can freely extend the behaviour of an object, adding new behaviours, or updating existing ones. By changing the script of existing objects, the user specialises existing classes. These modified classes are called *shared classes*. A shared class can be subsequently refined to produce other shared classes, that record the differences from the original. The shared classes are defined in terms of their *differences* from the base class from which they grew. New instances of these shared classes are made by copying existing instances.

Level 5: After creating shared classes, the next level is to create new base classes (termed *plug-in* classes). These are classes which are written totally in PdB [12], in files external to HyperNeWS. They should be used with caution, as the introduction of plug-in classes means that interfaces which use these new classes are no longer as portable as those using only shared classes. Objects which are instances of shared classes contain all the information required to define their behaviour, and thus can be freely cut and pasted, or passed on to other HyperNeWS users. However, objects based on added plug-in classes know only how they differ from the plug-in class. The actual definition of the plug-in class has to be passed

166

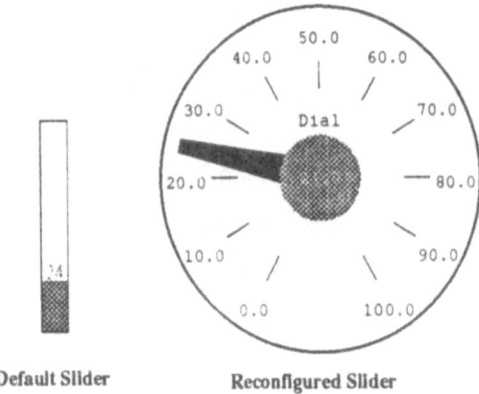

Default Slider   Reconfigured Slider

Figure 15: The Changes to presentation possible using scripting

around with the object. Sharing of interfaces is still possible, but more difficult, when using plug-in classes.

4 Conclusions

By generalising the way in which objects can be combined within HyperNeWS, it has been possible to increase the range of interfaces that can easily be constructed. This generality has been extended to include better communication with underlying applications. However, the new power has *not* been gained at the price of ease of use. The interface to HyperNeWS has been constructed to provide levels of access to the internals of the objects. These levels range from restricted designs, which are easily constructed to powerful, un-restricted designs, which require programming.

Further research is required to increase the number of designs that can be implemented using levels 1 and 2 for both presentation and behaviour. Specifically, some task analysis is required to discern which tasks are common (such as generating links between objects), so that particular support can be provided to allow high level specification of these tasks.

The design of HyperNeWS shows how it is possible to produce a user interface environment that can be easily used to build interfaces which conform to a standard (such as OPENLOOK). By making use of the default components, a user can quickly build a OPENLOOK conformant interface, mainly using direct manipulation. However, HyperNeWS does not restrict the user to solely OPENLOOK interfaces, but offers the freedom to design and implement a wide range of interface styles.

5 Acknowledgements

This paper covers work carried out by the HyperNeWS project at the Turing Institute. The group consists of Arthur van Hoff, Tim Niblett, Cathy Waite and Jim Rudolf. We would like to thank Rafael Bracho, Owen Densmore and

Don Hopkins of Sun Microsystems for useful input to the design and information about TNT, and OPENLOOK, and Wim Janssen of Philips for helpful discussion.

References

[1] Apple Computer, Inc. *HyperCard User's Guide.* Apple Computer, Inc., Cupertino, Calif., 1987.

[2] Peter Clark. Representing knowledge as arguments: Applying expert system technology to judgemental problem-solving. In T. R. Addis and R. M. Muir, editors, *Research and Development in Expert Systems VII*, pages 147–159. Cambridge Univ. Press, 1990. (Proc. ES90, the 10th BCS Specialist Group on Expert Systems).

[3] Joelle Coutaz. PAC, an Object Oriented Model for Dialog Design. In *Human-Computer Interaction -INTERACT'87*, pages 431–436. Elsevier Science Publishers B.V, 1987.

[4] M. Green. Report on dialogue specification tools. In *User Interface Management Systems*, pages 9–20. Springer-Verlag, 1983.

[5] Sun Microsystems Inc and AT&T. *OPEN LOOK Graphical User Interface Application Style Guidelines.* Addison-Wesley, 1989.

[6] Sun Microsystems Inc and AT&T. *OPEN LOOK Graphical User Interface Functional Specification.* Addison-Wesley, 1989.

[7] The Turing Institute. *The HyperNeWS 1.4 User Guide.* 36 North Hanover Street, Glasgow, G1 2AD., September 1990.

[8] The Turing Institute. *The HyperNeWS 1.4 Reference Manual.* 36 North Hanover Street, Glasgow, G1 2AD., September 1990.

[9] T. Niblett. The Object in HyperNeWS. In *UK Unix systems user group 1991 summer technical meeting, Liverpool*, 15 - 17 July 1991.

[10] Open Software Foundation. *OSF/Motif Style Guide.* Prentice-Hall, Englewood Cliffs, NJ, 1991.

[11] Sun Micorsystems, Inc. *Open Windows Developer's Guide.* Mountain View, CA 94043, October 1990.

[12] Arthur van Hoff. The PdB Reference Manual. Technical report, The Turing Institute, 36 North Hanover Street, Glasgow, G1 2AD., April 1991.

[13] Arthur van Hoff, Tim Niblett, Cathy Waite, and Jim Rudolf. The Design of HyperNeWS 2.0. Technical report, The Turing Institute, 36 North Hanover Street, Glasgow, G1 2AD., February 1991.

Declarative Objects for User Interface Construction

Trevor P. Hopkins

Computer Science Department, University of Manchester

Oxford Road, Manchester, M13 9PL, U.K.

Steve K. Wallis

Computer Science Department, University of Manchester

Oxford Road, Manchester, M13 9PL, U.K.

Abstract

As part of a project developing a toolkit for simulation-based interactive Computer-Based Training (CBT), a declarative object-oriented programming system was devised. This paper starts by outlining this language, then goes on to describe its use for user interface construction. The interfaces created are specifically targeted at unsophisticated computer users, and the programming system and tools are intended for use by CBT authors with limited programming experience. The results of using this system, together with the problems encountered, are also reported.

1 Introduction

This paper describes a toolkit for the development of interactive user interfaces, based on a composite object/functional programming system. This system has been used for the construction of realistic Computer-Based Training (CBT) applications.

1.1 Aims and Objectives

The aim of this work was to create and evaluate a prototype toolkit for building CBT applications. CBT has something of a reputation for being a rather boring medium of communication, mainly because the style of interaction is often very constrained. An important objective for this work, however, was to enable the construction of CBT packages which could be as open, or as constrained, as was required by a CBT author. This would make it possible to build highly interactive, exploratory learning packages.

Another objective was to allow the construction of simulation-oriented training material. The system should allow the construction of a 'deep' model of some machine or system, and then allow a learner (via an appropriate interface) to explore and interact with the simulated system. One important kind of training problem addressed by this approach is diagnostic or fault-finding training, where the underlying simulation can model a faulty machine. As an example, one package actually constructed using this toolkit modelled a hydraulically-operated steel press, and faults in individual components, such as valves or switches, could be introduced. The learners task was to find and rectify such faults, given diagnostic displays from (simulated) mimic panels, in the minimum amount of time.

Another aim was to make the toolkit usable by as wide a range of programmers as possible. Courseware authors are not usually sophisticated programmers, and it was hoped that an author could build complex courses without difficulty. However, the system should also be considered satisfactory by more sophisticated programmers, such as those building complex simulations, or those implementing specialised user interface components (called *gadgets* – see section 3.3).

1.2 Definition of Terms

A number of terms are used in a slightly unusual fashion in this paper, so a few definitions are required. Also, some of the terms used may not be familiar to those outside the CBT area. A *learner* is an individual actually undergoing training, and is therefore the 'end user' of the application. A *trainer* is typically either a manager responsible for training within an organisation, or another (such as a course teacher) who is responsible for a group of learners. Since the focus of the project was on the construction of interactive training material, the term *courseware* is used synonymously with *user interface* in this paper. The term '*courseware author*' (or just *author*) is used synonymously with *user interface constructor* although, strictly speaking, a courseware author is also heavily involved with specific training requirements analysis. The terms *model* and *simulation* are used synonymously to indicate the part of a system which provides the 'deep' behaviour, as opposed to the user interface part. Finally, the term *modeller* refers to an individual primarily concerned with the construction of the simulation component of a training package.

1.3 Approach Taken

A number of important decisions were taken early in the project. The first was to demand a clear, strong separation between the courseware and the underlying model. Although it was felt desirable that simulations and learner interfaces should use the same programming language, and (as far as possible) similar tools, they should be kept separate. This allowed learner interfaces and simulations to be developed separately, by different people, and furthermore would allow the same simulation to be used for several different (but related) training packages.

It was also decided to use a strong *object-oriented* metaphor throughout. Courseware authors (and modellers) are encouraged to design and use *objects* by describing *classes*, and composing complex objects from simpler ones, thus forming a *component* hierarchy. Objects have static connections, and definite inputs and outputs, so that objects can be 'plugged together', much like LEGO(TM) blocks. The object-oriented approach was also used by the implementors of the system, and Smalltalk-80 [1] was used for the prototype implementation.

1.4 Project Structure

This was a 14 month project, terminating at the end of March 1990, and was funded by the UK Training Agency (part of the Department of Employment). The project was treated as a user-centered design exercise, with involvement from several institutions. The prototype environment and tools were developed at the University of Manchester Computer Science Department. Much of the courseware was developed by authors at Mentor Interactive Training (Bradford), using the prototype tools; Mentor also collaborated with the University of Manchester on the development of the simulations. Specific training problems, together with trainers and learners, were supplied by British Steel (Rotherham) and Crosfield Electronics (Watford). CBT consultants from the Universities of Surrey and London, as well as independent consultants, advised on the progress and direction of the work. There was also an independent project manager, who coordinated activities on the multiple sites.

1.5 Structure of this Paper

The remainder of this paper is organised as follows. Section 2 provides an introduction to the programming model used for both courseware and simulations. Section 3 elaborates on those objects specifically intended for courseware construction, and Section 4 describes the window-based tools to support simple and rapid development. Section 5 gives a brief overview of the implementation approach used. Finally, section 6 outlines the post-prototype evaluation, discusses the advantages and disadvantages of the system implemented, and considers possible future directions.

2 Programming Model

This section describes the object-oriented programming model which is used by both the modelling and user interface tools. This programming model is unusual in that it combines a functional (declarative) and an object-oriented approach to program construction.

2.1 Objects and Classes

All user interface entities are represented by *objects* (also known as *components*), which are *instances* of *classes* in the usual way. A conventional class-based single inheritance scheme is used, with *subclasses* inheriting properties from their *superclasses*. Classes need not have a superclass, so that multiple disjoint class hierarchies can be created. Note however that changes made to classes are propagated immediately to their subclasses, and to instances of these classes, so that objects already in existence can be modified without losing their internal state.

Objects can be described by their classes in one of two ways. *Composite* objects are described entirely in terms of completely encapsulated *sub-objects*, connected together as described below. A complete model is a single (typically rather complex) composite object, usually without any kind of external connection. The sub-object hierarchy, which is a strict tree, can be as deep as necessary.

At the leaves of the sub-object tree, *primitive* objects are used. Classes describing primitive objects will define *attributes*, corresponding roughly to data members or instance variables in other languages. A major difference, however, is that most attributes are simply names for *values* which are the results of functions; these functions can be described in a number of ways (see below). Note that primitive objects will typically be rather more complex than composite objects; the latter are often simply containers for primitive objects.

Both primitive and composite objects have explicit *inputs* and *outputs*: an input can be connected to at most one output, while an output can be connected to as many inputs as is required. The connections between inputs and outputs cannot change while the simulation is running. It should be noted that this is a very 'static' object model, and is quite different from that provided in many object-oriented programming languages, such as Smalltalk-80 [1] and C++ [2].

2.2 Attributes and Connections

Five kinds of attributes are available:

Fixed attributes represent values which can never change. These are used like conventional program constants.

Variable attributes represent values which depend in some (pure functional) way on the values of other attributes. A variable attribute may depend on other variable, input, fixed and timed attributes to this object.

Timed attributes support the notion of sequential state changes, which is not otherwise available in a declarative language. Timed attributes therefore introduce an explicit notion of time. A timed variable can depend on the old value of itself, as well as both the old and current values of other attributes. This allows operations in conjunction with changes in variables to be described.

Input attributes correspond to connections from other objects, which will be be output attributes.

Output attributes provide connections to other objects. Apart from the fact that output attributes cannot be used within their defining object, they behave exactly like variable attributes.

All categories of attributes have a type (or *unit*) associated with them, and there is a type hierarchy which is quite independent of the class structure. The basic types are *numeric*, *enumerated* and *list*; user-defined units (sub-types) can include *boolean* (true or false), voltage, pressure, and so on. Similarly, all attributes have a default or initial value, which is useful both for defining the initial state of the simulation, and to allow unconnected inputs and undefined outputs (in a partially complete model) to be controlled.

2.3 Describing Object Behaviours

In order to completely describe what functionality is available within particular objects, classes specify a *behaviour* for each of its variable, timed and output attributes. The most general way of defining the behaviour of an attribute is to write a first-order function, in a simple functional language designed and implemented as part of the project. A large number of pre-defined built-in functions are provided, including list manipulation operations, as well as sophisticated functions for manipulating the elements of pictures.

While writing complex functions is straightforward and natural for experienced programmers, another means of describing behaviours was provided for less experienced modellers and courseware authors. This is done in two parts. First, the attributes which can affect a particular attribute are identified; these are termed the *determiners* for the *dependent* attribute. These determiners provide the headings for a table which can be filled in to describe the relationship between these attributes. Range specifiers may be used in these tables; also, the two notations can be mixed, so that arbitrary functions can be used within tables. In the cases where classes are already defined, it is possible to construct simulations graphically, merely defining the connections between inputs and outputs.

In summary, the programming model provided here has most of the features of a general-purpose object-oriented programming language. Note however that there are several important restrictions: connections cannot be determined dynamically, and new named functions cannot be introduced. It is *first-order*: objects cannot be used as the values of arguments to functions. Despite these restrictions, which were deliberately introduced to simplify the language for the benefit of non-programmers, it is our experience that this system is adequate for the intended purpose. Later extensions [3] remove most of these restrictions.

3 User Interface Objects

The programming model described in the previous section is used directly in the modelling environment. In this case, the modeller defines classes appropriate for the application domain, and connects together instances of these classes as appropriate. For the construction of user interfaces, however, a large selection of pre-defined objects is made available. The basic classes and the gadget library are described in this section, while the tools used by courseware authors to build a user interface are described in the next section.

3.1 Functional Areas

The class of objects used as the basis for all courseware authoring is the *Functional Area* (FA). This represents a rectangular screen area, with programmable visibility. An FA may have a background picture, which is visible at all times the FA itself is visible; if no background is specified, the FA is effectively transparent. Each FA also has associated with it a list of pictures, which are displayed in an order given by a 'current pictures' list. An FA may have one or more 'sub-FAs', so that logically different parts of an interface may be divided up appropriately. A 'top-level FA' representing the physical screen of the computer system.

3.2 Interaction Elements

Functional areas are output-only; for user input, a further class of objects known as *Interaction Elements* (IEs) are provided. IEs add access to mouse and keyboard input, and provide some special outputs which control various aspects of the interaction – the cursor shape, for example. By convention, IEs do not usually have sub-FAs. Normally, however, user input is handled by much more sophisticated objects known as *gadgets* (see section 3.3).

For screen output, a number of special units (types) are defined. These include *colour*, which is just an enumerated type containing the names of the colours available, and various *picture* types. Picture types include *fills*, which fill a rectangular area with a particular colour, with an optional border in another colour; *texts*, which are displayable strings with associated font, style, size and colour; *bitmaps*, which are simple coloured images produced using conventional painting tools, and *arcs*, which are coloured sections of an ellipse, again possibly with a coloured border. As mentioned previously, special functions for manipulating attributes of these types are provided.

3.3 Gadgets

To facilitate the rapid construction of user interfaces, a large library of pre-defined, specialised FAs known as *Gadgets* is made available. A library browser (see section 4.1) is available to allow the courseware author access to these gadgets. Although these gadgets are actually implemented as specialised subclasses, the appearance presented to the author is that of a library of gadget 'prototypes'. Certain 'fixed' variables are made available as *parameters*. For example, there is no input which allows the colour used to display text in a push-button gadget to be altered. However, it is reasonable to allow the courseware author to set up the colour to be used, for each new push-button instantiated. Some parameters are automatically set by the graphical manipulation tools (see section 4.2).

It should be noted that the gadgets are entirely implemented in the language described in the paper. Most gadgets support some interactive input operations, and therefore contain an *Interaction Element* (see section 3.2). Gadgets are regarded as 'sub-courses', and new gadgets of any degree of complexity can be created by a courseware author, using the normal mechanisms. A large number of gadgets are available; these include normal user interface components such as buttons and switches, sliders and scroll bars, and composeable menus, as well as more unusual items such as pie and bar charts, graphs and gauges, oscilloscopes and magnifiers.

4 Author's Interface

The interface provided to the courseware author is based on the familiar notion of windows. Window-based tools are provided for defining classes, with separate subwindows for defining attributes and behaviours. Other windows allow composite objects, including the entire user interface, to be composed from other objects. Changes to classes and inter-object connections can be made incrementally. Graphical tools for viewing and manipulating both the sub-object hierarchy and the inter-object connections are also available, allowing a naive user to compose an interface from pre-defined classes readily. Interactive tools for tracing and debugging are also provided. These allow the internal state of any particular object to be monitored, and changed if appropriate, while the simulation is running. Each tool is described in a little more detail below; further details of the use of the tools can be found elsewhere [3, 4]. Some of these tools are illustrated in Figure 1.

The general approach taken is that, at any one time, there is a single course (user interface) under construction. All tools operate on this course. To minimise the risk of unnecessary clutter on the screen, it is not possible to open more than one instance of certain of the tools discussed below. Attempting to open a second Library Browser, for example, will result in the currently active Browser being brought forward, deiconifying as necessary.

4.1 Library Browser

Since a large number of gadgets are made available, a browsing tool is provided to control access to a gadget library. The same library browser is also used to access

174

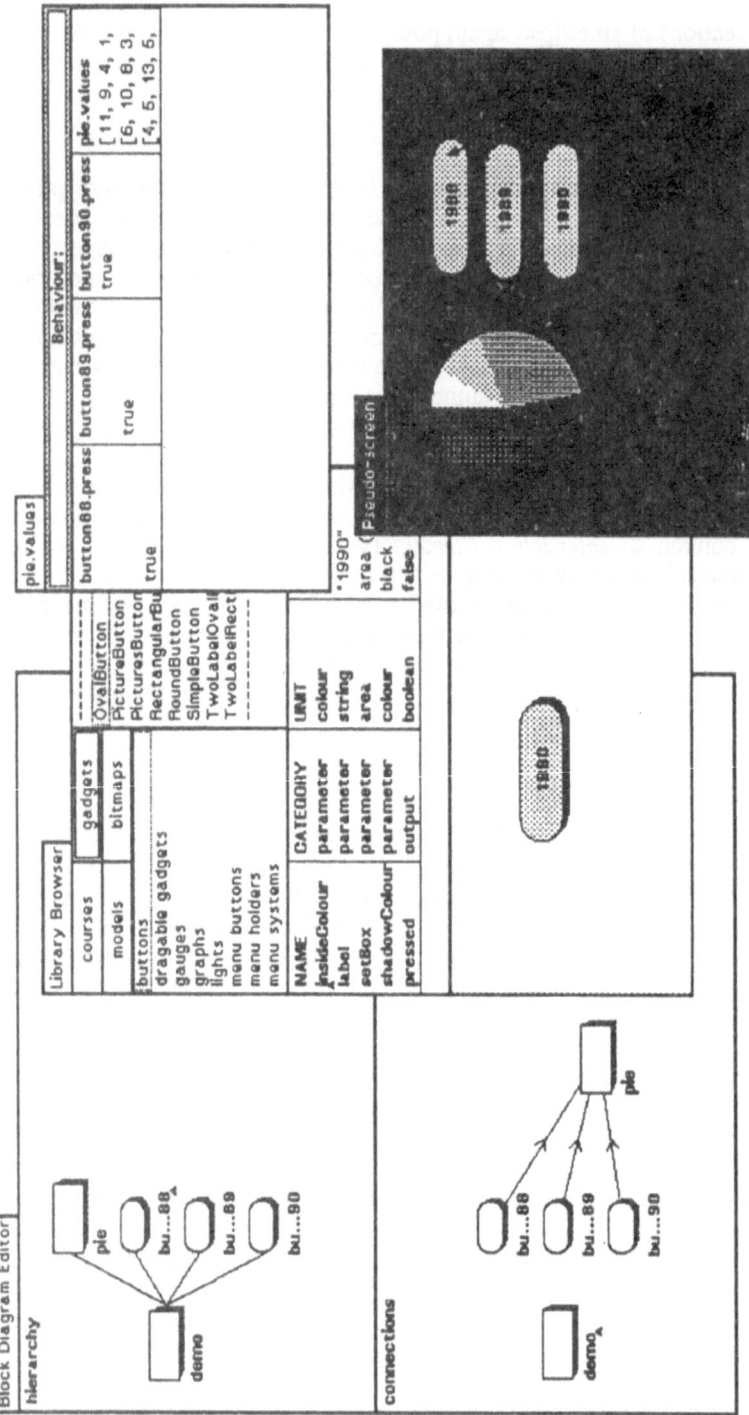

Figure 1: User interface tools in action

complete courses or work in progress, simulations and bitmaps. The library is shared over a network of workstations and PCs, so that users on different machines can have instant access to updated simulations, courses or gadgets. The library browser also supports multiple versions of gadgets, so that older versions can be used, if required.

In this description of operation, it will be assumed that the library browser is being used to access gadgets. Access to other kinds of library items is similar. The browser is structured so that first a 'category' of gadgets is selected (such as 'buttons' or 'gauges') in the top-left subwindow, then a particular gadget can be selected by name in the top-right subwindow. Once selected, the gadget is displayed in the lower part of the browser, together with a table (see later) of its input and output attributes, and any settable parameters. The browser display is interactive: for example, if a switch gadget is selected, pressing the mouse button over the switch causes it to operate. This allows the user to view the operation of an individual gadget before incorporating it into a course. The gadget can also be customised, by setting or altering parameters; these changes are also effective immediately.

4.2   Display Editor

Normally, the first action of a courseware author is to decide on the location and size of various Functional Areas (FAs) and gadgets. The relative position and size of these components can be determined graphically, using a tool known as the *Display Editor*. Gadgets and FAs can be placed inside other FAs; hierarchies of such components can be manipulated using the usual cut and paste operations. This tool also allows static pictures, including filled areas, static text and bitmaps, to be created and positioned. For complex user interfaces, the number of FAs and gadgets used may be large – possibly many hundreds. To make it easier for the user to manipulate such a complex structure, the Display Editor allows portions of the FA hierarchy to be temporarily 'hidden'.

4.3   Block Diagram Editor

Once the visual layout of the functional areas and gadgets has been determined, interconnections between inputs and outputs may be required. For simple connections, these may be made graphically, using the *Block Diagram Editor*. For applications constructed entirely from gadgets, this is all that is required. If somewhat more complex functions relating inputs and outputs are desired, then the Block Diagram Editor can be used together with Behaviour Templates (see section 4.5.3); alternatively, all these functions can be programmed using a Class Template (see section 4.5.1).

The Block Diagram Editor also allows the FA and gadget hierarchy to be edited. New FAs and gadgets can be added using this tool, rather than using the Display Editor. The usual cut and paste editing operations are available for individual FAs, as well as for complex structures.

In practice, of course, the Display Editor and Block Diagram Editor are used together with the other tools, making modifications to both the interaction and visual appearance as appropriate. Since all the tools are in independent windows, the courseware author is not constrained to any particular style of working.

4.4 Learners Screen

Once both the visual layout and logical connections of the FAs and gadgets have been determined, the operation must be tested. Normally, a running application takes over the entire screen of the machine. However, for development purposes, it is desirable to be able to test the operation of a course, while still having the tools available. To facilitate this, a *Learner's Screen* (or *Pseudo-Screen*) window is provided. Usually, the Learner's Screen window will be smaller than the real screen, so that the scrolling of the window over the operating interface is supported.

4.5 Templates

As noted in section 2.3, the operation of a user interface can be described as a table. The tools for constructing such tables are known as *templates*. A wide variety of template windows are available, some of which are described below.

Syntax analysis of information input in a template, together with some error check-ing, is performed immediately. Errors are highlighted, but need not be corrected im-mediately, since they may be the result of an incomplete user interface; an interface can be 'run' at any time. Running an interface entails compiling any parts which have been modified since the last run, initializing all attributes to their default value, and then propagating changes to values as time passes. The implementation of this is briefly discussed in section 5.

4.5.1 Class Template

More complex connections between input and output attributes, as well as internal behaviour for FAs and gadgets, can be described using *Class Template* windows. This template allow new attributes (including inputs and outputs) to be defined; as described in section 2.2, all attributes have a unit (or type), as well as an initial (or default) value. Attributes corresponding to the outputs and inputs of sub-FAs and gadgets appear as named inputs and outputs respectively. The value of an attribute may be defined in terms of a function of other attributes (see section 2.3). This tool allows either a table-oriented form, or a function definition, to be used.

4.5.2 Instance (Debug) Template

Once a user interface is running, it is frequently desirable to be able to see the values currently associated with inputs, outputs or other attributes within a particular object. For this purpose, *Instance Template* windows are provided. An Instance Template can be opened on any object, displaying the current value of all attributes of that object. The Instance Template window is continually modified, as the user interface operates. For example, if a particular switch gadget has an output which is either `true` or `false`, the change from `false` to `true` as the switch is operated can be observed. Instance Templates also allow the value of unconnected input attributes to be modified. This is particularly useful in the case of partially-complete user interfaces, or where the underlying simulation is not yet available.

4.5.3 Behaviour Template

Behaviour Template windows are primarily used in conjunction with the Block Diagram Editor (section 4.3). They allow a *single* function of one or more outputs to be used to give a value for an input attribute. Again, the function may be defined in terms of a table, or as an arbitrary expression.

4.5.4 Model/Courseware Interface Template

Although this is not described in this paper, this environment and language can also be used to build sophisticated models of real-world machines or systems. A simulation, and any courseware which might be used with it, are regarded as separate entities. This means that a particular simulation can be used with several different courses, for different training purposes. To be used in this way, a simulation will usually have input and output attributes which are not connected within that simulation; a corresponding course would also have unconnected inputs and outputs. For example, a simulation might have an input which causes it to start operating; this would need to be connected to the output of a push-button in the user interface. The *Model/Courseware Interface Template* window allows external connections to a simulation or user interface to be defined, and allows connections between a model and a user interface to be described.

4.5.5 Unit Template

As noted in section 2.2, all attributes and connections are 'typed', by including a 'unit' as well as a value. The *Unit Template* window allows new types to be defined. This template also allows a default value to be defined for an attribute of a particular type. For user interface construction, useful pre-defined subtypes include boolean values, two-dimensional points, colour and area. It is rarely necessary for courseware authors to define new types, although this facility is much more useful for simulation purposes.

4.5.6 Other Tools

A variety of other tools were also made available, and integrated into the system. These include conventional drawing and painting tools, as well as other tools to manipulate the colour display system [5]. Further tools were provided more for supporting the construction of simulations; these support direct access to the class hierarchy, and to complex composite objects.

5 Implementation

The current version of the simulation system should be regarded as a prototype, and is implemented using the **Smalltalk-80** [1] system. The language outlined previously is compiled into Smalltalk-80, although other versions [6] can also generate **Prolog** and C. The basic functions required for the language were defined in Smalltalk-80; since it was occasionally necessary to define a new function, either for convenience or for performance reasons, a simple interface to the underlying Smalltalk-80 system was provided.

The interactive tools were based on those provided by Smalltalk-80, although one version of the system made the tools available in colour, using a home-grown colour Smalltalk-80 system [5]. Extensive use was made of the Model-View-Controller

(MVC) mechanism [7], although some modifications were necessary to ensure that only one window of certain kinds could be active at a time. The current version runs on Sun-3 machines, using Smalltalk-80, version 2.3 (colour or monochrome), and on 386-based PC machines using Smalltalk-80 version 2.4 (monochrome only).

5.1 Representations

To maintain consistency within the system, for example, between a visual presentation in a window and the underlying data structures, or between classes and their instances, a general scheme known as *representations* [8, 9] was used. For example, the relationship between the 'source code' in a template, and the underlying representation (which might be either Smalltalk-80 (source) code, or a Smalltalk-80 compiled method) is handled using this scheme. Thus, small changes in behaviour or connections within objects cause only small parts of the code to be re-compiled, thus giving the advantages of incremental compilation for a language with entirely static runtime semantics.

This same representation mechanism is also used to ensure that when a change is made to a particular class, it is propagated to all subclasses and instances of all of those classes. As a final example, when an Instance Template (see section 4.5.2) is opened, the consistency between the window and the underlying object is ensured using the representation system. Using this system instead of the 'dependency' mechanism normally used in Smalltalk-80 applications meant that it was very straightforward to ensure that updates made using one window were immediately reflected in other windows, with no manual 'update' operation required. Further developments in using these techniques can be found in [6].

6 Evaluation and Conclusions

In this section, the evaluation process used during this project is outlined, and problems which came to light but were unresolved are discussed.

6.1 The Evaluation Process

Since this project was intended to use a user-centered design approach, evaluations by users of all kinds was considered very important. In fact, there were some fairly formal post-project reviews, as well as a continuous review process during the normal operation of the project.

The tools and programming system were designed in close collaboration with CBT authors, and many aspects were changed or modified in the light of their critical remarks. The tools and programming system were developed in parallel with the CBT authors attempting to use the system; while this led to some difficulties at the time, it did ensure that the tools were refined so as to maximise their appeal to the authors. There were also regular review sessions during the development period, with systems developers, CBT authors and external consultants offering their opinions.

The system developed was used by authors at Mentor Interactive Training to develop a training simulation of a hydraulically-operated steel press. This was a fault-finding training exercise. The resulting system was evaluated by trainers and learners from British Steel at Rotherham, with generally positive results. The system was also used to construct a prototype course for Crosfield Electronics; again, this training was structured as a fault-finding exercise. A number of other small courses were developed as demonstrations, and trainers at British Steel Open Learning Development Unit (Rotherham) also experimented with the system.

6.2 Problems Encountered

A number of design-related problems came to light during the evaluation period. One issue has to do with the visibility of gadgets in the Display Editor (section 4.2) tool. When a gadget is placed using this tool, the statically-determined background picture is displayed. If there is no background picture, then an outline only is drawn, so that the courseware author can see where it is located. Unfortunately, most of the gadgets in the library are interactive, and so necessarily generate most (or all) of their pictures dynamically. Thus, for most of the gadgets implemented in the library, only an outline box can be seen in the display editor; this is especially true for the more sophisticated gadgets. To address this deficiency, it would be particularly desirable if the display editor could partially execute a gadget before it was placed in the interface under construction. This would ensure that the display editor would at least display the default or initial state of the gadget.

Another question remaining at the end of the evaluation was the nature of the interactions between the separate tools, especially between the Display Editor, the Learner's Screen, the Block Diagram Editor and the Library Browser. At present, all of these tools are 'loosely-coupled', and work largely independently. This kind of operation was liked by some users, but others disliked it and found it confusing. The latter users would like a closer coupling between tools so that, for example, selecting a particular FA or gadget using the Block Diagram Editor would also select the corresponding FA visible in the Display Editor. It was not possible to resolve the dichotomy between these groups of users; perhaps a user-selectable 'mode' could be introduced. A similar question arose with the Display Editor and Learner's Screen: should these really be just one tool, with two different modes. Again, no clear answer was forthcoming.

A different kind of issue discovered with the prototype is that of runtime performance. The incremental compilation technique used allowed a large number of checks on correctness to be performed statically, but also avoided long compilation times when only a small change was made. Unfortunately, this led to two problems: firstly, the large and complex object structures required by the representations mechanism used (see section 5.1) meant that when a large change is made, necessitating an extensive re-compilation, the time taken to update all these structures is very large. Since some compiles were rather quick, and others very slow, this led to a certain amount of user frustration and confusion. The second problem was that the inter-object communication mechanism used was not particularly fast; consequently, for very complex user interfaces, certain interactions were annoyingly slow.

A related performance issue was the size of the Smalltalk-80 *image*[1] in use. The representations mechanism proved to be rather expensive in image space, with two consequences. Firstly, on workstations with virtual memory systems, both compile-time and run-time performance dropped quickly as larger user interfaces were constructed. Secondly, on PC machines with a fixed maximum real memory size, the development system would run out of memory when larger systems were being developed. These problems were exacerbated when the colour Smalltalk-80 system was

---

[1] In Smalltalk-80 terms, the 'image' is the memory space occupied by the objects.

in use, as this tended to increase the memory size required by pictures.

6.3 Future Work

At present, work on this system has stopped, although it is hoped to move toward a commercially-available CBT toolkit eventually. In view of the performance problems described in section 6.2, it is likely that a production version would use different implementation techniques to that used in the prototype. As an intermediate step, however, it is proposed to port the implementation to a more recent version of Smalltalk-80 (Objectworks/Smalltalk Release 4), although this has not yet been started. This Smalltalk-80 implementation is available on much faster workstations, and would help to address some of the performance-related problems discussed previously. Another advantage of this port is that Objectworks uses the window system provided by the underlying operating system, so that it would then be easy for other tools (word processors, drawing tools, and so on) to be used with the CBT development environment.

In the longer term, a production-quality system would require a re-think of the implementation techniques used. The choice of whether Smalltalk-80 should be used as the implementation language is not clear: it is difficult to determine whether significant gains in performance would really be achieved by a move to a lower-level language such as C or C++. Perhaps more importantly, it may be that the full power of the representations mechanism might not be necessary, and that a simpler consistency-keeping approach would be adequate. Further work on the basic programming model, and the representations mechanism, can be found in a forthcoming Ph.D thesis [6]. This thesis also describes later extensions to this approach for a range of object-oriented programming and knowledge representation problems, and also outlines further work on implementation techniques which address some of the problems encountered.

Acknowledgments

Stephanie Wilson designed and implemented the interactive tools described in this paper. The work described in this paper was in large part supported by the Training Agency. Steve Wallis was in part supported by a postgraduate studentship from the Science and Engineering Research Council.

References

[1] A. Goldberg and D. Robson, *Smalltalk-80: The Language and its Implementation*, Addison-Wesley, 1983.

[2] B. Stroustrup, *The C++ Programming Language*, Addison-Wesley, 1986.

[3] S. K. Wallis, S. Wilson and T. P. Hopkins, *FOOD: A Declarative Object-Oriented Framework*, Internal Report, Computer Science Department, University of Manchester 1990.

[4] S. K. Wallis, S. Wilson and T. P. Hopkins, *Declarative Objects for Simulation and User Interfaces*, The Society for Computer Simulation Western Multiconference, Anaheim, California, USA, pp 143–150, January 1991.

[5] T. P. Hopkins, *A Colour System for Smalltalk-80*, Technical Report UMCS-89-10-5, Computer Science Department, University of Manchester, October 1989.

[6] S. K. Wallis, *Integrating Object-Oriented Programming and Knowledge Representation* (working title), Ph.D thesis (in preparation), Computer Science Department, University of Manchester, 1991.

[7] S. Burbeck, *How to use Model-View-Controller (MVC)*, Technical Report, Softsmarts, 1987.

[8] S. K. Wallis, *An Object-oriented Semantic Network System*, Internal Report, Computer Science Department, University of Manchester, 1990.

[9] S. K. Wallis, *An Object-Oriented Approach to Semantic Networks*, Transfer Report, Computer Science Department, University of Manchester, September 1988.

X-Designer - Abstraction and Visibility in Graphical User Interface Design

Alistair George

Imperial Software Technology Limited
Reading, UK

Abstract

X-Designer is a graphical user interface (GUI) builder for the OSF/Motif toolkit. Like other tools in its class, it allows the developer to create the GUI for an application graphically, and then generates the code needed to implement the interface. Unlike other tools, however, it does not merely present the visual abstraction of the GUI - that is, this is how it looks - it also makes explicitly visible the internal structure - that is, this is how it is.

X-Designer uses a variety of simple techniques to control the amount of detail of the internal structure which is visible to the tool user. This allows the tool to present both a simple view for naive users and at early stages of development, and a more complex but complete view when required.

This provides considerable benefits in terms of designer support. This paper discusses these benefits, and shows how an appropriate set of tool functions can provide the advantages of abstraction and re-use, particularly at the early stages of development, and yet still allow tight control and the use of a familiar paradigm in the implementation stages.

1 Introduction

A graphical user interface (GUI) builder is a tool which supports the developer in building a GUI for an application. The level of support offered can vary widely. A typical GUI builder will:

Allow a GUI to be constructed using direct manipulation techniques (eg "drag and drop").

Give an essentially instantaneous "what you see is what you get" (wysiwyg) view of the GUI under construction.

Relieve the developer of at least some of the coding work which would otherwise be involved in building the GUI.

This is not intended to be the start of a debate about the nature of GUI builders. These three functions are commonly found, and serve to distinguish GUI builder tools from, say, pencil and paper (the cheapest way of obtaining an instantaneous wysiwyg view using direct manipulation).

Many GUI builders treat the external visual representation of the GUI (the wysiwyg view) as the fundamental representation used by the developer (for instance, Builder Xcessory from ICS, and Sun Microsystem's dev/Guide). Components are added by dragging them from a palette onto the wysiwyg view; the GUI builder then determines the internal structure of a GUI which will have the same appearance as that which the developer is creating, and generates code to implement this GUI.

X-Designer takes a different approach. X-Designer presents both a wysiwyg view and a view of the GUI structure. All development is performed on the structure view. This may seem to be a regressive step, in that the developer needs to be aware of the implementation structure from an early stage. In fact, it offers significant advantages, especially in the later stages of development.

2 GUI Development According to MIT

X-Designer is based on the Motif toolkit, itself built on the X toolkit and its intrinsics. In Motif (and other Xt intrinsics-based toolkits) the developer creates a GUI by:

> Creating a hierarchy of widgets (GUI components).

> Setting the resources (attributes) of each widget .

> Associating callback functions with user actions on widgets.

The application behaviour is contained in the callback functions. A hierarchy of widgets with no associated callbacks will display some behaviour - that which is programmed into the widgets by the toolkit supplier. For instance, pressing a button in a menu bar will cause a pulldown menu to be displayed. Pressing the "Open" button in the "File" menu will not open a file, unless the callback function to do this has been written and linked in.

The standard toolkit provides an API which allows the developer to create GUIs - that is, create widgets and the widget hierarchy, set resources and associate callback functions. A major difficulty in writing any GUI is simply the volume of code which has to be written. There are many pitfalls for the unwary, and a coding error may simply lead to failure of the application, rather than the helpful error message we would hope for.

3 X-Designer as an Implementation Tool

X-Designer fully supports the representation used by Motif. In particular, X-Designer provides:

A palette of icons representing the widget classes.

A design area in which the widget hierarchy is constructed.

Resource panels for each widget class, which allow the resources of each widget instance (including callback function names) to be set.

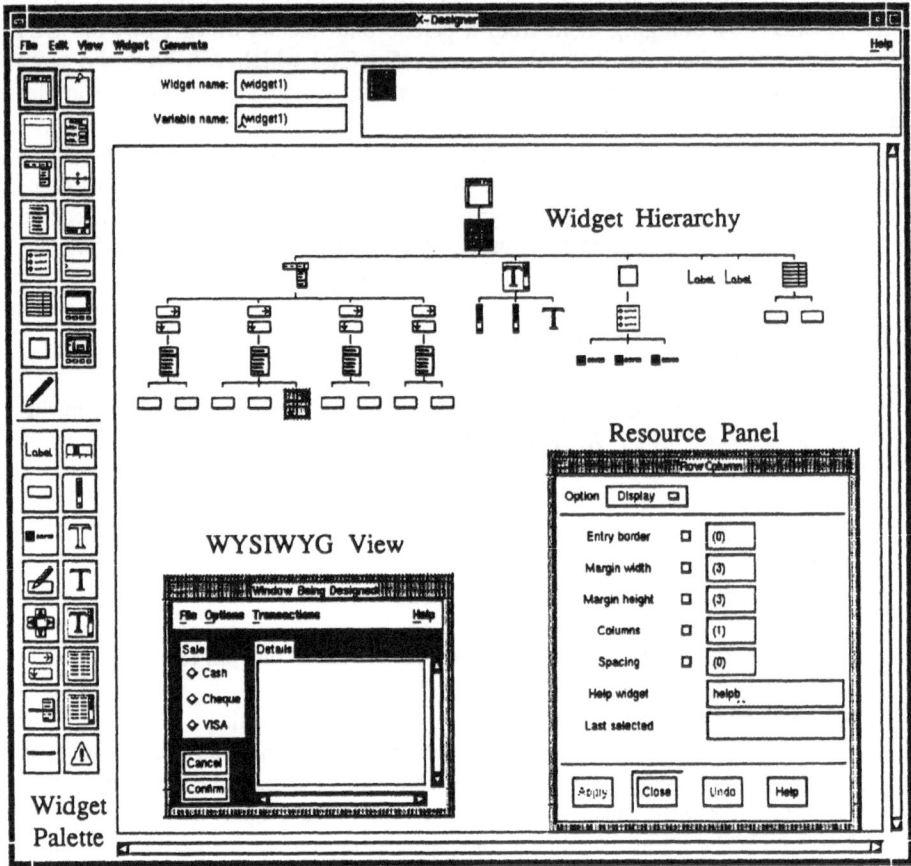

Figure 1: X-Designer

Clicking on a widget icon in the palette adds it to the hierarchy as a child of the currently selected widget. Clicking on a widget icon in the design area makes that the currently selected widget (shown highlighted), and double-clicking brings up a resource panel appropriate to the class of the widget.

The tool also presents the wysiwyg view of the GUI in a separate window. Since the GUI is constructed by operating on the hierarchy in the design area, the wysiwyg view always looks and behaves as the eventual GUI will - there is, for instance, no need to switch from build mode to test mode to try the effect of pressing a button.

At the most basic level, X-Designer is simply an interactive tool for defining a user interface dialog (in hierarchy/resources/callback terms), with an associated code generator. This alone gives several advantages over hand-coding:

> The generated code is syntactically correct. X-Designer does not need three tries to get the correct spelling of XmNmnemonic.

> Common errors (setting a non-existent resource, creating an invalid widget hierarchy) are barred by the tool.

> The wysiwyg view of the GUI is updated to take account of design changes immediately. There is no need to compile and link to see the effect of a change. This means that rapid prototyping is possible; it is also a considerable help in learning Motif. The questions "What does this do?" and "How do I do this?" can be answered by experimentation.

At this level, the abstractions presented by the tool to the developer are (almost) the same as those presented by the API. That is, the tool is readily understood by experienced Motif developers, and the understanding developed by using the tool can be applied to the task of writing the callback functions.

4 Object Types Supported by X-Designer

One of the benefits of abstraction is that it simplifies the semantics of a type - the developer only has to deal with the public interface of the type. There is a general tradeoff between complexity and the number of different types - between a small number of powerful, generic (but complex) types and a larger number of simple, specific types.

Not all of the abstractions supported by the Motif toolkit API are supported by X-Designer. For instance, an application warning message is usually displayed in an warning message box. To create such a message box, the developer must create a two-widget hierarchy, with dialog shell parent and message box child, and set the message box type resource to 'warning'. This is such a common requirement that the Motif toolkit provides a convenience function (XmCreateWarningDialog) to do it. There are similar convenience functions for other types of message dialog (error, information...).

X-Designer does not support this. To create an error message dialog in X-Designer, the developer creates the hierarchy and sets the type of the message box via the resource panel. This process requires four clicks of the mouse button. If X-Designer supported the warning dialog as a (pseudo-)widget, it would require only one. The point here is simple. If the construction facilities are sufficiently easy to use, the benefits of some kinds of abstraction are outweighed by the costs - in this case the addition of six extra functions to the API. Further, by avoiding this abstraction (and similar dialog creation convenience functions) we gain an important unification - that every widget hierarchy has a shell at its root.

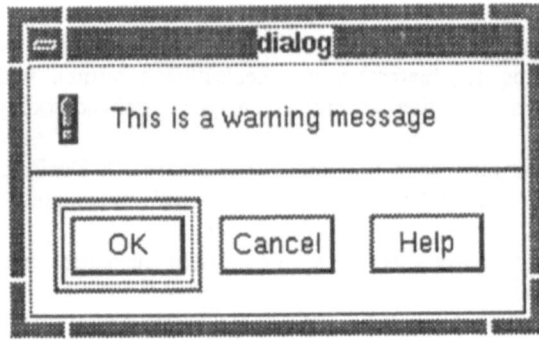

Figure 2: Warning message dialog

An additional simplification provided by X-Designer is that widgets and gadgets (less capable but less expensive versions of some classes of widget) are treated as configured instances of the same object. To create, say, a push button gadget, the developer creates a push button, and then uses a toggle in the resource panel to convert it to a gadget.

In all, the 49 creation functions in the Motif API (XmCreate*) are replaced by 32 icons in X-Designer. The tool facilities give a one-third reduction in the number of types of object the developer has to deal with (in respect of object creation) without loss of functionality or ease of use.

The avoidance of abstractions is not a design principle - it is design pragmatism. X-Designer does not treat the different types of message dialog as distinct. However, it does distinguish the types of row column widget. Menu bar, radio box, popup menu and so on are all treated as different types of object. The decision as to whether to support objects as distinct is a matter of judgement, and is, I would suggest, not intrinsic to the problem. X-Designer presents only a single-level view of the basic objects (the widget palette), and therefore aims to keep the number of different object types small. If the tool presented an object type hierarchy on multiple levels, so that clicking on a widget icon brought up a menu of its subtypes for selection, then a much larger set of types could be supported. That is, the set of types is influenced by the presentational characteristics of the tool, as well as the problem (Motif GUI building) which is being solved.

5 Composite Widgets

Some of the widgets provided by the Motif toolkit are primitives - button, text field, scroll bar, etc. These are single objects with no internal structure. Others, such as the message box, have children which are created when the parent widget is created. These are sometimes called composite widgets (strictly, only some of the composite widgets have automatically created children).

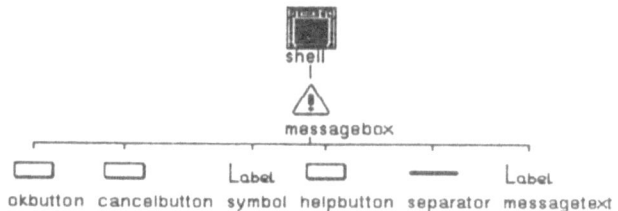

Figure 3: Internal structure of a message box

Typically, a composite widget will have resources which allow a subset of the children's resources to be set. For instance, a message box has a label string resource. Setting the message box label string changes the message displayed in the box, by changing the label string of its message label widget child. However, the message box widget does not have a resource which allows, say, the font or colour of the OK button to be changed separately from the fonts or colours of the other buttons. That is, the message box does not show all the details of its construction at its primary interface.

There are occasions when it is necessary to set resources which do not appear at the primary interface of a composite widget. The Motif toolkit developers recognised this, and (in many cases) provided function calls which let an application get handles on the children of a composite widget. Given these handles, the resources of the children can be set.

X-Designer also provides this facility. When a composite widget is added to the design hierarchy, X-Designer determines its children (known as abstract widgets) and shows them in the hierarchy as well. From the developer's point of view, these are just more widgets which are part of the design. Their resources can be set, and callbacks associated with widget events. The only difference is that the internal structure of the composite widget cannot be changed in X-Designer - that is, the abstract widgets cannot, in general, be deleted. In this, X-Designer is merely respecting the toolkit.

The developer can choose whether or not to set resources on the abstract widgets. Indeed, since any part of the design hierarchy can be folded, the developer can choose to fold a composite widget, hiding its abstract children, and both view it and treat it as a primitive widget. Typically, a composite widget may be treated as primitive at an early stage of development, and only unfolded later if it is necessary to set resources which cannot be accessed via the resource set of the composite parent.

The facility to hide and reveal details of an object's structure allows the tool user to ignore detail at one stage of development, and exploit it at another. This is the best of both worlds - simplicity when wanted, tight control when needed.

6 The Cost of Visibility

One of the benefits of abstraction is that implementation details are hidden from the developer, and can be changed without impact. A good example of this is provided by the Motif file selection box widget. This is a complex composite widget which gives the user a list of filenames from which to make a selection. In version 1.0 of Motif, it looked like this:-

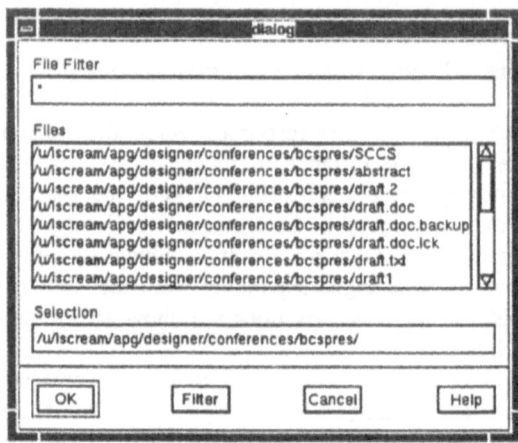

Figure 4: Motif version 1.0 File Selection Box

The hierarchy of abstract widgets which constitute a Motif 1.0 file selection box is:-

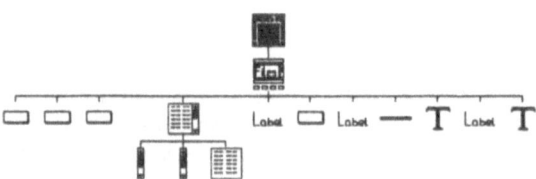

Figure 5: Internal structure of a Motif version 1.0 File Selection Box

In Motif 1.1, everything changed. The widget became more complex, both in appearance and in structure. An extra scrolled list widget was added to hold a list of directory names.

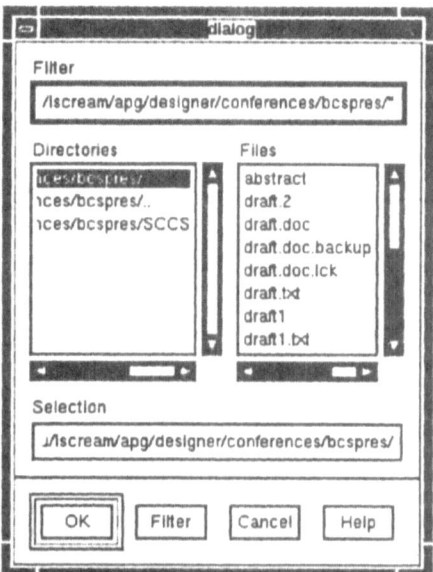

Figure 6: Motif version 1.1 File Selection Box

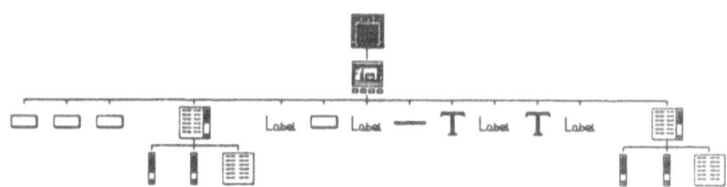

Figure 7: Internal structure of a Motif version 1.1 File Selection Box

The developer who had made use of only the file selection box resources to customise an instance of a Motif 1.0 file selection box was (reasonably well) insulated from this change. The same code could be built against Motif 1.1, and show reasonable results. However, if the developer had set resources on the abstract widgets, then this insulation was lost. For instance, if the font for the filename list had been explicitly set on the list widget, under Motif 1.1 the file selection box would display the filename list in the selected font, but the directory list in the default font.

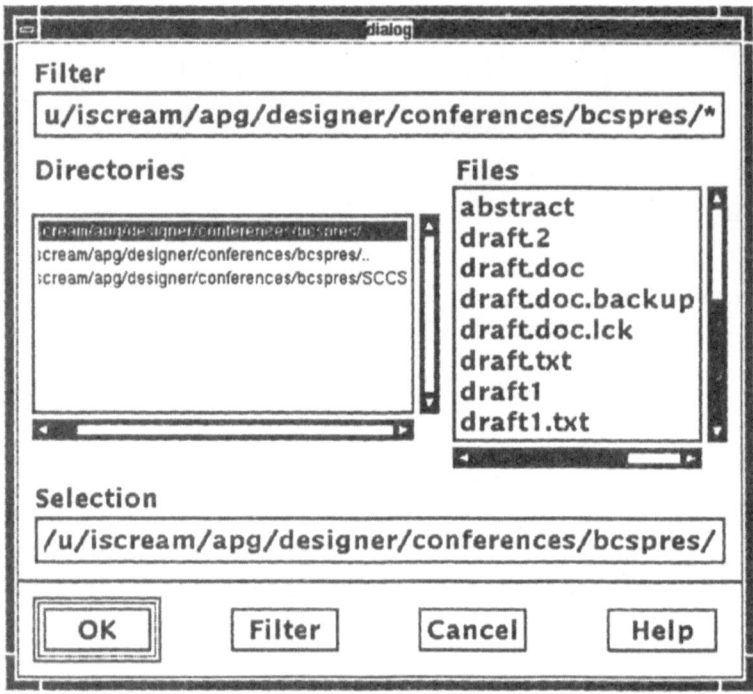

Figure 8: Moving up from Motif 1.0 to Motif 1.1

This problem is not characteristic of X-Designer. In allowing the developer to access and modify abstract widgets X-Designer is simply providing the same facilities as the Motif toolkit. The problem arises not because X-Designer goes beyond the published interface of the file selection box (in this case it does not), but because that interface was not preserved between Motif 1.0 and Motif 1.1. However, it does demonstrate that there are costs in providing visibility of the internal structure of objects, as well as benefits.

If an application has only a few instances of a file selection box of this sort, the problem is readily resolved. It is simply a matter of making the appropriate change to every instance, and then regenerating the code. The tool facilities make this straightforward, but it is time-consuming if there are many instances.

Ideally, only one change would be needed. Rather than taking instances of the file selection box class, and setting the filename list font on each, the developer would create a 'file selection box with filename list font' class, and take instances of this. The implementation of this derived class would have to change when the file selection box implementation changed, so that the same font was used for the directory list as well, but this change would be centralised. The cost of this would, of course, be a proliferation of types. Better facilities for the management of the widget class hierarchy would be needed, and this would inevitably lead to an in-

crease in presentational complexity. A new widget type is probably only appropriate when the required functionality cannot be provided at reasonable cost by composing existing widgets.

7 Invisible Objects

As we have seen, X-Designer provides a graphical technique for composing widgets, and makes visible to the user some of the internal structure of composite
widgets (which has an associated cost for both tool user and tool developer when
the structure is changed by the widget developers). It also makes the wysiwyg
view - the 'face' - of the widgets visible in the design window.

Many widgets have no face, or changing faces. For instance, a widget which
is used to control layout, such as a form, is visible only in the gaps between its
children. If the wysiwyg view is used as the primary means of selecting widgets
so as to set their resources, special techniques may be required to select layout
widgets - after all, a form may have no gaps between its children, and so have
nothing visible in the wysiwyg view to select. Similarly, menus, which are invisible in the wysiwyg view until the user presses a mouse button, may requires special-purpose menu editors.

Since X-Designer uses the internal structure as the access route, layout widgets and menus can be treated in the same way as any other widget. The resources of a layout widget can be accessed by clicking on the relevant widget in the hierarchy. Buttons are added to a menu by selecting it in the hierarchy, then clicking
on the button icon in the widget palette, once for each button. The user model
('menus contain buttons' rather than 'menus have menu items') is simple and consistent, and the extension to provide submenus (cascading menus) is obvious.

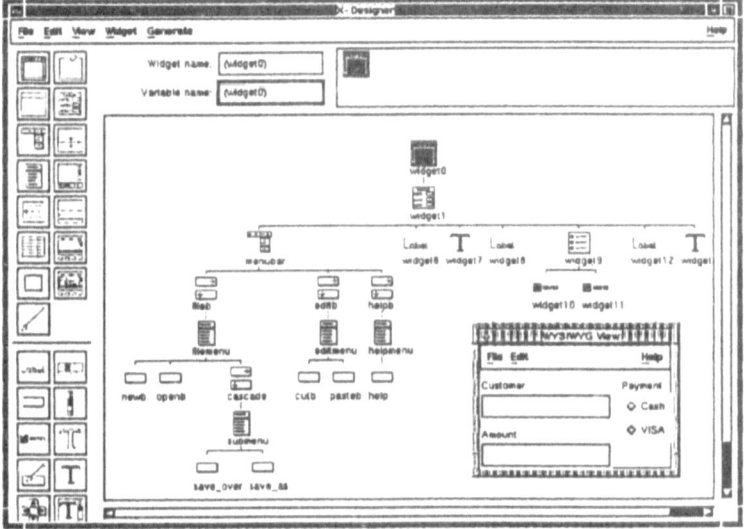

Figure 9: Dialog with menus and cascading menu

Although X-Designer was originally developed to work with the Motif toolkit, it has now been extended so that it can be configured to work with any widgets based on the X toolkit intrinsics (Athena, OLIT, or extra application-specific widgets). These are, at least nominally, user interface objects. There is, in principle, no reason why X-Designer should not be extended to support other kinds of object. The X toolkit intrinsics do not provide the ideal basis for, say, a database object, and a more general model which supports the intrinsics as a special case will be required. In addition, the idea of an application as a set of object hierarchies (each corresponding to a user interface dialog) may need to be extended. However, there is the prospect of a smooth transition from a user interface building tool to a more general application building tool.

8 Re-use in X-Designer

X-Designer allows the user to compose objects taken from a pre-defined (but extensible) set, the widget set. The user is free to create new widgets from existing ones, and add them to the widget palette. Widget building is still the blackest of black arts, and subclassing widgets is not a task which a typical application programmer would relish.

X-Designer has a number of features which promote reuse at a level which is manageable without detailed knowledge of the technology. In particular, it supports reusable design fragments, and effective ways of modifying existing designs.

Any part of a widget hierarchy can be saved as a clipboard item. A clipboard item can later be retrieved and pasted into a new design at an appropriate point in the hierarchy. Of course, this is similar to reusing existing code, using the cut and paste facilities of a text editor. However, an X-Designer clipboard item is a single object. The code required to implement it has, typically, half a dozen sections. To reuse the code, each section would have to be cut from the existing code file and pasted in at the appropriate point in the new code file.

The clipboard mechanism provides a way to define, say, a project standard menu bar. The developer can paste this in to a new design, and need only populate it with extra items which are specific to the application. This is useful where there is a common base which needs to be extended for particular purposes. Another situation which commonly occurs is that of a number of similar objects, but with no obvious common base. In this case, the need is to take an existing object, and modify it with the least possible effort.

Again, the internal view of the design hierarchy is used. Conventional cut and paste facilities are provided, and any widget in the hierarchy can be moved to a new position by dragging it with mouse button 1, or copied by dragging with mouse button 2. These operations work on the dragged widget and all its children, so entire sub-hierarchies can be moved or duplicated in a single operation.

Both of these techniques - clipboard items and dragging - rely on visibility of the internal structure. In the wysiwyg view, it is much harder accurately to identify a part of the design - there is no clear visible boundary between objects, and some objects may not be visible.

9 X-Designer and the Widget Class Hierarchy

Any widget toolkit consists of a number of classes of widget, derived in the usual way in a class hierarchy. Each child class inherits the resources of its parent class.

In the Motif toolkit, this class hierarchy is, in some sense, imperfect. In particular, there are instances where a child class inherits resources from its parent which have no function in the child class - the documentation marks them as "not applicable" in the child class. There are also instances where the parent class has resources which have no function in the parent, but have a function in some classes derived from it. For instance, the Label widget class, which is used as the basis for a number of different classes of button, has resources which are used by some buttons, but not all. In addition, there are resources which are only useful in some circumstances - a pushbutton can have a keyboard accelerator if it is in a menu, but not otherwise.

X-Designer provides resource panels which allow the resources of a widget instance to be set. The design of these panels is critical to the usability of a GUI builder, and there are a number of different approaches.

9.1 Core Resource Panel

The most obvious approach is to have a resource panel for each widget class, which includes all the resources of that class. However, there are many resources which a widget class inherits from remote ancestors, and which are only rarely set by application programmers. For instance, the unit type, which specifies whether dimensions are given in pixels, 100ths of a millimetre, etc is rarely set and, if it is, it is likely that the value will be the same for all widgets in the design, and so should be specified in an X resource file.

In X-Designer, these resources are grouped together into a Core resource panel. Resource panels for each widget class contain only those resources which are not in the Core resource panel. Normally, a user will set resources in the class-specific resource panel. However, the Core resource panel is available when required. In this way, X-Designer hides detail which is irrelevant most of the time, but allows access to it when required.

Note that the Core resource panel is also used for gadgets, which are not derived from the Core class. In this case, inappropriate resources are greyed out, and cannot be set.

194

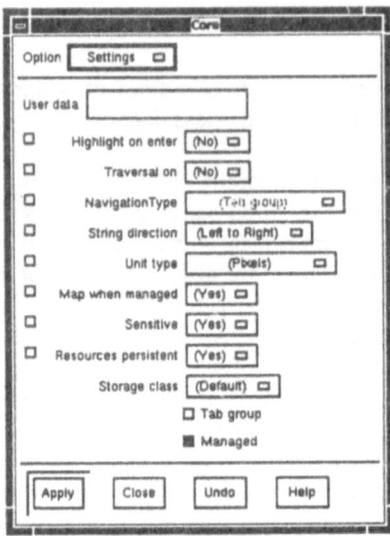

Figure 10: The Core resource panel

9.2 Subsidiary Resource Panels

This technique is carried through to lower parts of the class hierarchy. The resource panels for derivatives of bulletin board do not include the bulletin board resources, but provide access to the bulletin board resource panel via a button in the class-specific resource panel. Bulletin board resources which are 'not applicable' to a child class of bulletin board are greyed out in the bulletin board resource panel when it is being used to set resources of an instance of that child class.

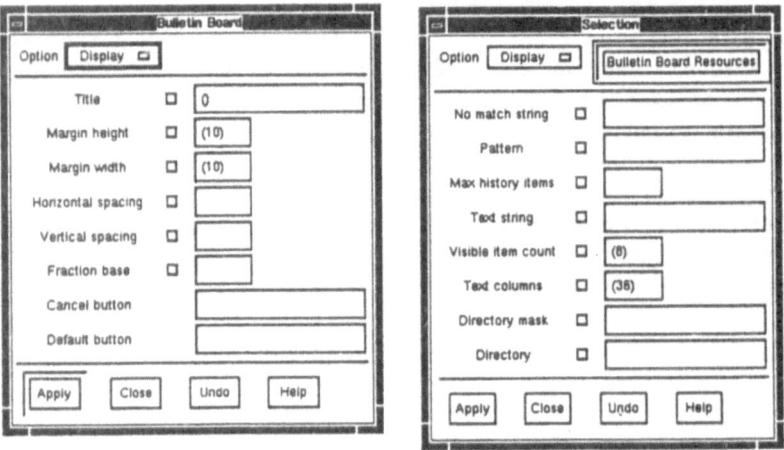

Figure 11: Resource panels for Bulletin Board and Selection Box
(a Bulletin Board derivative)

Where the user has extended X-Designer to support a new widget which is not in the standard Motif toolkit, X-Designer builds a class-specific resource panel for it on the fly. This includes only those resources of the widget which are not resources of its first known (Motif) ancestor. Access to the Motif ancestor is provided via a button in the class-specific resource panel (of course, if the new widget is not derived from a Motif widget, the class-specific resource panel will contain all those resources which are not in the Core resource panel).

9.3 Multi-Purpose Resource Panels

Although class-specific resource panels have been mentioned, it is not the case that every widget class has its own resource panel. Where there is a sub-hierarchy of classes which inherit from a common parent, the same resource panel may be used for them all. A case in point is the label class and its derivatives, which all use the same resource panel. Since the classes in the label subhierarchy have different resource sets, inappropriate resources are greyed out according to the class of widget whose resources are being set.

Inappropriate may mean one of three things:

> The resource is not a resource of the selected widget. For instance, Arm Colour is not a resource of label, but is represented in the label resource panel so that the panel can be used for setting resources of pushbutton. It is only enabled in the resource panel when the currently selected widget is a pushbutton.

> The resource has no function in the currently selected widget. For instance, the label class has resources related to keyboard mnemonics, but these only have a function for certain of the button classes derived from label.

> The resource has no function in the selected widget under the current circumstances. The mnemonic resources of a button are only enabled if the button is a child of a menu bar, pulldown menu or popup menu.

There are two advantages in reusing resource panels. First, the number of resource panels in the tool is reduced, so the tool uses fewer machine resources (in particular, less memory). Second, the tool user has to learn fewer different tool dialogs, and there is less clutter on the screen.

As well as cases where the same resource panel is used for all the classes in a subhierarchy, there are cases where a single resource panel is used for all the subtypes of a given class. The various subtypes of the row column widget (menu bar, menu, radio box, etc) all use the same resource panel.

196

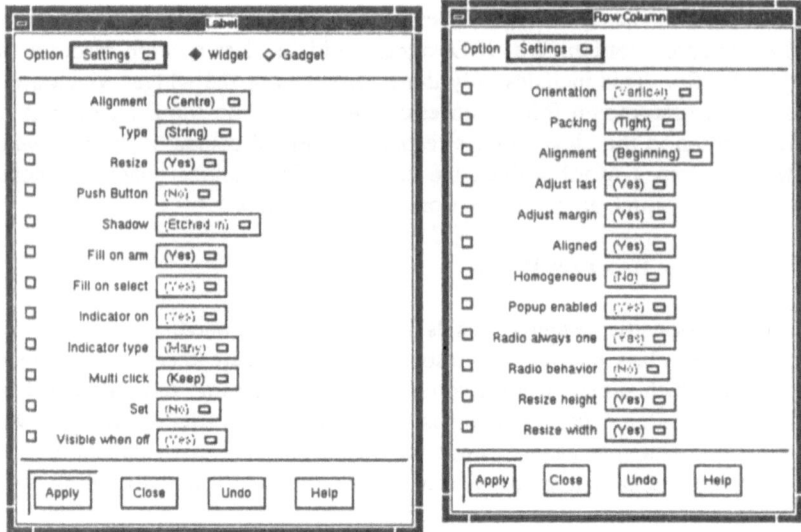

Figure 12: The Label resource panel (as applied to a push button)
and the RowColumn resource panel (as applied to a menu bar)

Note that some of the resources in the Row Column resource panel are greyed out not because the selected widget is of a particular class, but because it is of a particular type (its type resource has a particular value). For instance, since menu bars can contain only cascade buttons as children, the homogeneous resource (which specifies that all the children must be of the same class) is never enabled for menu bars (instances of the row column class where the type resource has the value menu bar). The tool user cannot see the difference between this and the case where the same resource panel is used for instances of different widget classes. That is, the fact that the Motif toolkit uses types of the same class where distinct classes might have been appropriate is hidden from the tool user.

9.4 Special-Purpose Resource Panels

Most resource panels consist of lists of resources with a means of setting the resource value (by entering text, selecting from a list of alternatives or setting a toggle, as appropriate). For some resources, this is not adequate. In particular, the form widget imposes constraint resources on its children which are used to specify the form layout. The mapping between the desired result and the resource values required to achieve it is not obvious, even to an experienced user of the Motif form.

X-Designer provides a special layout editor which lets the developer define the layout graphically. To maintain the principle that the external wysiwyg representation should always look and behave as the final application will, layout, like hierarchy editing and resource setting, is done using a separate representation. This shows the children of the form as rectangles, with lines and circles to represent form attachments and position constraints.

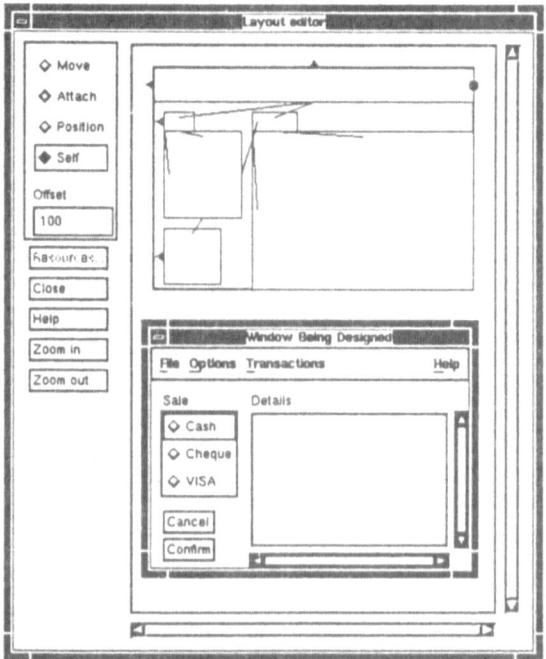

Figure 13: Form Layout Editor and corresponding WYSIWYG View

In this case, there is no question of X-Designer using a more abstract representation, or hiding unwanted detail. The layout editor uses a different, more usable, representation, but it contains the same information as is contained in a list of constraint resources and their values (apart from offset values, available from a separate resource panel).

10 Modelling the Application

X-Designer provides facilities for a developer to create user interface dialogs. To complete the application, the developer must also define the behaviour of the user interface and, at some point, that of the core application.

X-Designer provides only very limited support for these. To create a complete application, the developer will use X-Designer to design dialogs, and to associate callback function names with user actions and other events. The code generated by X-Designer includes these associations, but does not include the callback functions themselves. These are written by the application developer, using whatever development tools are available and appropriate. The callback functions are then compiled and linked with the code generated by X-Designer to create the final application.

Since X-Designer uses essentially the same model as the implementation toolkit, it is straightforward for the developer to make the transition from the design phase to implementation. Code generated by X-Designer looks like the code which the developer would have written to do the same job, but is easily related back to the design hierarchy. To the developer, working with the generated code is just like working with code written by another programmer (one who has an exceptionally consistent style, and who always writes code which corresponds exactly to the design!).

Although the behaviour of the final application is determined by the callback functions, it is often convenient to be able to demonstrate the behaviour of a system before all the code which implements it has been written. X-Designer supports this using a mechanism known as 'links'. Links are simply actions to be taken when a button is pressed. There are four sorts of action - hide, show, enable and disable - and a single button press can invoke multiple actions on many different widgets.

Figure 14: The Links Dialog

Although this model verges on the trivial, it is sufficient to prototype behaviour of the application. The prospective end-user can see not only what the application will look like, but also the major paths through the application.

The behaviour defined using links can optionally be passed through into the generated code, although it is more usual to replace the simple link actions with callback functions in the final application. However, there is at least one significant application built using X-Designer which uses links to implement all the dialog behaviour.

11 Summary and Conclusions

The design of X-Designer attempts to reconcile the need for simplicity and ease of use with the requirement to provide access to and control of the very rich facilities of the underlying Motif toolkit. In order to do this, it uses a number of techniques which either hide that richness, or make parts of it unnecessary. In the course of development, a number of points arose which may have general relevance to the design of software development tools.

First, the most obvious abstraction (in this case the wysiwyg view) is not necessarily the most appropriate. A more concrete representation can bring benefits in terms of:

Consistency (no special purpose menu editors).

Extensibility (support for invisible objects other than user interface layout objects).

Easy reuse (clipboards and dragging).

Transition from design to implementation .

Second, the set of basic object types which the tool has to support is not intrinsic to the problem being solved, but can be influenced by (quite minor) aspects of tool functionality and presentation.

Finally, where the set of types exists in a derivation hierarchy, the tool user interface can profitably be used to conceal complexity (both the internal structure of objects and the many uninteresting attributes an object inherits from its distant ancestors), yet still provide access to the full facilities of the underlying toolkit types. It can also be used to conceal or mitigate idiosyncrasies in the structure of the underlying technology.

SIRIUS: An Object-Oriented Framework for Prototyping User Interfaces

Separation, Integration and Specialisation: Issues and Mechanisms for Object-Oriented User Interface Construction

Peter Windsor

Logica Cambridge Limited
Betjeman House, 104 Hills Road
Cambridge CB2 ILQ, England

Abstract

The object-oriented approach to software construction is well suited to the development of graphical user interfaces with their rich state and complex behaviour. We have re-appraised how user interface and application software can be structured in an object-oriented context and developed a framework architecture which defines a standard organisation based on abstract superclasses which are specialised for an application. Our SIRIUS prototyping system is an implementation of this architecture and has been successfully used in the design of new user interfaces for the Oceanic Air Traffic Control Centre.

1   Introduction

It is practically impossible to design the user interface to a complex system and get it right first time [9]. We believe that a fundamental process in developing usable computer applications is the construction of realistic prototypes of proposed user interfaces and their evaluation through trials with their eventual end users. In our work as an industrial human computer interaction group, we have built prototypes while designing user interfaces for application areas such as control and monitoring, job shop scheduling, insurance and banking and customer support and other office systems. In many cases, existing tools have been sufficient. However, where the important user interface design issues derived from the complexity and dynamics of the application, or the volume and variability of its data, we have found that these tools suffered from a number of limitations. Our work for the Civil Aviation Authority to develop the user interface for the Flight Data Processing System at the Oceanic Air Traffic Control

Centre (hereafter, called 'OACC') is an example of an application where these concerns arise [12, 13].

The first problem with user interface tools is that they only have a limited capability to model the application domain. For all but the simplest domains, a user interface prototype needs to be a convincing, if incomplete, replica of the final system. When the prototype is for an application that does not yet exist, or, as in the case of Air Traffic Control, is not accessible, the application has to be simulated. It is important that the tool allows at least a data model and some core functionality to be implemented with the minimum of effort. With many user interface tools, considerable effort is then required to map between the application entities and semantics and the facilities of the toolkit. To take a simple example, an application involving maps may use latitude-longitude coordinates. Unless the tool explicitly supports this type of data, the prototype builder has to set up a translation between the application representation and the user interface elements provided by the tool. With the rich semantics of real applications these translations can become cumbersome and unwieldy. The Iconographer toolkit tackles this problem directly, but does not attempt to construct complete systems [5].

Secondly, the tools lack flexibility in the kinds of user interface they support. Toolkits implemented in conventional programming languages (e.g., the X toolkits) are difficult to customise, while UIMS style tools (e.g., Teleuse) are constrained by the capabilities of their definition languages. Further, it is not uncommon for a tool to work well within its intended context, but, as soon as a developer steps outside these bounds, the effort required increases by an order of magnitude or more. This 'trapdoor effect' is typified by moving from assembling a user interface using standard controls (widgets) to generating new widgets from scratch. Another related problem is that tools will lag behind the state of the art simply because of the time taken to integrate innovations into an existing system. These problems are partially addressed by parameterisation and templating facilities, but remain a serious handicap when using a tool for rapid prototyping.

Finally, most commercially available user interface tools are delivery vehicles, not design tools. As a consequence, they do not meet the requirements of the design process. One major requirement is to be able to evaluate two or more alternatives for part of the user interface. With many tools this can be difficult. If a tool does not allow the interface definition to be partitioned, it has to be duplicated, with the usual consequences for configuration management. Further, while tools will often allow different user interfaces to be examined using a definition (layout) editor, it is typically necessary to shut down and restart the system to see the variations in a running system.

In this paper, we will present the design of our SIRIUS prototyping tool which aimed to address these problems. We took an object-oriented approach because it provided the basic technology to solve them. Specialisation allowed us to extend the basic toolkit and incorporate application semantics in the user interface while polymorphism supported flexibility. In combination with encapsulation, they provide the means to partition and vary the user interface. An object-oriented language with an established class library gave us a rich medium in which to work; this was especially necessary as we needed our prototypes to simulate applications. Lastly, by using an incremental development system[1] we looked for a highly productive environment for constructing complete prototypes.

In order to realise this potential, it was necessary to develop an appropriate architecture within which the technology could be exploited. In the following sections we will review the concerns that led to the SIRIUS architecture and explain the structure and mechanisms of the framework itself. We will also discuss the extent to which SIRIUS solves the problems described above and suggest how the lessons might influence the development of future User Interface Design Environments.

2   The Structure of an Interactive Application and its User Interface

2.1   Separation of Concerns in an Interactive System

Software systems are inherently complex. This is especially true of interactive systems with graphical user interfaces. In the development of the SIRIUS framework, an important goal was to design a generic architecture for interactive systems. We wanted to find an approach to decomposing such systems and support this decomposition with standard abstractions and hierarchichal organisations. Using Booch's terminology for the 'canonical form for complex systems' [1] we wanted to specify the architecture in terms of the structure of the class and object hierarchies we would expect in any interactive application. We could then implement a 'framework' of standard classes and mechanisms that would allow a prototype system to be assembled simply and quickly.

Prior attempts to produce such a generic architecture have followed the Seeheim model [10] and started with a functional decomposition into Application and User Interface

---

1   The primary implementation of SIRIUS uses Objectworks™/Smalltalk, but we also have a Lisp version. It would be straightforward to implement SIRIUS in C++ or another hybrid language, but some of the flexibility would be lost.

sub-systems. The user interface is then further sub-divided into components such as Presentation, Dialogue and Application Linkage, as shown in figure 1.

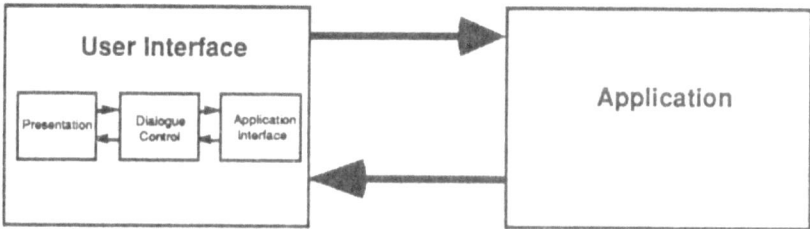

Figure 1 Simple functional decomposition

Clearly, in any interactive system, we can distinguish application and user interface elements especially at the 'extremes' of the system. It is certainly possible to produce display device drivers, graphics packages and windowing systems that are independent of any application. Likewise, database systems and core application algorithms can be completely separate from the user interface. We can also describe the dialogue between the user and the system at an abstract level. Such a description would encompass commands that the user gives to the system, information that the user retrieves from the database and the application 'telling' the user when its database changes.

However, this separation by functional decomposition breaks down when we consider the interactive system as a whole. First, the design of the application software is constrained by the requirements of interaction. Genuine batch systems legitimately take their complete instructions and re-order them for efficient processing. An interactive application, however, may need to be interruptable, provide progress reports and generally sub-divide its processing so that the user can retain control. Further, some parts of the application may not be able to proceed without intervention from the user. For example, Macintosh applications take control of the user interface when they ask the user to supply a floppy disk.

Similarly, the user interface software needs to take the application semantics into account. Application 'objects' need to be mapped to names or visual representations (for example when presenting a set of files), parameters and options need to be derived from the state of the application data and semantic checks need to be applied to entered data. An especially demanding case is found in direct manipulation systems which require fine-grained semantic feedback. For example, 'desktop' applications using 'drag & drop' interaction typically give semantic feedback about what operations are valid; documents can be dropped into folders but not vice versa.

Even at the extremes of the application–user interface split, separation is not always appropriate. Performance requirements may demand that device drivers have customised features. For example graphics firmware for radar often includes primitives for displaying data blocks. Similarly, it may be necessary to support application specific input devices. At the application end, the database may need to maintain user interface related data: images, colour and font data and user preferences.

Finally, and most importantly, in any interactive system the nature of the interaction is characterised by how the system lets the user access objects in the domain. The system will have a 'state' which is defined by the domain objects that are active in the user interface. For example, a word processor will typically have one or more documents active (open) and a current position for each. One document will be current, and new text is implicitly added to that document. This 'access model' is the essential state of the interaction and is effectively independent of the details of the user interface. In the Seeheim model and its derivatives, these aspects of a system are placed in the dialogue control sub-system or in the application interface. However, the interpretation of the access model is inseparable from the application semantics; the presentation of the user interface is largely the presentation of the active objects and the system's response to user input depends heavily upon the interactive state.

For the SIRIUS architecture we wanted to partition our system so that application and user interface were largely separated for the database and device elements but integrated elsewhere. We were particularly concerned that the access model and the organisational aspects of the user interface were explicitly identified. The model we developed assigns each of the classes of an interactive system to one of five major categories arranged in layers, as shown in figure 2 (a more abstract version of this model was presented in [13]). The classes within a category are closely coupled and will depend on each other. Classes in one category will interact with those from an adjacent category more frequently than with those 'further away'. For any given class, the software will include both application and user interface functionality, but, as the figure indicates, the upper categories are predominantly concerned with the former while the lower categories are biased towards the latter.

The domain model classes hold the application data and provide the core functionality. They will provide services to meet the requirements of the user interface. Conversely, the physical user interface classes provide the interface to the display and input hardware. Where necessary, they will provide application specific functions.

The three intermediate layers deal with the interactive aspects of the system at distinct levels of abstraction. The access and actions layer specifies the interaction in a highly abstract fashion in terms of operations on objects from the domain. The structural level extends this by identifying a number of 'views' or components of the user interface and describing the rôles they fill. It is still abstract; the functions of the components are defined but not their realisation. This is provided by the concrete presentation layer which specifies the user interface as perceived by the user: windows, controls and menus for a GUI, or commands, messages and screens in a non-graphical context.

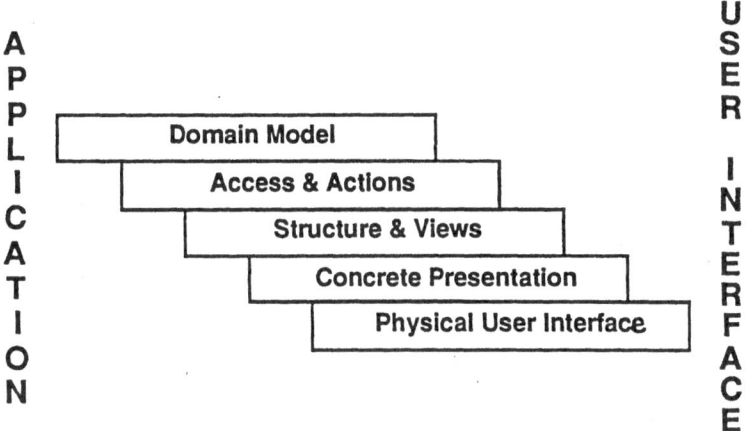

Figure 2 Aspects of an Interactive System

Although we have presented the five layer model after a discussion of architectural and implementation concerns, its main function is as a user interface design model. Each layer specifies a distinct part of the user interface, moving from the abstract description of the domain, to the characteristics of the physical devices. An important property exhibited by the model is the fact that it defines the consequences of changes to the system specification. 'Application' changes (new functionality / new presentations) will percolate down the model. 'User Interface' changes (new devices) will diffuse up.

2.2 The Notion of a Framework

The limitations of functional decomposition led us to the five layer model for the organisation of an interactive system. In addition, we needed a technology that would allow us to partition our software in a standard way into cohesive, independent elements and yet retain the capability to incorporate application specific functions. The obvious candidate was an object-oriented approach where we could use specialisation to add application software to standard classes and exploit polymorphism to implement standard mechanisms. The standard, abstract classes form a 'framework' upon which the system may be built [2, 4].

The SIRIUS framework is a 'sandwich' model with classes divided into three groups. The topmost layer, shown in figure 3, specifies the architecture for an interactive application. It defines a set of abstract superclasses plus 'rules' for how an application may extend and modify them. An actual application will typically use a small number of objects from these classes to form the backbone of the system. The framework defines a canonical structure showing how these major objects are connected. The abstract classes implement standard interfaces and mechanisms that will be needed by any application. Where application information is necessary, the framework places requirements on application subclasses to supply specific methods. Finally, rules and conventions dictate what parts of the application functionality should be placed in those subclasses. There are typically few of these 'superstructure' classes – the SIRIUS framework has seven – and their principal purpose is to manage and coordinate the operation of the system.

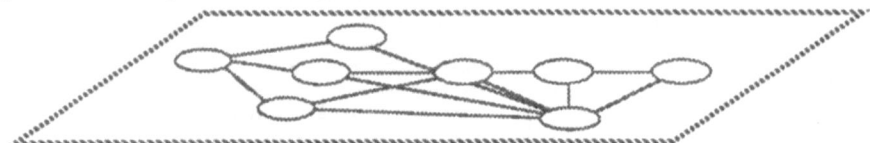

Figure 3 The Abstract Superstructure

The middle layer of the model, illustrated in fgure 4, is application specific. The application specialises the superstructure classes and instantiates them to form its structure. For some of the classes the application will use multiple subclasses and where appropriate there will be a class hierarchy with common aspects of the application abstracted out. For example in the OACC prototypes, there are a number of queue and log windows and the ComponentModel classes for these windows have a common intermediate superclass. Similarly, there may be multiple instances of some classes. The rules for the SIRIUS framework specify that some superstructure classes only have a single instance, while others occur multiply.

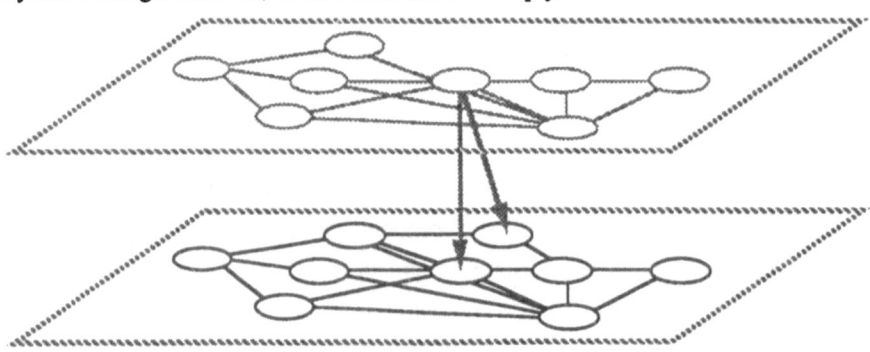

Figure 4 The Application Superstructure Subclasses

To turn the framework into an application, the interfaces between the superstructure classes are defined following existing conventions, state variables are added to manage the application state and methods written to implement the application functions. Typically these methods will invoke the standard mechanisms supplied by the framework classes. The application might also introduce additional superstructure classes that are not generic but fulfil a comparable rôle, typically managing a part of the system state that is sufficiently complex to demand encapsulation.

The base layer, added in figure 5, consists of utility classes that support the construction of the complete system. The Smalltalk `Collection` and `Magnitude` classes are examples of universally applicable utilities. SIRIUS includes support classes for object graphics and for the interface with the display devices. It also has a library of utilities for Air Traffic Control data: air speeds, flight levels, aircraft types etc. Usually, these utilities are used in their vanilla form but subclasses are an important mechanism for adding application specific facilities to the standard mechanisms.

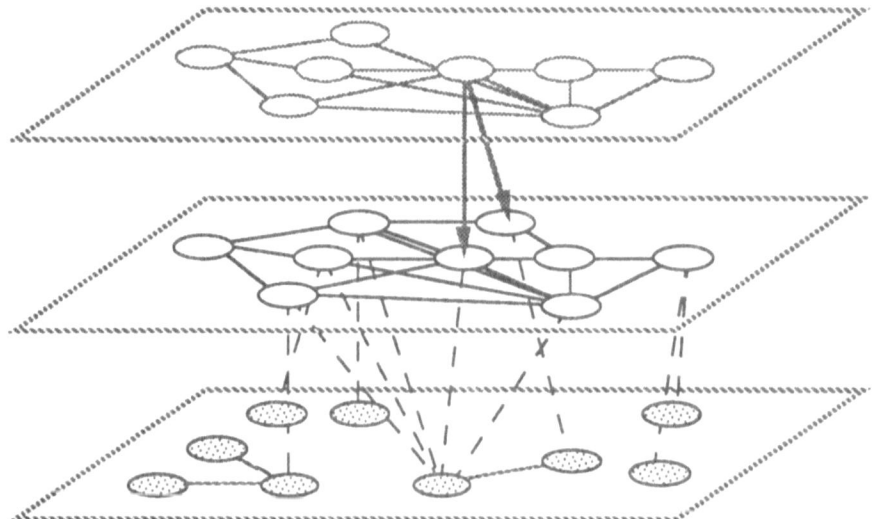

Figure 5 The Complete Sandwich Model

The separation of the framework software into superstructure and utility classes is not exact. Classes that form the superstructure for part of the system can be viewed as utilities in a broader context. For example, as we will discuss below, SIRIUS has a superstructure class `ControlApparatus` whose subclasses are the controls (buttons, sliders etc) that appear on the screen. Although the use of application specialisations of the various control classes is an important aspect of the framework, there is also a library of standard controls that are used as utilities.

A framework is not a complete recipe for a system. There will still be many application specific classes that are not part of the framework structure. With SIRIUS it is still necessary to model the domain, although utility classes can simplify this. The importance of the framework notion is that it provides the organising principle for Object-Oriented systems. In the long term, we and others expect to see a variety of both generic and domain-specific frameworks developed and we believe that they will prove to be a major facilitator for software re-use [4].

2.3 A Framework for an Interactive System

How, then, can we combine the framework notion with our layered model? From the concerns we voiced in introducing the five layer model, a number of observations suggested the shape our superstructure might take.

Starting with the 'naturally separable' aspects of the system, we expected to have a group of 'device interface' classes that encapsulate the functionality of the workstation hardware. In the context of modern window managers, these classes might include windows, sub-windows, menus, input events, fonts and colours. The process that receives events might also be represented as an object. In our sandwich model, these are utility classes, used in vanilla form, although they do fulfil a structuring rôle. In addition to these fundamental classes, we wanted to extend the capabilities of the device interface with utilities to support display lists (object graphics), named styles giving an indirect, and hence flexible, way of specifying display attributes and device independent descriptions of fonts and colours.

Next, we expected to have classes for the domain entities themselves. For example, in the Air Traffic Control domain these would include flights, routes and sectors. Although these classes would primarily be 'application' rather than 'user interface' software, their interfaces would be 'coloured' by the interaction requirements. We also saw a need for 'database' objects to keep track of the domain objects. Although in a simple application it is reasonable to treat a class itself as the collection of all its instances (as well as being their template), this is not sufficient for more complex systems.[2] The database objects would form part of the superstructure, while the domain objects are outside the framework. Depending on the application, there might also be classes that implement particular algorithms or functions, coordinating the functionality encapsulated by the individual domain objects.

Then, we needed classes to take information from one or more domain objects and display it using the facilities of the device interface. These classes also needed to respond to input events and interpret them in application terms. Again, in a simple object-oriented system it may be possible for domain objects to present themselves with

---

[2] For example, in our OACC prototypes, we have several 'databases' each of which contains a different air traffic scenario. It is important that the system kept them distinct, not least because the 'same' flight is in several databases but at different points in its journey.

straightforward display methods, but in practical applications, there is usually a requirement to present the same object in a number of different ways. For example, an aircraft's route might be displayed in tabular form, a 'flight plan' and on a map. Similarly, we wanted to support a variety of interaction techniques for entering commands and data. To meet such requirements we chose to use presentation objects that translated between the application and device worlds. An important point, though, is that we expected the presentation objects to access the domain objects directly, not via some additional interface. At the basic level, each presentation object would hold references to the domain objects with which it worked. The framework could provide superstructure classes for such objects and utilities for displaying common data types. We would expect an application to use many specialised presentation objects according to the variety of the domain and the user interface demands.

The device interface, domain modelling, database and presentation classes are necessary building blocks for a framework for interactive systems, but its major concern is to provide the superstructure to coordinate those objects and manage the activities of the system as a whole – the central layers of the five layer model. The first part of this structure was to support the 'access model' that tracks those domain objects that are active in the interaction. Thinking about a graphical user interface with a number of windows suggested that we should have a single 'model' object that maintained the global access model, common to all windows[3], plus one object for each window holding its local state. If necessary, for example when one window has sub-windows, we could extend this structure and have a hierarchy of model objects.

As the access model is the basis for the interaction, it was appropriate that the models should implement the dialogue at an abstract level. The framework model classes could provide mechanisms to support the interactions between the model objects while conventions would assist in deciding how the total state should be partitioned and what interfaces should be provided. In the SIRIUS framework, the central model plays the pivotal rôle in the system. As well as maintaining the global access model and controlling the dialogue, it manages the component (per window) models and provides access to the database objects and application functions. The hierarchy of model objects forms the backbone of the system and significantly determines its character.

---

[3] For historical reasons, this central model is called the dialogue manager; it has also been called the interaction manager. Neither name is particularly appropriate; in this paper we will use 'central model' when talking about the framework concepts, but revert to `DialogueManager` when referring to the class.

The notion of a model that holds the interactive state and mediates between the domain and presentation classes is not new, coming originally from Smalltalk's Model-View-Controller framework [6]. This also suggested another element for the complete framework: to split the abstract part of the interaction from its concrete presentation. This would allow us to provide different concrete user interfaces with the same basic semantics. A familiar example occurs in the Macintosh finder; the contents of a folder can be 'viewed' in a number of ways, but each form supports the same notions of selecting documents and invoking functions.

In SIRIUS, we incorporated the model-view split, but with the more elaborate hierarchy of models providing the abstract level. However, the monolithic View-Controller organisation did not offer the flexibility we required; we wanted to use a network of individual, cooperating presentation objects. Coutaz' Presentation-Abstraction-Control paradigm [3] suggested an approach. Although PAC was intended as an overall architecture, we used it for just the concrete presentation part of the superstructure. The presentation objects could be organised into a hierarchy and each object would combine input and display methods and provide an abstract interface to the rest of the system.

The concrete presentation layer would also need to manage the distribution of input events. We did not want to restrict ourselves to a simple geometry-based system with events dispatched to the leaves of our PAC hierarchy. For example, in a graphical editor with a variety of tools – selection tool, line drawing tool, text tool etc – a geometry-based distribution would mean that each presentation object would have to know about the currently selected tool. Therefore, we chose to pass input events to the root objects of the PAC hierarchy and then distribute them according to context. The framework would provide geometry-based distribution as a standard mechanism, but it could also support 'tool' objects and other techniques.

Returning to the access and domain layers, it was also important that the framework should coordinate access to the application functionality and provide mechanisms to manage the system's response to changes in the domain. There were two major concerns. First, we felt that if the presentation objects were allowed to initiate changes to domain objects directly, this would rapidly become unmanageable. In particular, it would be difficult to provide standard mechanisms that ensured that every part of the user interface that needed to respond to a change did so in a systematic, co-ordinated manner. Second, we did not want commands, enquiries and responses to be implemented as methods in some object interface; such an approach would lead to large, unwieldy interfaces to the model objects which would be hard to maintain. In addition, the common GUI device of dialogue boxes for setting command arguments had a clear analogy with the relationship between presentation and domain objects.

Thus, we decided that 'commands', 'enquiries' and 'results' should be objects in their own right and that the framework should have superstructure classes for them. It could provide standard mechanisms for handling these 'action package' objects with small, straightforward and flexible set of interfaces in the models. A similar approach is used in Apple's MacApp framework [11] which demonstrates how command objects provide a basis for undo. We have also used them for command logging and to support progress (percent complete) indicators.

The action packages would be created within the concrete user interface, passed through the models and then 'processed' under the auspices of a single 'application' object or transaction manager. This object would not perform any application functions itself; it would instruct the action packages to execute themselves and they in turn would invoke the appropriate methods of the domain objects. In addition, the transaction object could provide an interface for the action packages to declare what changes they had made to the domain model. This information would then be passed to the central model which would coordinate the response of the user interface components.

Figure 3 shows the major SIRIUS superstructure. Although it can be viewed as a hierarchical organisation with the transaction manager as the root and the presentation objects as the leaves, the structure should be regarded as a flat graph with the all the objects having equal prominence. Further, the functions of the classes and the mechanisms that they provide are distinct; each layer fulfils a different rôle.

In fact, SIRIUS is best described as two frameworks, one responsible for the organisation of the total system and a subsidiary one that supports the internal workings of the concrete presentation. As we will discuss later, this split allows us to consider extending SIRIUS by using other frameworks in this rôle. In the next sections, we will first describe the superstructure and utility classes of the organisational part of the SIRIUS framework and then explain how the concrete presentation is supported.

212

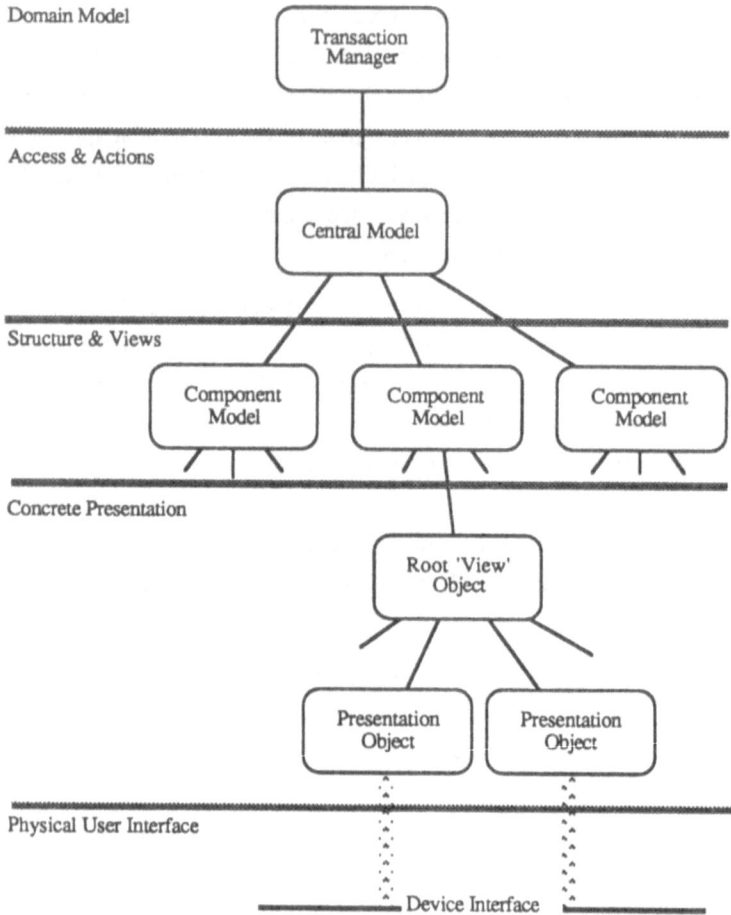

Figure 7 The Major Elements of the SIRIUS Superstructure

3   The SIRIUS Architecture for Interactive Systems

3.1   The SIRIUS Device Model

The first part of SIRIUS we will consider is the device interface classes that encapsulate the facilities of the workstation and its window manager. SIRIUS considers that a workstation has one or more screens, a keyboard and a pointing device. There is a normally a single 'connection' to a workstation, but in a networked environment, there can be multiple connections. On any workstation screen, there can be any number of 'windows' – independent, virtual displays. Note that we use the term window for the 'top-level' window, managed by the window manager and with label, resize and other decorations, rather than the X11 sense of any member of the virtual display hierarchy.

Each window is tiled with panes and associated with each pane is a 'drawing surface'. This is illustrated in figure 8.

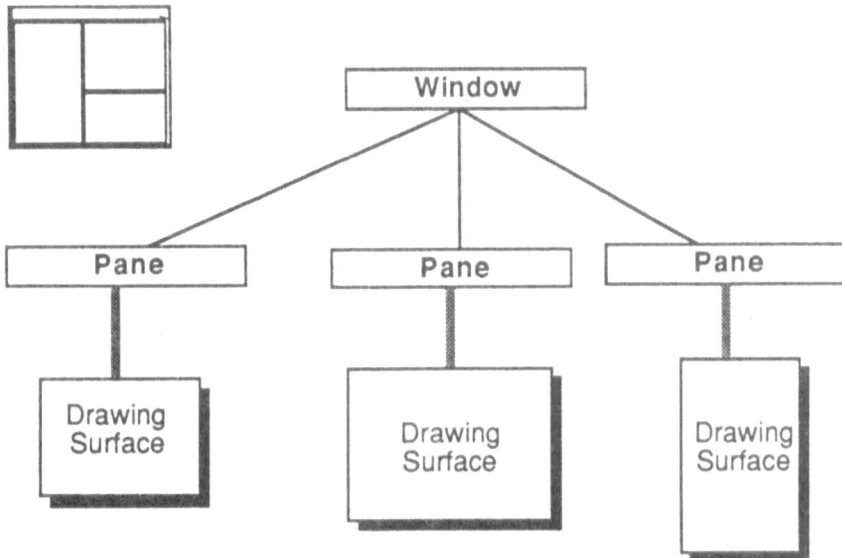

Figure 8 Windows and Panes

The Window and Pane classes serve several purposes. First, they keep track of the window manager resources and provide an interface to the associated functions: resizing, moving etc. Second, they hold references to the objects responsible for the concrete presentation and provide the mechanisms through which those objects gain access to the display functions. Finally, they are part of the input distribution chain.

Drawing surfaces are implemented by the Paper class and provide device independent graphics. Each instance of Paper has its own, 'world' coordinate system of arbitrary size and orientation and maintains a mapping from part of that space onto the pixel coordinates of the pane as shown in figure 9. Then, Paper provides a rich graphics interface including line, shape and text drawing functions, a 2-d transformation stack and control over clipping.

The second part of the device interface is the input model. For each workstation connection, SIRIUS has an 'input manager' that receives events from the window manager. It splits events into groups: pointer events, key events and window management events.

Pointer events are generated for the press and release of pointer buttons, window entry and exit and pointer movement. The movement events are split into motion events when no pointer buttons are down and drag events when one or more buttons is being pressed. Pointer events are generally passed to the pane containing the cursor, but the events for a 'drag sequence' (press, drag, release) are all passed to the same pane.

Drawing Surface

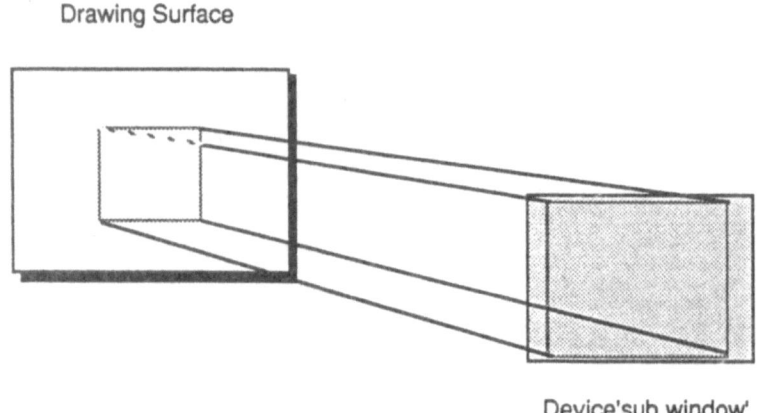

Device'sub window'

Figure 9   Mapping from World to Pixel Coordinates

Key events are generated when keyboard keys are pressed. They are split into alphanumeric keys, control keys and function keys. The first two are distributed either to an application-controlled 'input focus' or to the pane containing the cursor. When an input focus is used, it will be a 'field' (a presentation object) displayed in a pane. Function key events are always sent to the central model.

The final event category is those events generated by the window manager to control the multi-window environment. They include damage events, and events notifying the system of window moves and resizes. Window manager events are passed to the Window instance which will respond directly and inform the underlying model object.

Event distribution is managed by an instance of the InputManager class. It converts the window manager data into an instance of the appropriate subclass of InputEvent and tells the event to process itself. The event determines its recipient and then sends a message to that object. The low level state of the interaction, particularly dragging and any input focus, are maintained by the input manager but used by the event specific methods.

Although events are distinguishable objects within the framework mechanisms, they are passed to presentation objects as messages in the usual object-oriented programming sense. The protocol for input events is an important part of the framework conventions within the concrete user interface and the appropriate superstructure classes implement a default, 'do nothing', response.

The event distribution policy is arbitrary. It was chosen to suit our prototype user interfaces. It is possible for a particular application to provide its own policy by subclassing the `InputManager` class. This is facilitated by each application having its own workstation connection(s) and by the way the distribution mechanism is split between `InputManager` and `InputEvent` methods.

The device interface also includes support for pop-up menus.[4] Menus are defined using a number of superstructure classes (described in §4.8) but implemented in the device interface. In particular, the graphics do not use the device independent drawing surface approach, and during menu tracking events are passed directly to the menu. This retains some flexibility in definition, but allows a simple interface and an efficient implementation.

The SIRIUS device interface is a 'strong' model. As we will see in the subsequent sections, the framework is strongly influenced by the window and pane structure and that does limit its capabilities. This may seem inflexible when compared with a 'soft' model such as that provided by X11's window hierarchy. It is our contention that the functions for which that flexibility is used are much better implemented in the concrete presentation software where application semantics can be applied.

3.2   The Model / View / Control Panel / Drawing Surface organisation

For each window used in the device interface, SIRIUS insists on a single 'component model' object. These objects provide the structure and views layer of the system and implement the abstract form of the user interface. The superstructure classes provide the mechanisms to lay out the panes of the window and for managing the device interface objects. Note that the pane layout can be defined as simple fractions of the complete area or a more complex scheme can be achieved by using 'framing blocks' that calculate the areas according to an application algorithm.

---

[4]   The original implementation of SIRIUS used Sun Microsystems' NeWS which supported menus in the server. Instances of a `Menu` class then managed the server resources in the same fashion as `Window`. The current implementation is based on X11 and so menus are implemented in the client, but the device interface implements them directly.

216

Figure 10 shows the part of the graph of objects for a window with two panes.

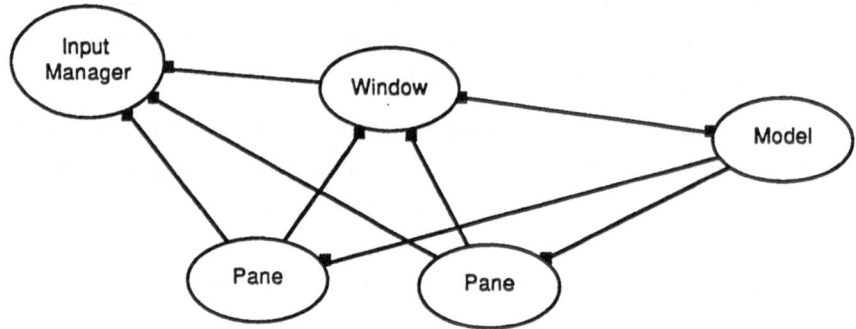

Figure 10   Windows, Panes and Models

It is also expected that some windows will be subsidiary to others. For example, a window displaying graphical data may have an associated dialogue box which is used to set display properties. In such a case, SIRIUS has a hierarchy of model objects, but the windows are independent within the device interface.

There are two model superstructure classes. WindowModel provides the basic mechanisms for constructing the window and panes. It can be subclassed directly for simple systems with a single window. For example, the test harness for SIRIUS consists of a number of such tiny applications. ComponentModel extends WindowModel for use within the complete SIRIUS framework. It adds the links to the central model object plus the support for submodels. These classes are subclasses of Smalltalk's Model class so that the Smalltalk dependency mechanism can be used efficiently.

```
Model
    WindowModel
        ... <standalone model classes>
        ComponentModel
            ... <application model classes>
```

For each type of window that an application uses, it will create an appropriate subclass. These objects will define their windows and maintain the local part of the access model. More importantly, they will implement the abstract user interface and supply the pane with the presentation objects for the concrete user interface. When the model lays out panes on its window, it is specifying the 'views' through which the user will interact with the model. The pane and its drawing surface provide the device interface for the view, and the pane will ask the model to supply a 'control panel' object to form the view contents. The control panel takes a set of domain objects and constructs the required presentation objects for display. It is also the recipient of input events and maintains its appearance after user or application initiated changes.

Figure 11 shows the graph of objects for a 'view'. Note that the control panel does not hold a direct reference to the drawing surface but has to ask the pane for access to it. This makes it straightforward for control panel methods to be written to work when the control panel is not an active part of a view.

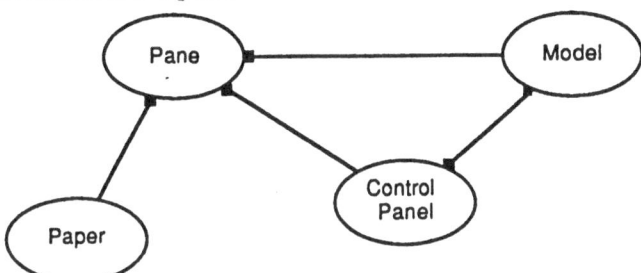

Figure 11   A Control Panel forms the contents of a Pane

Model objects persist as long as they are needed by the system, regardless of whether their windows are present and displayed. The window, pane and paper objects are created when the window is displayed and do not change their organisation once it has been established. Control panels, however, are dynamic. As the interaction proceeds, one control panel can be replaced by another, possibly to display different domain objects or to present a different view of the original ones. It is possible, although not necessarily desirable, that a single view may have radically different contents at different times.

3.3   Two representations and their maintenance

As we have seen, SIRIUS has two major representations for each component of the user interface: the abstract version maintained by a component model and the concrete one presented as one or more views. Perhaps the most important mechanism in SIRIUS is that for the management of these two representations. It has three elements: the interface provided by a component model for its control panels, the complementary interface provided by the latter for the former and the mechanism for replacing a control panel.

The first interface is the actual abstract user interface. It defines the operations a control panel may invoke and what information it can access directly. Obviously, this protocol depends on both the application and the user interface and cannot be defined by a framework. However, SIRIUS does have conventions that guide its specification plus standard control panels that use such interfaces. In particular, for a 'list' view (presenting a set of objects and allowing the user to select one) there should be a single 'select' method and for a 'command' view (typically a row of buttons which invoke operations) there will be a method for each operation. In addition, where the control panel is expected to generate action packages, there should be a single method for 'sending' these commands. The only general guidance we can offer is to consider two or more concrete presentations and design the abstract user interface to encapsulate the underlying semantics.

The remaining mechanisms are concerned with updating the concrete presentation to reflect changes in the interactive state or in the domain. If the system changes so that it needs to present a different set of domain objects, or so that it needs a different presentation, it is necessary to replace an active control panel with a new one. SIRIUS uses the Smalltalk dependency mechanism to achieve this. The model 'announces' that it has changed a particular view. The panes are dependents of the model and the appropriate one responds. It releases the previous control panel and asks the model for the new one. The drawing surface is cleared and reset for the required coordinate system and the control panel instructed to draw itself. This mechanism is similar to the Model-View-Controller system, but there the model supplies the view with the data (domain objects) to be displayed and the view does the presentation itself. In SIRIUS the model creates a control panel which forms the contents of the view while the pane retains the organisational rôle.

This 'wholesale' mechanism is inappropriate for changes 'within' the domain entities being presented. For example, if we have a view showing a flight plan and the aircraft's expected time of arrival at a beacon changes, we only want to update that piece of the presentation. SIRIUS supports this by allowing the model to communicate directly with its control panel. Again, the interface that the control panel provides for the model depends on both the application and the user interface and there are conventions associated with standard views. For the list views, the model can tell the control panel to add or remove an item from the set and to change the availability of individual items. The interface to a command view control panel allows the model to enable or disable commands and to substitute one command for another. Note that for both the interfaces between component models and control panels, an application should define its own conventions in addition to the general purpose ones. For example, in the Oceanic prototypes we have a standard protocol for a model to pass changes to a flight record to those control panels which display flight data. This helps ensure that we can exploit polymorphism both by substituting one control panel for another and by using the same control panel class with more than one model.

Other developers have extended the basic MVC approach by employing a hierarchy of view objects and using the dependency mechanism for all changes. We did not take this approach for a number of reasons. Firstly, as we have already indicated, we wanted to integrate the view and controller functions in presentation objects. Then, we wanted to separate out the static part of the structure, represented by the pane objects, from their dynamic contents. These are, perhaps, cosmetic differences; more importantly, we felt that the dependency mechanism became cumbersome when we had rich application semantics. This is partly because it is 'hidden' and partly because it would be difficult to manage the mapping between the model's structure and that of the presentation objects. We decided it was better that the model software was aware of its views and explicitly instructed the control panels through an abstract specification of their capabilities. In taking this decision we were potentially losing the useful property that a model was independent of its views and could have multiple views without change. In fact, SIRIUS retains this property by separating the central model from the individual component models. Our approach is that the component models define the structure of the user interface and each model knows what views it has to support. The central model manages the user interface as a whole, and as far as possible does not distinguish between its components.

3.4   The Central Model Object

The focal point in a SIRIUS system is the 'central model' object, also known as the dialogue manager. Its purpose is to maintain the global access model, to coordinate the user interface and to provide the sole access route between the component models and the transaction manager (and hence the domain functions). Figure 12 illustrates how these objects are connected.

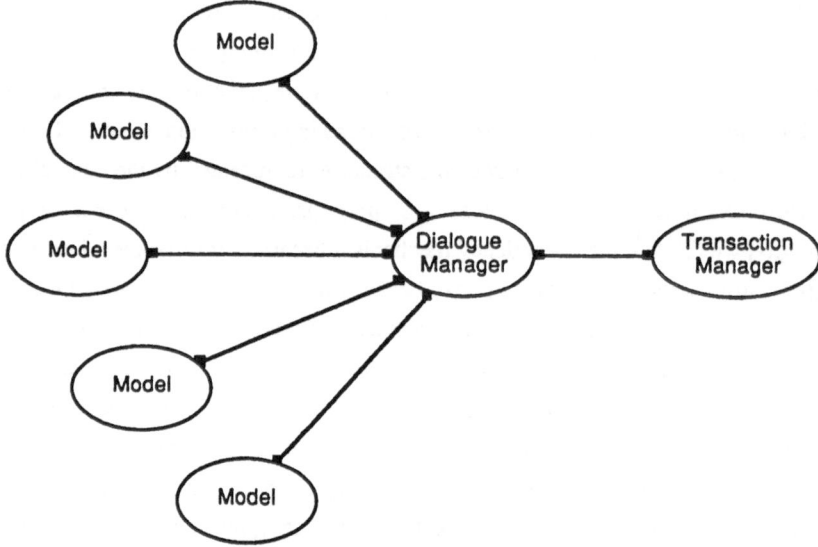

Figure 12 The Dialogue Manager and the Component Models

The application is required to provide two interfaces in its central model class: one for use by the models and one for use by software within the domain model layer. As with the component models, these interfaces depend heavily on the application and the particular access model underlying the interaction.

The interface for the component models allows them to access and change the interactive state and to pass action packages through to the transaction manager. The conventions for this interface are sparse. There should be a complete set of atomic operations on the interactive state and a rich enquiry protocol. There should be a single interface for passing action packages to the transaction manager, but it may be supplemented by 'command' methods that create and send objects for important commands taking the domain objects in the access model as arguments. Note that the component models are not allowed to interact directly. One model can only affect another as a consequence of invoking a dialogue manager method.

The interface for the domain model allows information about changes in the domain to be passed to the user interface. The interface must encompass the creation and destruction of domain entities, changes within an entity and changes in the relationships between them. The granularity at which changes are described is a balance between keeping the interface manageable while allowing the changes to be distinguished. Generally, we have used individual interfaces to notify creation and destruction of domain objects. For changes to a specific domain entity, we have classified possible changes into a small number of groups and then passed a 'change description' identifying which categories have been affected.

To support these application interfaces, the DialogueManager class can only provide some basic mechanisms. It keeps track of the components of the user interface by recording the models in a table by name. Then, it provides the means to 'broadcast' a message to those models, that is, to send the same message to each in turn. The application software in its DialogueManager subclass uses this mechanism to inform the component models both of changes to the global access model and of changes in the domain. Normally, every component model object is notified of every change, but only needs to respond to those that affect it. This is achieved by using an application superstructure class between ComponentModel and the individual model classes. Occasionally, the user interface semantics will require that a message is only sent to a specific component, for example to bring its window to the front. In general, we avoid this as it reduces the flexibility to vary the user interface.

DialogueManager also provides part of the mechanism to control the interaction between the central model and the transaction manager. We will return to this after discussing the action packages and the transaction manager itself.

3.5 The Transaction Manager and Action Packages

SIRIUS does not allow arbitrary objects to invoke 'application processing'; that is, anything that changes domain objects or requires significant processing. It insists that these operations must take place under the auspices of a transaction manager object. Further, the transaction manager does not perform any processing itself. This is delegated to a variety of action package classes. The application must subclass TransactionManager and provide an interface for action packages to declare what changes they have made to the application. This interface is comparable to that provided by the central model. We considered allowing action packages to notify the central model directly, but the extra level was needed to allow parts of the system to act asynchronously as we will discuss below.

The application transaction manager may also provide functions to support 'structural changes' to the domain, that is, adding and removing objects and relationships. These methods ensure that relationships among several domain objects (e.g., consistency rules) are maintained. For example, in the Oceanic prototypes, rather than change a filed flight plan directly, a 'copy flight' is made and updated. Only a single copy is allowed and ultimately it will either replace the original flight plan or be discarded. The transaction manager for the Oceanic prototypes has methods that implement these rules centrally so that the action packages that update flight plans do not duplicate the logic concerning copies.

As well as the transaction manager, SIRIUS has a single 'database' object. This keeps track of all the domain objects and provides searching functions as needed. Note that component models and control panels may acquire a reference to the database (via the central model) and hence retrieve domain objects directly. This means that the relevant interfaces do not have to be duplicated unnecessarily.

The `TransactionManager` class provides two basic mechanisms. First, it provides a standard interface through which the central model passes it action packages. Secondly, it provides a queueing mechanism for buffering change notifications prior to sending them to the central model. The `Database` class is purely a place holder; there are no standard functions that are appropriate for SIRIUS to provide.

The superstructure classes for action packages are `ActionPackage` plus three subclasses:

```
ActionPackage
    Command
    Enquiry
    Reply
```

`ActionPackage` does not provide significant functionality, but defines standard interfaces to be used in various parts of the system. It also provides default implementations for these methods. The important interface is that an action package class can specify the control panel class to be used as its user interface. This makes it possible for a model to include a view on an action package (essentially a dialogue box for the command) without knowing any details of what that command does. In this way, action packages integrate pieces of user interface and application function, inverting the separation of many user interface tools.

As SIRIUS is primarily a prototyping tool, it does not attempt to support an application with complex internal processes. We recognise that for many applications the simple model of a transaction manager, a database and action packages will be inadequate. In our Oceanic prototypes, the simulated application is somewhat more involved. A complete implementation would need many classes to support the message switching, monitoring, recording and calculation services needed in an ATC system. We hope to see comparable frameworks developed for other categories of application. The appropriate application framework would be combined with SIRIUS to form an expanded superstructure. We expect that SIRIUS would still see the application as a single object, but it may be that a more elaborate model is needed.

3.6   Asynchronous operation & Distributed Processing

The final element of the organisational part of SIRIUS is the way in which it manages the execution of its various elements. We wanted the user interface and domain processing to operate asynchronously so that the user interface was always active and so that the user could interrupt the application. We were also concerned to check that our user interface designs would work when the application processing was not local to the workstation. To achieve this, SIRIUS uses three concurrent processes, one each for the input manager, the central model and the transaction processor.

We described the input manager process as part of the device interface. It is the 'top level loop' which takes events from the window manager and initiates their processing. It is this process that executes in direct response to user actions. For example if the user presses the mouse button with the cursor over a screen button control, the software that makes the button look 'pressed' is run within the input manager process.

The other two processes control the interaction between the central model and the transaction manager. Each object has a 'job queue' on which the other places instructions and a process that consumes elements from that queue.   The transaction manager places its change descriptions on the central model queue and the process belonging to the central model is responsible for initiating the system's response to each change. Similarly, the central model places action packages on the transaction manager's queue and the transaction manager process controls their processing. Figure 13 illustrates these two processes.

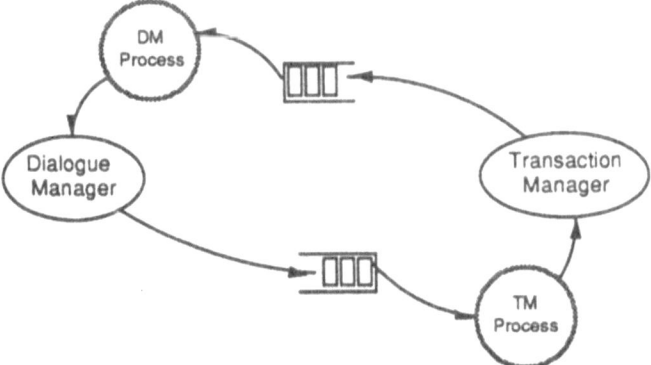

Figure 13 The Central Model and Transaction Manager Processes

The central model and transaction manager processes do not interfere. However, the input manager and central model processes both execute software which can change the state of the system in any layer outside the domain model. In particular, both processes share the resources of the device interface. Therefore, access to the device interface is via a semaphore, held by the input manager. Either process must acquire this semaphore before it can run, and the input manager will hold it across a drag sequence so that the user interface cannot change during a low-level interaction.

In addition, SIRIUS has two conventions for controlling application processing. First, action packages are kept small so that the complete processing of a single 'command' is accomplished quickly. Then, the software that is invoking the command, typically within a component model, generates a stream of action packages to perform a larger task. It may generate and dispatch these objects en mass, but normally the reply from the processing of one command (passed back through the central model) will be the trigger for sending the next.

The second approach is that an action package will complete a 'step' in its execution and then tell the transaction manager to re-queue it for further processing. If another part of the system has retained a reference to the package, it could then receive instructions to modify its subsequent behaviour. Most often, the action package would be told to terminate. We have generally used the technique of multiple action packages as we have found it simpler for providing feedback to the user.

The central model–transaction manager split is not true distributed processing, as the two processes are in the same address space. However, it is sufficient to demonstrate that a SIRIUS-based system could be distributed, with the constraint that 'read-only' copies of domain objects would need to be available in the workstation.

3.7   The Complete Framework

To sum up, the major part of the SIRIUS framework imposes an organisation on an interactive system. The main features are:

- The domain is modelled as a network of individual objects.

- There is a single database object which records all the domain objects.

- The database and the domain objects can be accessed directly by any part of the system, but changes can only occur under the control of a transaction manager.

- Action package objects are used to pass commands and enquires to the transaction manager and for it to pass back replies.

- There is a single 'central model' that maintains the access model references to the domain objects that are active in the user interface.

- The user interface is split into components, with a 'component model' holding the interactive state for each component and defining the abstract user interface.

- The concrete user interface for each component is organised as 'views' with a 'control panel' forming the contents of each view.

- The device interface provides windows tiled with panes, input events, device independent graphics and pop-up menus.

Figure 14 summarises the structure of a SIRIUS system.

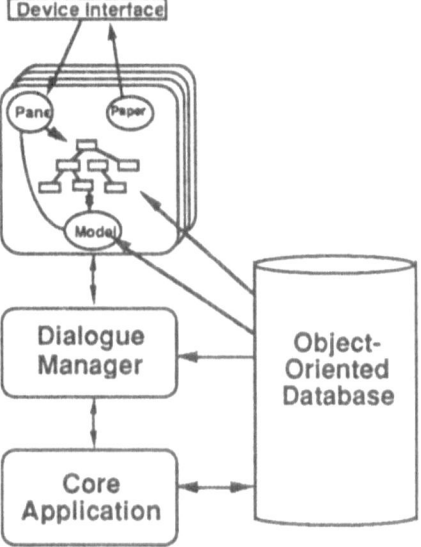

Figure 14   The SIRIUS Framework

4   The SIRIUS 'Micro-Architecture' for the Concrete User Interface

4.1   The Standard Control Classes

The second half of SIRIUS is concerned with the concrete presentation and behaviour of the user interface. We have already explained that a control panel creates and manages a set of presentation objects, called 'controls', which implement what the user actually sees. SIRIUS has a rich library of standard controls, so it is possible, and sometimes desirable, to use the organisational part of the framework with the control classes as utilities. The control panel superstructure class specifies a definition method to be provided by each application subclass which instantiates and parameterises library controls as required. The interfaces to the control objects using the control panel are standardised and kept abstract, so it is straightforward to vary the details of the user interface by substituting one control for another functionally compatible one.

Note that these interfaces are in terms of domain objects. For example, a selection control (such as radio buttons or a scrolling list) is given the list of domain objects from which the user is to select. The 'label' that is used to represent the domain object is either obtained by the selection control asking the domain object for its default label, or supplied as a parameter by the control panel. When the user makes a selection, the control panel is given the actual domain object as the argument of the selection message (the message selector is a parameter). This approach of specifying interfaces in terms of domain objects and only switching to display terms (text strings, pictures) when absolutely necessary at the device interface is an important principle. It maximises the flexibility of the framework and makes it possible to achieve fine-grained semantic feedback in the concrete user interface.

When using the control library, the concrete presentation layer of SIRIUS is essentially a conventional widget toolkit. However, for the complex prototypes which are the framework's raison d'être, it is expected that a developer will create his or her own controls using the superstructure classes for the concrete user interface. These can vary from simple specialisations which set up standard uses of the library classes to full developments of highly specific presentation and behaviour.

4.2 The PAC Approach

SIRIUS' superstructure classes for the concrete user interface use a variation of Coutaz' Presentation-Abstraction-Control paradigm [3]. The external interface of each control object is split into three parts: presentation, abstraction and control. The methods invoked through these external interfaces communicate through a private 'update' protocol which maintains the internal state of the object.[5] Figure 15 illustrates this arrangement.

The presentation protocol is concerned with displaying the control. Its major interface is the method that responds to a 'draw yourself' instruction from its superior. Although some controls are implemented to use the drawing surface functions directly, we normally use the object graphics system described below. When the control is first activated, it constructs its picture which can then be displayed and re-displayed as

---

[5]   In Coutaz' scheme, what we term Presentation and Control are combined into a single protocol and her Control corresponds to our internal Update methods. The mis-naming was due to sloppiness on our part.

necessary. The internal update methods invoke the necessary (private) portion of the presentation protocol to change and redraw the picture when the state changes.

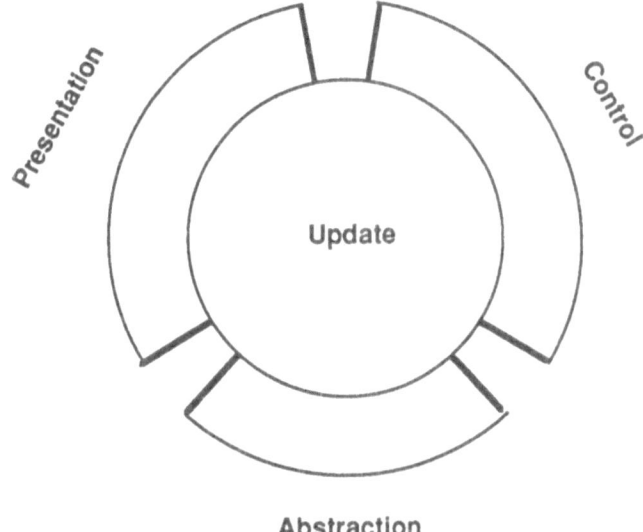

Abstraction

Figure 15   The Interfaces to a Control Object

The control portion of the interface provides the methods that respond to input events. For some controls these will process 'raw' events as defined by the device interface, but for controls that form part of a larger structure, the events will have some semantic interpretation. For example, a control which represents one element in a selection display (a single radio button) will receive 'select' and 'deselect' messages from the control that manages the complete selection.

The abstraction interface is used to define and manage the control object without reference to it appearance or interactive behaviour. For example, the abstract interface to a toggle control (such as a check box) includes methods for switching it to the on or off state, for enquiring its current state and for specifying the message to be sent when the user changes the state. Typically this interface will be used by the application specific software in the control panel subclass which is using a control object.

On a small scale, the PAC approach is the opposite of the Seeheim decomposition; rather than separate the elements of an interactive system, it integrates them into a cohesive unit. To construct larger systems, the control objects are organised as a hierarchy with the control panel as the root. All activity, whether presentation, abstraction or control, commences in the control panel and is propagated down the hierarchy as required. Note that presentation methods in a parent control only send presentation messages to its offspring and similarly for the other protocols. Figure 16 shows the object network for a simple control panel.

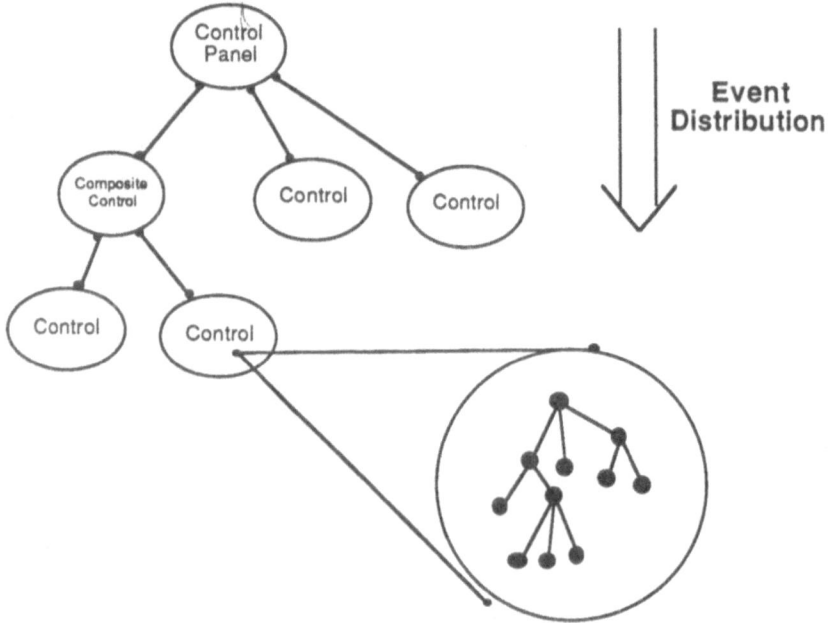

Figure 16 A Hierarchy of Presentation Objects

The figure also shows the object graphics structure attached to a root control. Some toolkits have used a single structure with both control objects and graphical objects treated uniformly. We chose not to do this because we saw a clear distinction between them. Controls are aware of the domain objects for which they provide the concrete user interface, play an active rôle in responding to user input and may incorporate application semantics. Graphic objects, however, are purely display objects and are universal. A SIRIUS control is responsible for maintaining the mapping between a part of the domain and its portion of the display.

Coutaz proposed PAC as a complete architecture, but we have only applied it to the concrete user interface. We felt that PAC was not sufficient for constructing large interactive systems. It does not provide support for managing which domain objects were participating in the user interface – our access model, nor does it explicitly allow the split between abstract and concrete representations of a user interface. These were two features of the model-view-controller approach that we needed to retain with their associated mechanisms. Further, the PAC approach implicitly allowed changes to the domain to occur at any point within the hierarchy; we wanted to introduce action packages and a transaction manager so that domain changes could be controlled. It is possible to describe a complete SIRIUS system as a PAC-like hierarchy, but we prefer to see the layers as a cooperating network of objects.

4.3   An Example: SIRIUS' Selection Controls

The value of the PAC approach in the concrete user interface is that it combines with inheritance and polymorphism to form the basis for an extensible widget system. To illustrate this, we will describe SIRIUS' selection controls that allow the user to choose from a set of objects. From the abstract viewpoint, these controls fall into two major categories: exclusive selections from which the user may make a single choice and non-exclusive selections which allow any number of choices. Figure 17 shows some of the possible 'look and feel's for selection controls.

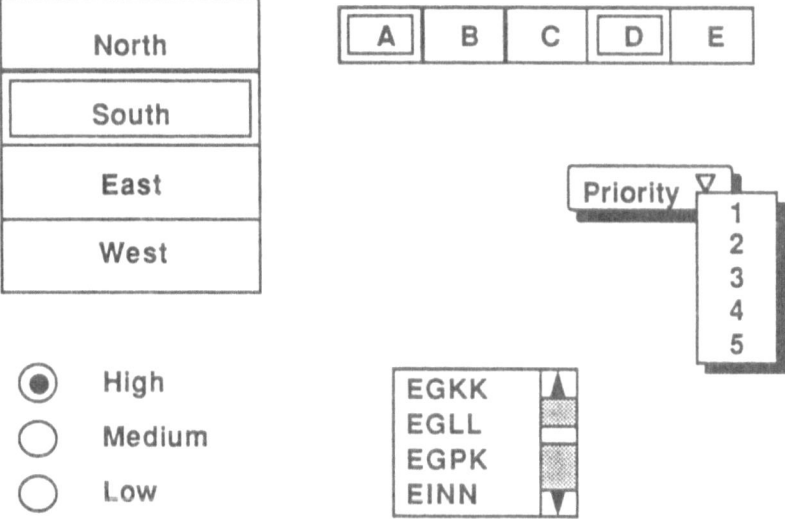

Figure 17   Various Selection Controls

SIRIUS uses a hierarchy of control objects for a selection control. The root object handles the semantics and layout and has one child control, a 'selection button', for each choice. Note that in the case of the scrolling list, all these offspring are present, but only a subset are visible.

In the exclusive case, the root object 'knows' which domain object is selected and hence which child. When the user 'clicks' on the control, the root object determines which child was pointed at, sends a deselect message to the previously selected child and a select message to the newly chosen one. It then sends its selection message to the control panel (or other nominated receiver) with the chosen domain object as an argument. The message selector for the selection message is a parameter defined when the control is added to the control panel.

Similarly, for the non-exclusive case, the root control holds a set of selected objects. In response to a user click, it checks if the identified object is already selected and sends a select or deselect message as appropriate. It also sends an added or a removed message to the control panel.

The individual selection button objects are independent of whether they are being used in an exclusive or non-exclusive context. Further, the interface between the root objects and the selection buttons is independent of the 'look and feel' of the buttons. Thus it is possible to use various look and feel styles by making the class of selection button to use a parameter of the root control. For convenience, SIRIUS has subclasses of its main selection control classes that default to the common styles (Motif, OpenLook etc). Figure 18 shows some of the objects involved in selection controls (most of the selection button objects are omitted).

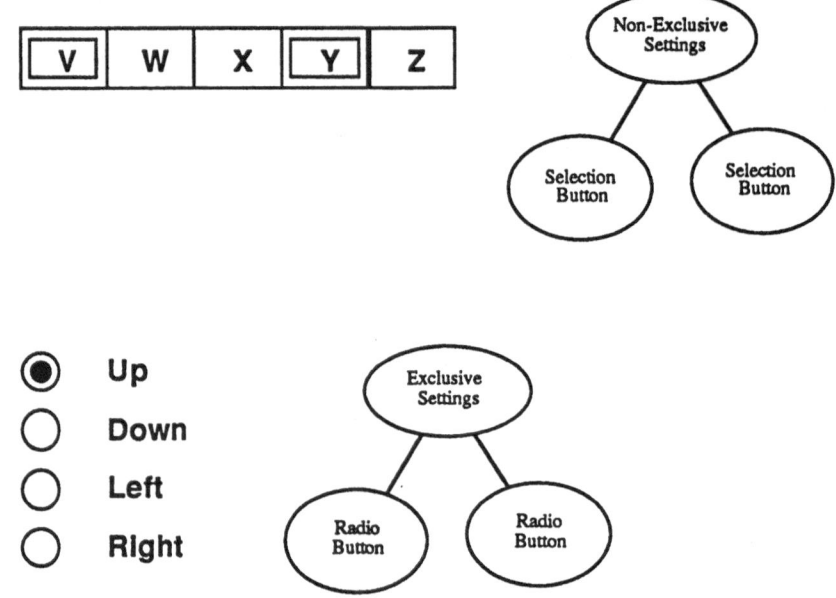

Figure 18 Alternative Semantics

Much of the internal workings of the two forms of selection are also common. The root control has to identify which child is under a given point, and, when it is set up, it has to lay out its offspring. These common elements have been teased apart with the PAC organisation as a guide. Between the exclusive and non-exclusive controls, the presentation aspects are common, with variations in the other protocols.

We also wanted to vary the presentation. This can be controlled by the superstructure class with the details implemented in subclasses. Figure 19 shows an example of two alternative layouts. The software which initialises the control will create its offspring and then invoke an internal method to tell them where they appear.

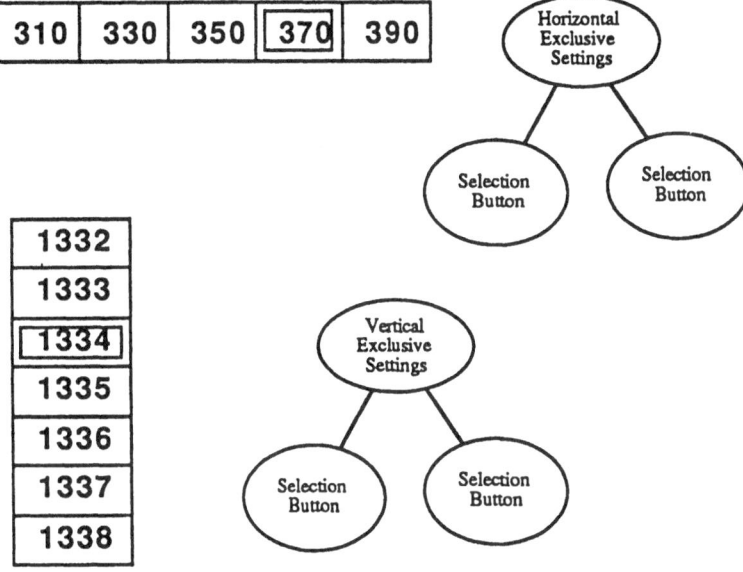

Figure 19 Alternative Layouts

Multiple inheritance would be useful here to define the layout techniques once for both the semantic forms. However, we have found it sufficient to provide distinct methods for the standard layouts in the superstructure class and have the subclasses 'indirect' to the appropriate one.

4.4 Adding Application Semantics to Controls

We expect applications to subclass the standard controls. Figure 20 shows two simple examples from our Oceanic prototypes. Our user interface designs had conventions for standard selection devices, particularly in the 'dialogue box' control panels for action packages. To make sure that the conventions were implemented once and to give a simple interface when setting up the control panel, we used subclasses of the selection control classes. The subclasses illustrated only changed the abstraction aspects of the controls.

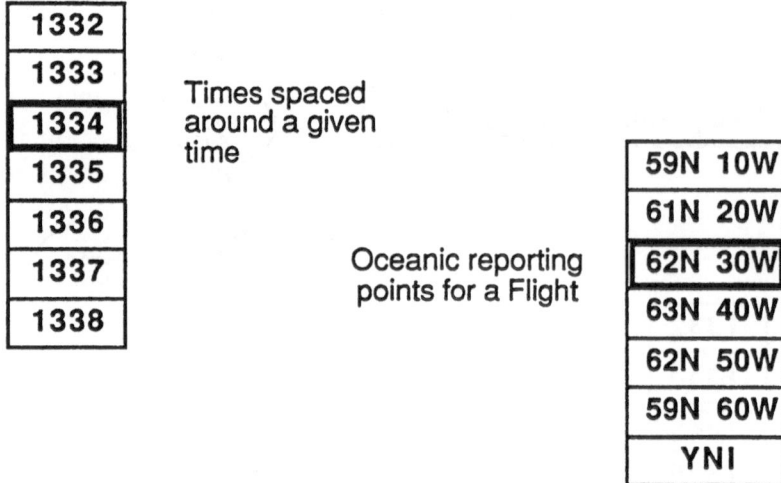

Figure 20   Application Specific Selection Controls

Similarly, when we wanted graphics rather than simple labels in the selection buttons we subclassed selection button classes and specialised the presentation methods. Outside the selection classes, another example is the use of specific parsing methods in application subclasses of the standard input field classes. In that case, the principle of hiding the specific concrete presentation within the control meant that a control panel could use either a text field or a graphical device (slider or dial) for entering a value interchangeably. This could then be exploited using a hierarchy of control panels providing different concrete interfaces to the same functionality. In our Oceanic prototypes we made full use of this flexibility.

4.5   Menus

As well as the controls that are displayed directly as part of a view, SIRIUS supports two forms of pop-up menu: command menus and choice menus. For a command menu, the selection of an item invokes an associated method on some nominated object. In the simplest case, the menu is defined from a list of method names, each with an associated label. Similarly, a standard choice menu is constructed using a list of objects from which the user is to make a selection, plus a label for each. When an item is selected, there is a single method which is invoked with the selected object as an argument.

Menu definitions are actually represented as a shallow hierarchy with a menu item object for each entry. The standard constructions set up this structure automatically, but more complex menus can be built piecemeal. In particular, there is a menu item for a 'sub-menu' allowing hierarchical menus to be defined. Menus can be edited by adding and removing menu items, and, as with the rest of SIRIUS, application specific menu-items are expected.

Menus can be activated by any software within the concrete presentation layer. The menu is then handed over to the device interface for the duration of the interaction. `ControlPanel` has standard methods for responding to the 'menu button' (right mouse button) to activate the menu for a pane. This mechanism tries three potential sources for the menu to use. First, it looks for a (context specific) menu from the control under the cursor, then it checks for a menu defined for the control panel. If neither of these is present, it requests a menu from the component model.

4.6 Event distribution

The `ControlPanel` and `ControlApparatus` classes provide standard mechanisms for distributing input events. Of the event types distinguished by the device interface, pointer and key events (bar function keys) are dispatched to control panels and their offspring. SIRIUS' default policy for passing these events to the appropriate control is intended to support 'dialogue box' style interactions, but there is also software to facilitate implementing 'diagram editing' with direct manipulation.

The standard policy for distributing pointer events is geometry-based. The control panel identifies the control under the cursor for a 'down' event and makes it 'current'. All the messages for events in a single 'drag sequence' are sent to the current control. This leads to the familiar logic that 'pressing' on one control, say a button, and then dragging the cursor outside it causes a 'no-op' regardless of whether the cursor is over some other control when the button is released. Note that composite controls (such as the selection controls) are seen as a single control by the control panel. The semantics of the composite determine how the input sequence is interpreted.

This simple mechanism, however, is inappropriate for diagram editors or other sophisticated contexts. For example, in an application such as MacDraw, when a 'definition' tool is selected, it is irrelevant what object the cursor is over. It would be poor engineering if the software for individual controls had to check the global context while processing each input event. SIRIUS supports this form of interaction with 'tool objects'. A control panel using this mechanism has a current, or 'active' tool to which it sends all pointer events. The tool applies its own semantics, but asks the control panel when it does need to know what object / objects are under the cursor.

SIRIUS has superstructure classes for tool objects including a selection tool class, skeleton definition and edit tools and a 'zoom and pan' tool. The tool objects from these classes are PAC objects, but their 'presentation' is to the set the cursor shape for the appropriate pane. Then, during a drag sequence, they provide an 'echo' overlaid on the display. The device interface provides a mechanism for drawing and erasing an echo without 'damaging' the underlying display.

As with the other presentation objects, an application is expected to implement tool object subclasses. Here, above all, is the place were SIRIUS allows fine-grained semantic feedback. For example, in the Oceanic prototypes, there is a 'route editor' for changing the proposed route for a flight. When the tool is used to drag a point on the route, it normally applies a 1° (lat-long) grid and echoes the modified route with a 'rubber band' plus a text label. However, the exit points at the west edge of the Flight Information Region are restricted to specific 'beacons'. If the user is modifying such a point, the route editor recognises this and 'snaps' the point to the next beacon in a north-south sequence.

The default policy for distributing character events is largely implemented in the device interface. The input manager sending key event messages to an 'input focus', a specific control, is usually, but not necessarily, a text field. However, each control panel has a list of which offspring are 'fields', that is, able to be the input focus, and `ControlPanel` provides mechanisms for 'tabbing' between fields. Switching the input focus between control panels is usually driven by the component models, or possibly the central model[6]. A control panel is notified when the input focus moves into or out of its territory. If it is necessary for the control panel to intercept key events, this can be achieved by making the control panel the input focus and maintaining a 'current field' locally.

An additional mechanism that we have found to be useful, allows the control panel holding the input focus to ask to be notified when the next key event is dispatched to one of its fields. We use this in 'dialogue boxes' as follows. We have a control panel with fields and other controls for entering the parameters of a command. When all the fields have valid data, an 'enter' button is enabled. If the user alters the contents of a field by typing into it, it is necessary to disable the 'enter' button (and enable a 'check' button). The notification mechanism makes it straightforward for the control panel to implement this logic without having to intercept every key event.

4.7 Styles for Display Attributes

In many graphics systems and user interface toolkits, controls/widgets have parameters that determine their 'display attributes', that is which colour, font, line style, and so on,

---

[6] Here, the concrete presentation does infringe on the software implementing the abstract user interface. We think this is unavoidable, but try to keep a degree of abstraction by using 'names' for the field involved, not direct references to the objects themselves.

to use when rendering the object. However, such a system is unwieldy when a developer wishes to make systematic changes to related objects in a system. SIRIUS, therefore, uses a system of named 'display styles' which specify display attributes indirectly, (this is similar to the Primitive Representation Numbers of GKS [7]). A drawing method tells a drawing surface the name of the style it wishes to use, the drawing surface looks up the actual style object and sets up the display attributes accordingly. The use of names makes it straightforward to refer to styles in source code or in a definition database.

Each style object actually holds three sets of display attributes, and the drawing surface is told to use a style with a 'display status' of 'normal', 'highlight' or 'dimmed'. This parameter is then used to select the appropriate attributes. Although the same functionality could be achieved using multiple styles we have found that we typically change the display attributes for groups of objects in order to reflect their status in the interaction. The status parameter makes it straightforward to achieve this when those objects use different styles.

We have also found that it is useful to use a proliferation of styles, but then managing styles becomes a problem in its own right. In the original implementation, each style held its display attributes independently, but we have recently modified this so that styles have a definition hierarchy. In this scheme, attributes not defined specifically for style are 'inferred' from an ancestor.

4.8   SIRIUS' Object Graphics Utilities

To support the construction of control objects, SIRIUS has a simple 2d object graphics system, similar to, but less sophisticated than, PHIGS [8]. This allows a 'picture' to be defined as a hierarchy of objects totally independent of the display. The leaves of the hierarchy are 'graphics primitives': lines, arcs, text displays etc, while the nodes are 'graphics segments' which structure the picture. Each segment has an associated transformation matrix (by default the identity) which defines the 'local' coordinate system for that part of the picture. In addition, a segment is marked as 'visible' or 'invisible' and has a display status of 'normal', 'highlight' or 'dimmed'. Each primitive holds its own definition data plus the name of a display style; the display style plus the segment's status determine the display attributes which will be used when the primitive is rendered in the device interface. Figure 21 shows an object graphics hierarchy for a 'sketch' of an aeroplane.

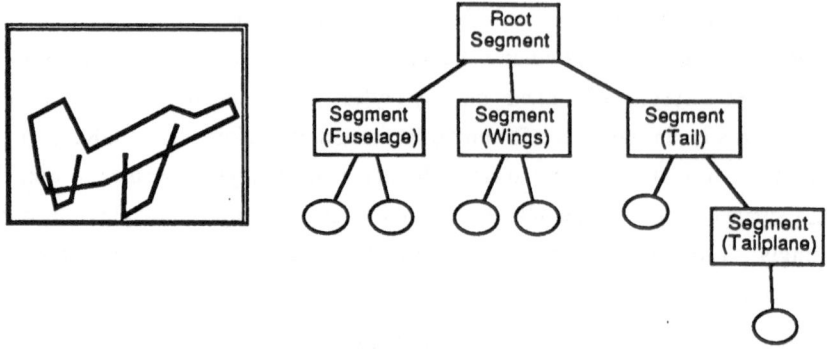

Figure 21 An Object Graphics Picture

The standard SIRIUS controls each have an object graphics 'picture' to define their appearance. The pictures are not independent, and each root segment defines the local coordinate system for its control relative to the 'world' system of the control panel. This usage of object graphics provides two benefits. First, it is both efficient and convenient. The calculations for a control's appearance are performed once and stored in the picture. The appearance can then be modified by making a segment visible or invisible, or by changing its display status as well as by 'primitive editing'. Second, if families of controls use the same organisation of segments, much of their behaviour can become common. For example, consider selection buttons and toggle controls. These objects all have two forms of presentation, an 'on' and an 'off' state. SIRIUS uses a 'background', an 'on' and an 'off' segment for each of these controls. The picture construction methods remain specific to the subclasses, but all the behavioural software is in the common superclass.

The SIRIUS object graphics system is not particularly sophisticated. In particular, unlike PHIGS or GKS, it does not automatically update the display when a picture is changed. It is left to the control that 'owns' the picture to manage the re-display, telling the appropriate parts of the picture to erase or draw themselves on the drawing surface as required. This approach was chosen for simplicity of implementation, but has proved to be very flexible as, once again, it allows appropriate semantics to be added. Similarly, we have not needed a 'hit search' ('pick') mechanism for the object graphics, but have handled geometry searches within the control hierarchy. Conversely, because of the object-oriented approach, it is straightforward to introduce custom primitives (or even segments) as subclasses of the object graphics superstructure classes.

We believe that there is an important lesson here. If we were to use a display system such a PHIGS (or even an X11 window hierarchy), we would need significant software to track our use of its resources and to manage the parameters that control its various algorithms. With a customisable server, the client-server interface can easily become unwieldy or else much of the system is 'sucked' into the server as customisation. Vendors of display systems are keen to add functionality to their 'servers' and offer improved performance via hardware support. The price for this is both a loss in flexibility and a more complex application.

5 Frameworks, Toolkits and Development Environments

5.1 Sirius' Development Cycle

In developing and using SIRIUS, we have learnt a number of lessons about what makes a usable user interface prototyping tool. The first lesson came from an unexpected direction. We chose Smalltalk-80 as our implementation platform for two reasons: because it was a pure object-oriented system with a rich class library and because it had a productive incremental development environment. What we have realised is the value of incremental development in user interface prototyping.

The key feature is 'suspended-time editing', that is, the ability to change a running system without having to shut it down and restart it. Suspended-time editing immediately saves development time because it eliminates the old 'edit-compile-debug' cycle. This is why we wanted an incremental development environment. Almost as a side effect, this has meant that SIRIUS remains productive despite not having an interactive layout tool. We could define the layout of a control panel in a Smalltalk methods and see the effect of changes immediately. Note, however, that in our experience, the selection of controls and their layout is at most 10% of a user interface definition; the productivity gains apply to all of it.

A more important property of suspended-time editing is that it allows us change the user interface of a running system. This is crucial if want to evaluate alternative user interfaces in user trials. An incremental development environment does not necessarily provide this ability. Many tools make it difficult, either by using monolithic definitions, or by attaching user interface semantics to objects that are only instantiated at start-up time. The SIRIUS structure, however, distinguishes between static and dynamic parts of a system and localises different aspects of the user interface in individual objects. In particular, the standard mechanism for 'wholesale' update of a view replaces one control panel with another, giving suspended-time editing automatically. Similarly, component models can be added and removed without impact on the structure as a whole. SIRIUS owes much of its power as a prototyping tool to this capability.

5.2   Using an Object-Oriented Language

The second lesson is the utility of a uniform object-oriented language for user interface development. SIRIUS makes no pretence of being an end-user tool; it is fundamentally a programming system. While it is possible to conceive 'non-programmer' tools for prototyping simple user interfaces, defining the behaviour of a user interface is inherently a programming task and developing its structure is akin to software design.

We chose an object-oriented approach as best practise in software engineering. As we expected, having an expressive, powerful language available to define any part of the system has contributed to its flexibility and capability. Our much emphasised insistence on using abstract interfaces and making domain objects available in concrete presentation software has ensured that any part of the system can exploit the power of the language to bring user interface and application semantics together.

In addition, where we have used definition data-structures, defined in one place and interpreted in another, we were simply able to build such definitions as object networks without having to design a special definition language. For example, we have a simple definitions database for the Oceanic prototypes that specifies the dialogue manager and component model classes plus the air traffic scenario to be used. Smalltalk may not be the ideal 'concrete syntax' for a high level user interface design language, but it is an excellent vehicle for storing and interpreting the resulting definitions.

Two further properties of Smalltalk are also worth noting. First, we made use of the fact that functions (Smalltalk Blocks) are first class objects as a parameterisation technique for utility classes. For example, the specification of each pane for a window includes a 'framing block' that is evaluated when the size of the window is known to yield the area for the pane. Similarly, we utilised the fact that classes are themselves objects in various algorithms for determining which class to use for a part of the system. Although we have not described it as part of the framework proper, SIRIUS has a system of configuration parameters through which we control variations in a user interface. Many of these parameters simply specify which class is to be used for a control panel or specific control.

5.3   Frameworks and Software Re-use

We think that SIRIUS has demonstrated that the framework approach assists software re-use. The utility classes such as the standard controls and the object graphics are potentially universal, but it is the framework that provides 'a place to put them' by guiding the development of the application. Further, we have found that perhaps 75% of what we have developed as 'application specific' is re-usable for similar systems in the same domain. From our Oceanic prototypes we now have a large library of air traffic control utility classes. Most of these are additions to the control library, but they include standard control panels, superstructure classes for map (radar) and flight strip components and domain modelling utilities. Some of these classes could be generalised for use in other control and monitoring applications.

However, there is undoubtedly a cost associated with the framework approach. A framework does not have a straightforward 'Application Programmers' Interface'. If a developer is to use a framework such as SIRIUS to its maximum potential, he or she has to understand not only its facilities but also its philosophy. It is possible to use SIRIUS as a conventional 'widget assembler', with comparatively little knowledge, although it could be made easier with appropriate tools. However, the system will only be productive if the developer understands the way that SIRIUS expects an interactive system to be structured and how to use the superstructure classes. We are sure this will be the case with any sophisticated framework. As SIRIUS incorporates much of our experience of building interactive systems, we think that ultimately the cost of understanding a framework will be regained through higher quality systems.

5.4 Requirements for a UIDE

Our experience with SIRIUS also suggests requirements for a User Interface Development Environment. First, SIRIUS' structure shows what a user interface definition must encompass and how such a definition could be partitioned. This is particularly important when we consider large scale developments with a team of user interface designers. It must be possible for members of the team to work together on the structure of the user interface and work independently on the details of its parts. As with any software development, this requires tools for version control and configuration management. In the prototyping context, this will need to support – not hinder – suspended-time editing.

Secondly, we found that the application classes we developed within SIRIUS, particularly the component models and control panels, were naturally organised in specialisation hierarchies. This suggests that user interface definitions should themselves use an object-oriented approach. This could be based on a hierarchy of parameterised templates that are instantiated and then assembled to construct the user interface. Hopkins and Wallis' FOOD system (see the paper in this volume) is an example of such an approach applied to widget hierarchies and electro-mechanical simulations. We believe that such a system combined with the SIRIUS organisation would yield a powerful, flexible definition tool.

Thirdly, we recognise that a prototyping system must have a smooth transition from straightforward systems built directly through high level tools to complex ones that require programming. Organising and partitioning a system such as SIRIUS does assist this in that each component model or control panel is separate and can be defined either through a tool or directly programmed. However, it will also be necessary to have hybrids that are partly specified through a high level definition and then completed by programming. We believe that there are two keys to achieving this integration. First, as we discussed above, the definitions should be held as object data-structures which could either be developed using design tools or be program generated. Then, the definitions should be essentially declarative, identifying which classes are to be used and specifying their parameters. At run-time, the definition interpreter creates and links the actual objects. These objects can be from application classes and there is no difference between a definition derived system and a purely programmed one.

5.5   Extending SIRIUS

Our experience with SIRIUS also suggests how it might evolve. Our next major development will probably be a definition system and tools as suggested above. We have the simple system we used for assembling the various Oceanic prototypes, but although this had the declarative structure, it lacked templating and only supported a fixed set of parameters. We are looking to design a general purpose system with flexible template and parameter handling taking the FOOD system as a guide.

A related development is to consider specialisations of the substructure classes that would support common user interface designs. Three candidates we have identified are form-filling dialogues, some form of hypermedia and extensions to our existing support for diagram editors. We also believe that Iconographer could be integrated in SIRIUS. Its domain filter would map onto a component model with the switchboard and presentation system as part of a control panel in the concrete presentation.

6   Conclusions

SIRIUS has met its major objective: it has enabled us to construct complex user interfaces with the minimum of effort. It has demonstrated what can be achieved in a wholly object-oriented system. The potential benefits from inheritance and polymorphism are real and can be exploited to build flexible systems with minimal performance costs. Similarly, the framework approach has led to re-usable software.

The architecture itself makes two specific contributions. First, the five layer model as realised in SIRIUS' superstructure shows how to organise a large interactive system. It separates those aspects that are genuinely independent so that alternative user interfaces are easily produced, but allows user interface and application concerns to be integrated to deliver semantically rich interactions. Second, the combination of the model-view-controller approach with widget hierarchies (control panels) shows how both an underlying abstraction and a much needed structure can be added to the now common widget systems.

SIRIUS weaknesses come directly from its strengths. It cannot easily be applied to non-object-oriented systems, nor is it straightforward to use it as front-end to an existing application. Similarly, it sits uncomfortably with toolkits for standardised 'look and feel'. It is quite possible to use such a toolkit in SIRIUS' concrete presentation layer, but much of the flexibility is lost. These are not problems for SIRIUS itself as a prototyping tool, but do arise when we consider the wider application of the architecture.

We intend to develop SIRIUS into a more complete User Interface Development Environment and we will continue to use it to support our user interface design work when its sophistication is required. We also use it as a 'reference model' for assessing commercially available tools for user interface implementation. By comparison with SIRIUS we can see how much of the problem a tool addresses and where the likely limitations lie. We hope that tool developers will take up some of the ideas incorporated in SIRIUS for the next generation of tools.

Acknowledgements

David Brazier, Kate Taylor and Colin Grant worked on the design and implementation of SIRIUS and they and others contributed not only to the design but also to the underlying ideas. The device interface and, especially, the object graphics system are based on the work of Robin Langridge and his team at CADCentre Limited. I would particularly like to acknowledge the contribution of my Logica colleague Ian Clowes who has challenged me to develop my ideas on interactive architectures for many years and who reviewed the drafts of this paper.

Finally, I would like to thank Phil Gray for the opportunity to write up SIRIUS in detail and his encouragement to do so.

References

[1]	Grady Booch. *Object-Oriented Design with Applications*. The Benjamin/Cummings Publishing Company, Inc, California, 1991.

[2]	*Communications of the ACM*, Vol 33, No 9 (September 1990). Issue on Object-Oriented Design.

[3] Joelle Coutaz. *Architecture Models for Interactive Software: Failures and Trends*. In Engineering for Human-Computer Interaction. Proc. IFIP WG2.7 Working Conference, Napa Valley, California. 21-25 August, 1989. North-Holland, 1990. pp. 78-93.

[4] L. Peter Deutsch and Adele Goldberg. *Smalltalk Yesterday, Today and Tomorrow*. Byte Vol 18, No 8 (Aug 1991) pp 108-115.

[5] S.W. Draper and K.W. Waite. *Iconographer as a visual programming system*. In D. Diaper and N. Hammond, eds., People and Computers VI. Cambridge University Press, 1991. pp. 171-185.

[6] Philip Gray and Ramzan Mohamed. *A Practical Introduction to Smalltalk-80*. Pitman, 1990.

[7] F.R.A. Hopgood, D.A. Duce, J.R. Gallop and D.C. Sutcliffe. *Introduction to the Graphical Kernel System (GKS)*. Academic Press, 1983.

[8] International Organisation for Standardisation, Information Processing Systems - Computer Graphics, Programmer's Hierarchical Interactive Graphics System (PHIGS), Part 1 - Functional Description. ISO IS 9592, 1988

[9] D. A. Norman. *The Psychology of Everyday Things*. Basic Books, Inc., New York, 1988.

[10] Gunther, Pfaff, ed. *Proceedings of the Workshop on User Inteface Management Systems*, Seeheim, Nov. 1983. Springer-Verlag, 1985.

[11] Schmucker, Kurt J. *MacApp: An Application Framework*. Byte 11,8 (August 86), pp. 189-193.

[12] G. Storrs and P. Windsor. *Prototyping for Requirements Capture*. In Stansilaw Wrycza, ed., Proceedings of the Second International Conference on Information Systems Developers Workbench, University of Gdansk, September 1990.

[13] P.N. Windsor. *An Object-Oriented Framework for Prototyping User Interfaces*. Proceedings of Interact '90. pp. 309-314.

Author Index

Burns, A. 56
Cockburn, A. 35
Cornali, D.J. 115
Davison, A. 85
Draper, S.W. 104
Duce, D.A. 69
Edmonds, E.A. 115
George, A. 182
Gray, P. 133
Heggie, S.P. 115
Hopkins, T.P. 168
Jones, S. 35
Mohamed, R. 104
Reid, I. 115
Rosner, P. 85
Slater, M. 85
ten Hagen, P.J.W. 69
Thimbleby, H. 35
Took, R. 6
van Liere, R. 69
Waite, C. 151
Wallis, S.K. 168
Williams, P. 23
Windsor, P. 200

Published in 1990

AI and Cognitive Science '89, Dublin City University, Eire, 14–15 September 1989
A. F. Smeaton and G. McDermott (Eds.)

Specification and Verification of Concurrent Systems, University of Stirling, Scotland, 6–8 July 1988
C. Rattray (Ed.)

Semantics for Concurrency, Proceedings of the International BCS-FACS Workshop, Sponsored by Logic for IT (S.E.R.C.), University of Leicester, UK, 23–25 July 1990
M. Z. Kwiatkowska, M. W. Shields and R. M. Thomas (Eds.)

Functional Programming, Glasgow 1989, Proceedings of the 1989 Glasgow Workshop, Fraserburgh, Scotland, 21–23 August 1989
K. Davis and J. Hughes (Eds.)

Persistent Object Systems, Proceedings of the Third International Workshop, Newcastle, Australia, 10–13 January 1989
J. Rosenberg and D. Koch (Eds.)

Z User Workshop, Oxford, 1989, Proceedings of the Fourth Annual Z User Meeting, Oxford, 15 December 1989
J. E. Nicholls (Ed.)

Formal Methods for Trustworthy Computer Systems (FM89), Halifax, Canada, 23–27 July 1989
Dan Craigen (Editor) and Karen Summerskill (Assistant Editor)

Security and Persistence, Proceedings of the International Workshop on Computer Architecture to Support Security and Persistence of Information, Bremen, West Germany, 8–11 May 1990
John Rosenberg and J. Leslie Keedy (Eds.)